# CLASSIC
# HORSE RACES

FAMOUS MOMENTS
FROM THE HISTORY
OF THE FLAT,
STEEPLECHASE
AND HURDLES

Anne Holland

INTRODUCTION BY
Julian Wilson

Macdonald
Queen Anne Press

First published for Marks and Spencer plc in 1989 by
Macdonald & Co (Publishers) Ltd
Updated edition first published in Great Britain in 1991 by
Queen Anne Press, a division of Macdonald & Co (Publishers)
Ltd, Orbit House, 1 New Fetter Lane, London EC4A 1AR

A member of Maxwell Macmillan Pergamon Publishing
Corporation

© Macdonald & Co (Publishers) Ltd 1989, 1991

ISBN 0 356 19708 5

A CIP catalogue record for this book is available from the
British Library

Typeset by Litho Link Limited, Welshpool, Powys, Wales
Printed and bound by **Kim Hup Lee Printing Co. Pte Ltd**

EDITOR: David Heslam
SENIOR ART EDITOR: Philip Lord
DESIGNER: Bill Mason
PICTURE RESEARCH: Caroline Thompson
SENIOR PRODUCTION CONTROLLER: Sonya Sibbons

The author and publishers would also like to thank the
following organizations and individuals for their kind
assistance:

The Jockey Club; The Timeform Organization/Portway Press
Ltd; Raceform Ltd (D. Corbett); Sporting Life (Andrew
Harrison); Messrs Weatherbys (G. Bivens, S. Cheney, Mrs
L. Moran, P. Palmer, P. Rees); Billy Hinshelwood; William
Hughes; F. Hyland; Aintree Racecourse Ltd.; Ascot
Racecourse; Ayr Racecourse; Cheltenham Racecourse;
Churchill Downs Inc.; Curragh Racecourse; Doncaster
Racecourse; Japan Racing Assoc.; Newmarket Racecourse;
New York Racing Assoc. Inc.; Phoenix Park Racecourse;
Société des Steeple-Chases de France; Triple Crown
Productions; United Racecourses; Victoria Racing Club.

The Publishers would like to thank the following collections for
allowing us to reproduce their photographs:

Front cover photograph: Allsport/Steve Powell; Page 1 Allsport/Oli
Tennant; 2/3 Allsport/Dan Smith; 7 Bridgeman Art Library/Private
Collection; 8 & 11 Gerry Cranham; 12 Copyright The Sir Alfred
Munnings Art Museum, Dedham/Bridgeman Art Library; 14 E. T.
Archive; 15 & 16 Sport and General Press Agency; 17 E. T.
Archive; 18 George Selwyn; 20 Allsport/Roger Labrosse; 21 & 22
Gerry Cranham; 25 Bob Thomas; 26 Fiona Vigors; 27 Sport and
General Press Agency; 28 Syndication International Ltd; 30 Mel
Fordham; 33 Allsport; 34 Fiona Vigors; 35 Sport and General Press
Agency; 37 Gerry Cranham; 38 Bridgeman Art Library; 39 Hulton-
Deutsch; 40 & 41 George Selwyn; 42 Sporting Pictures (UK) Ltd; 43
George Selwyn; 45 Allsport; 46 Sport and General Press Agency; 47
& 49 Gerry Cranham; 50 E. T. Archive; 51 t. The Bridgeman Art
Library, b. Gerry Cranham; 52 Gerry Cranham; 53 Sport and
General Press Agency; 55 W. W. Rouch & Co; 57 Allsport; 58 E. T.
Archive; 61 George Selwyn; 63, 64 & 66 Gerry Cranham; 67 Sport
and General Press Agency; 69 Gerry Cranham; 70 Tim Hannan
Photography; 73 Allsport/Chris Cole; 74 Gerry Cranham; 75
Popperfoto; 77 George Selwyn; 79 Topham Picture Library; 80
W. W. Rouch & Co; 83 Allsport/Mike Powell; 84 Gerry Cranham;
85 & 86 Kinetic Corporation; 87, 88 & 89 Allsport/Mike Powell; 91
Jill M Dodson; 92 Raymond Woolfe; 93 Jill M Dodson; 94 & 95 Bob
Coglianese Photos Inc; 97 Gerry Cranham; 98 Raymond Woolfe; 99
Hulton-Deutsch; 100/1 Bob Coglianese Photos Inc; 103 & 104
Allsport/Dan Smith; 105 The Mansell Collection; 107 Museum of
Victoria; 109 Gerry Cranham; 110 Japan Racing Association; 112/3
& 115 t. Sporting Pictures (UK) Ltd; 115 b. Allsport/Mike Powell;
116 Bridgeman Art Library; 117 Gerry Cranham; 118 Bob Thomas;
119, 120 & 122 t. Gerry Cranham; 122/3 Sport and General Press
Agency; 125 Sporting Pictures (UK) Ltd; 126 George Selwyn; 127
Sport and General Press Agency; 129 Alec Russell; 131 George
Selwyn; 132 Alec Russell; 133 Mel Fordham; 135 & 136 Sporting
Pictures (UK) Ltd; 137 W. W. Rouch & Co; 139 Popperfoto; 141
Topham Picture Library; 142 Bob Langrish; 143 Popperfoto; 144 W.
W. Rouch & Co; 145 Gerry Cranham; 146 George Selwyn; 148
Gerry Cranham; 149 Allsport; 151 & 152/3 Sport and General Press
Agency; 155 t. Allsport; 155 b. Copyright The Sir Alfred Munnings
Art Museum, Dedham/Bridgeman Art Library; 156 Gerry Cranham;
157 Allsport/Oli Tennant; 158 Sporting Pictures (UK) Ltd; 161 Tim
Hannan Photography; 162 Mel Fordham; 163 W. W. Rouch & Co;
144/5 Jim Connolly Photography; 167-171 Raymond Woolfe; 173 &
174/5 P Bertrand et Fils; 176 W. W. Rouch & Co.

**Front cover** shows the 1988 Derby field

**Page 1** shows *Desert Orchid* ridden by Simon Sherwood

**Pages 2 and 3** show *Little Polveir* winner of the 1989
Grand National

# CLASSIC
# HORSE RACES

# CONTENTS

Introduction 6

## CLASSIC FLAT RACES 8

## CLASSIC JUMP RACES 112

# INTRODUCTION

During the history of man the horse has been charger, carriage conveyor, corner-stone of industrial transport; and friend to countless people. However, it is the horse in sport that has become the aristocrat of the horse kingdom; and such has been the impact of the British thoroughbred, that horses with direct or indirect British pedigrees now race in almost 100 countries around the world.

Huge sums are spent worldwide by rich men in pursuit of the best racing bloodstock and it is the great races that act as the shop windows in which this expensive talent can be displayed. *Classic Horse Races*, in which the word 'classic' is used in its more general meaning as 'of the highest class', includes many of these great races and describes some of the greatest and strangest moments from their history.

The 'Sport of Kings' has always evoked extremes of emotion in its participants and spectators. It has witnessed on the one hand joy, elation and sentimentality and on the other skulduggery, greed and envy. It is a sport peopled at all levels by heroes and villains. Happily, the impact of the former far outweighs the disgrace of the latter.

The oldest British classic, the St. Leger, dates back to 1776. However, even in my lifetime, there have been several characters, human and equine, who have succeeded in keeping our sport on the front pages. The men I have in mind are Sir Gordon Richards, Lester Piggott, Bob Champion, Fred Winter and Jonjo O'Neill. The horses who, for different reasons, became immortal were Arkle, Aldaniti, Dawn Run, Mill Reef, Red Rum, Shergar and, more recently, Desert Orchid. All had that special quality or charisma that elevates sporting competition from the level of the humdrum to an altogether higher plane.

The truly epic and best remembered encounters on the turf have, like the greatest theatre, the ability to tug at the emotions in a way that weakens the fiercest self-control. There are several occasions that have forced a tear even from my professional eye.

In 1975, the epic battle between Grundy and Bustino left all who viewed it drained and breathless. Seldom have I witnessed horses dig so deep into reserves of stamina and raw courage. Two years later the Grand National success of the incomparable Red Rum was a fairy story of almost impermissible dimensions when, aged 12, he came back to Aintree to win for the third time. Most recently, there was that forever memorable occasion at Cheltenham when a grey prima donna battled his way up the muddy final slope lifted by the roar of 50,000 throats.

But perhaps the most poignant moment of all in my memory was the 1981 conquest of the seemingly unconquerable by Aldaniti and Bob Champion . . . a hopeless cripple and a courageous cancer victim. Never have I been more relieved to be covering Becher's Brook in the Grand National, rather than the uncontrollably emotional end of that race.

Of course, from time to time, the racing world has also been besmirched by scandal. In the 1844 Derby, a horse named Running Rein won by threequarters of a length but was later found to be a four-year-old called Maccabeus and was disqualified. In the 1963 Derby, Relko, the French-trained winner, returned a positive dope test, and was allowed to keep the race only after the lengthiest of enquiries.

In between times, and since, there have been many other 'causes célèbres'. Such is the rich tapestry of our great races. The racing world has always and will always, be peopled by saints and sinners. But though horses can be temperamental, stubborn and downright difficult they can never be villains in a human sense. And it is of them that this book speaks — racing's true heroes — the horses.

*Julian Wilson*

*The start of the 1830 St. Leger* by James Pollard

# CLASSIC

# FLAT RACES

*T*HE *'flat classics' may have evolved on the racecourses of England but top thoroughbreds worldwide have produced races their equal in quality and excitement. All the major racing countries have their Derbys, their Nijinskys and Mill Reefs, their champion jockeys and trainers. The years have witnessed their triumphs and tragedies from Longchamps to Louisville…*

THE DERBY
THE OAKS
THE 2000 GUINEAS
THE 1000 GUINEAS
THE DEWHURST STAKES
THE ST. LEGER
THE 'KING GEORGE'
THE ASCOT GOLD CUP
THE QUEEN ALEXANDRA STAKES
THE ECLIPSE STAKES
THE IRISH DERBY
THE CARTIER MILLION
THE PRIX DE L'ARC DE TRIOMPHE
THE GRAND PRIX DE PARIS
THE KENTUCKY DERBY
THE BREEDERS' CUP
THE PREAKNESS STAKES
THE BELMONT STAKES
THE MELBOURNE CUP
THE JAPAN CUP

# EPSOM

Racing was established on Epsom Downs by 1625, if a burial list of that year is anything to go by, referring to 'William Stanley who in running the race fell from his horse and brake his neck'. Charles II is said to have been a racing visitor, and Samuel Pepys, on a later visit to the Epsom Wells in 1663, refers in his diary to 'horsemen upon the hill where they were making matches to run'.

Twenty one years later in 1684, the track had its own clerk of the course, and from 1730 there were regular meetings in the spring and autumn.

Today Epsom hosts a Spring and August meeting as well as the Derby meeting in June.

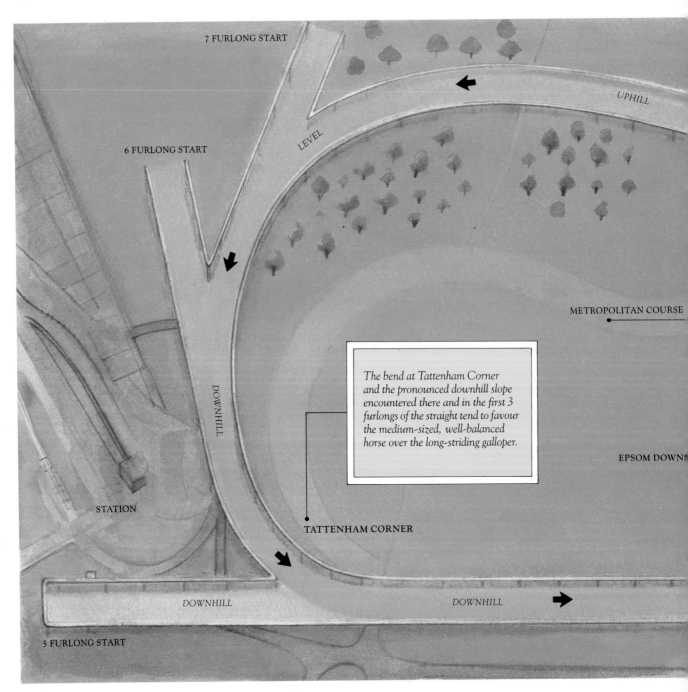

7 FURLONG START

6 FURLONG START

LEVEL

UPHILL

METROPOLITAN COURSE

DOWNHILL

STATION

*The bend at Tattenham Corner and the pronounced downhill slope encountered there and in the first 3 furlongs of the straight tend to favour the medium-sized, well-balanced horse over the long-striding galloper.*

TATTENHAM CORNER

EPSOM DOWNS

DOWNHILL

DOWNHILL

5 FURLONG START

**Right** *The Royal Party witness the parade of horses before the 1979 Epsom Derby won by Troy.*

THE DERBY AND OAKS
START (1½ miles)

UPHILL

The Metropolitan Course at Epsom comes into use in 2¼ mile races. These start at the winning post and leave the straight just before Tattenham Corner rejoining the course proper once again just over 8½ furlongs from the winning post.

WINNING POST

UPHILL

GRANDSTAND

## A COURSE FOR THE BRAVE

The Epsom course is truly unique, and although there are those who criticise it as unsuitable for deciding the best three year old in the world, nevertheless, the winner has to be not only fast, but also well balanced and brave, qualities which will do him no harm in reproducing the breed.

After the parade in front of the stands, the horses cross the downs to the start on the far side of the course. The first half mile rises 150 feet in height, and then falls in varying degrees a total of 100 feet sweeping left-handed round Tattenham Corner, until in the home straight there is a slight rise again to the winning post, the length, since 1784, being one and a half miles.

A total of five public roads are crossed during racing, and four of these are covered by coconut matting and the other by wood chippings. Entry to the course centre, called the Hill, is free to people but there is a car parking charge. A highly charged, colourful atmosphere emanates from here, with gypsies selling lucky heather and telling fortunes, a fun fair and stalls galore selling everything from ice cream and hot dogs to cockles and mussels, souvenirs and trinkets.

Trippers arrive by the coach load to enjoy their day out, their casual dress a contrast to the top hats and grey morning suits of those in the paying enclosures. It is estimated that about a quarter of a million people in total attend the races on Derby day.

# THE DERBY

IN 1780, the year after the first running of The Oaks, its two founders, Sir Charles Bunbury and Lord Derby, decided to introduce another race over the same course and distance but this time open to both sexes. It was decided to call the race after one of themselves — would it be called *The Bunbury* or *The Derby*? It is said that the toss of a coin decided the outcome, and so, in 1770, the Derby was born, the first race being won by Sir Charles' horse *Diomed* who netted for him the first prize of 1,075 guineas.

## HYPERION

As one drives out of Newmarket on the Snailwell Road, past the stables of Geoff Huffer and Pat Haslam, and towards the British Racing School, there is by the Woodland Stud a life size statue of one of the Derby's greats, *Hyperion*. He was bred and owned by the Earl of Derby, and it is beside his Newmarket stud that his statue stands.

*Hyperion* was by *Gainsborough* out of a neat little mare called *Selene* who foaled him in 1930, and to begin with he gave no signs of being anything exceptional, for not only was he small, but he was also lazy at home. Big horses often need extra work, but little *Hyperion* did, too.

It came as something of a surprise when he ran out an easy three length winner of his first race as a two year old; he was beaten next time out over five furlongs but made amends quickly when winning the 7 furlongs Dewhurst Stakes.

This obviously put him in contention for the 1933 Derby, and so he was trained with that object in mind. He showed that he was on course for it by winning the Chester Vase on his first run as a three year old, and he was installed favourite for the Derby.

### DERBY FAVOURITE

He was as lazy as ever at home, but his trainer, the Honourable George Lambton, did not lose faith in him, and gave the little colt the work he thrived on. He also arranged for a pacemaker, *Thrapston*, and so the scene was set.

On the morning of the race, Lambton was ill and could not travel to Epsom; of course, it was before such events were televised, but radio broadcasting had begun six years before.

Once a trainer has done his homework, there is little he can do to alter the race result on the day, and in *Hyperion's* case, Lambton had done all that was required of him; the horse was trained spot on, and let no-one down in the race.

*A portrait by Sir Alfred Munnings of the 1933 Derby winner, Hyperion. He also went on to win the St. Leger and was a great success at stud being Champion Stallion six times.*

There were 24 runners and *Hyperion* started an easy 6-1 favourite. Steve Donoghue did his work admirably on *Thrapston* being first to jump out of the gate in an excellent start. He forced the pace in front of *Coroado*, *Light Sussex*, *Madagascar* and *Raymond*.

This group was followed by another headed by *King Salmon*, *Hyperion* and *Manitoba* who began to lose his place after half a mile as *Thrapston* kept up a good gallop at the head of affairs.

Close behind the pacemaker were *Light Sussex*, *Scarlet Tiger*, *Hyperion* and *King Salmon*. Going down the hill towards Tattenham Corner *King Salmon* was on the inside, but Harry Wragg then pulled him to the outside as *Thrapston* was still setting a fast pace.

Down the hill he was pursued by *Light Sussex*, *Hyperion* and *Coroado* and sweeping round Tattenham Corner *Hyperion* only had his pacemaker ahead of him; *King Salmon*, *Raymond*, *Statesman*, *Scarlet Tiger*, *Solar Boy* and *Franz Hals* followed in that order, with *Scarlet Tiger* finding himself a little squeezed for room round the bend.

*Coroado* had shot his bolt and was the first to drop back beaten. Next to go was *Thrapston* who gradually fell away, his job magnificently performed.

For a few strides *Light Sussex* flattered but receded with two furlongs to run as *Hyperion* swept on. *King Salmon* moved into a threatening position but was unable to carry it through as *Hyperion* drew away to beat him by four lengths in a new course record with *Statesman* a length back in third. *Scarlet Tiger* finished fourth ahead of the gallant *Thrapston* who had 19 horses strung out in a ragged line behind him.

## CHAMPION SIRE

The course record stood for only three years when it was bettered by *Mahmoud*, but the crowds took *Hyperion* to their hearts, and he was a very popular winner, believed to be the smallest for almost a hundred years.

He went on to win the Prince of Wales's Stakes at Royal Ascot and, after a set-back, the St. Leger. His trainer was changed when he was four and he was beaten in both his runs, but he went on to be champion stallion six times, siring seven Classic winners; much of his blood moved across the Atlantic to America, too.

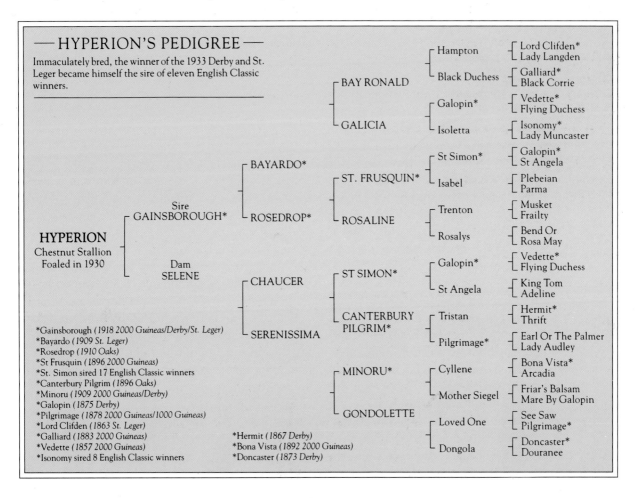

## — HYPERION'S PEDIGREE —

Immaculately bred, the winner of the 1933 Derby and St. Leger became himself the sire of eleven English Classic winners.

**HYPERION**
Chestnut Stallion
Foaled in 1930

Sire GAINSBOROUGH*
 — BAYARDO*
  — ST. FRUSQUIN*
   — St Simon*
    — Galopin*
    — St Angela
   — Isabel
    — Plebeian
    — Parma
  — ROSALINE
   — Trenton
    — Musket
    — Frailty
   — Rosalys
    — Bend Or
    — Rosa May
 — ROSEDROP*

Dam SELENE
 — CHAUCER
  — ST SIMON*
   — Galopin*
    — Vedette*
    — Flying Duchess
   — St Angela
    — King Tom
    — Adeline
  — CANTERBURY PILGRIM*
   — Tristan
    — Hermit*
    — Thrift
   — Pilgrimage*
    — Earl Or The Palmer
    — Lady Audley
 — SERENISSIMA
  — MINORU*
   — Cyllene
    — Bona Vista*
    — Arcadia
   — Mother Siegel
    — Friar's Balsam
    — Mare By Galopin
  — GONDOLETTE
   — Loved One
    — See Saw
    — Pilgrimage*
   — Dongola
    — Doncaster*
    — Douranee

BAY RONALD
 — Hampton
  — Lord Clifden*
  — Lady Langden
 — Black Duchess
  — Galliard*
  — Black Corrie

GALICIA
 — Galopin*
  — Vedette*
  — Flying Duchess
 — Isoletta
  — Isonomy*
  — Lady Muncaster

*Gainsborough (1918 2000 Guineas/Derby/St. Leger)
*Bayardo (1909 St. Leger)
*Rosedrop (1910 Oaks)
*St Frusquin (1896 2000 Guineas)
*St. Simon sired 17 English Classic winners
*Canterbury Pilgrim (1896 Oaks)
*Minoru (1909 2000 Guineas/Derby)
*Galopin (1875 Derby)
*Pilgrimage (1878 2000 Guineas/1000 Guineas)
*Lord Clifden (1863 St. Leger)
*Galliard (1883 2000 Guineas)
*Vedette (1857 2000 Guineas)
*Isonomy sired 8 English Classic winners

*Hermit (1867 Derby)
*Bona Vista (1892 2000 Guineas)
*Doncaster (1873 Derby)

*Nijinsky with Lester Piggott up painted by L. Sandys Lumsdaine. The first horse since the war to win the colt's Triple Crown of 2000 Guineas, Derby and St. Leger.*

## NIJINSKY

The sign of a truly great horse is one who handles different situations in his stride — courses, going, gradients, crowds — and still comes out the winner. Those blessed with a phlegmatic outlook, such as *Sir Ivor*, can stand many races and still come back for more, but the very nature of the thoroughbred racehorse means that he is likely to be highly strung if he is also to be brilliant.

Such a one was *Nijinsky*, and the only blot on his magnificent record was that he was perhaps taken to the well once too often.

### A QUESTION OF JUDGEMENT

*Nijinsky* was bought at the Woodbine Sales as a yearling in Canada by Vincent O'Brien on behalf of Charles Englehard, but he was not Englehard's own choice; O'Brien, nevertheless, felt the bay by *Northern Dancer*, bred by E. P. Taylor, was the better prospect, and paid top price for him.

There followed probably the greatest test of O'Brien's judgement throughout his distinguished career, for when he brought the colt home to Ballydoyle in Co. Tipperary he was so stubbornly

intractable that he was virtually unrideable.

At first he would not eat an oat, baulked at being led out of the stable and once he had been, would rear up frequently, pawing the air, and all too often refused to do any work. Not surprisingly, the staff were not altogether enamoured of him, in spite of his attractive heart shaped star, beautiful eyes and stunning good looks; but, they were a hand-picked lot who could be relied upon to do a competent job in caring for a horse without knocking him about, no matter what his prospects.

*Nijinsky* sweated so profusely even at home that he was bathed in lather and it must be true to say that in some hands he might never even have reached a racecourse, let alone become the only horse since the Second World War to win the coveted Triple Crown.

### FINE TUNING

It is a tribute to his skill and patience as a trainer that Vincent O'Brien not only calmed down the colt, but kept him sweet for two years, channelling his energies in the right direction instead of letting him boil over.

His ability on a racecourse was immediately apparent as a two year old. He had settled down sufficiently for Vincent to be able to reassure the owner, and once on the gallops would work well; even something like learning to go through the starting stalls went smoothly, and by the time of his first race, he was odds-on favourite. He not only won it, but did so in such style that suddenly the whole of Ireland was talking about him.

In all, he ran five times as a two year old and won every time. Not surprisingly, he was installed favourite for the 1970 2,000 Guineas.

He won his 'prep' race, beating *Deep Run* who became the phenomenally successful National Hunt sire, and then, amid a great deal of security, travelled to England for the Guineas, which he duly won at odds-on.

There were those who felt, however, that his

*Flecked with foam and shining with sweat after winning the 1970 Derby Nijinsky is led towards the winner's enclosure. Possessed of a volatile and nervous disposition he had been almost unrideable when first brought to the O'Brien stables.*

stamina might have limitations, and that the Epsom test could find him out. So it was that the Derby became the only race in his whole career for which he started at odds against.

## PRE-RACE SCARE

As it turned out, it was neither lack of stamina, nor faulty security that nearly undid him but, unbeknown to the waiting world, a colic scare. *Nijinsky*, who had been housed at Sandown Park in the early part of the week, completed his final work at Epsom the day before the race and returned to the stables.

There he started pawing the ground and sweating; it was a hot day; the heightened tension might be getting to him; but no, the signs were unmistakeable: the most valuable horse in the world at that moment had a debilitating stomach ache. And because it was so close to the race, he could not be given the normal injection of a drug that relaxes muscles and allows the pent up gases to be released in such cases.

*Nijinsky* and his close entourage could only sit it out and hope for an improvement. It was probably the longest one and a half hours of Vincent O'Brien's life; then thankfully it was through, the colic had passed, the crisis was over.

## THE BLUE RIBAND RACE

It is easy for a horse to look great if all he beats is moderate opposition, but the Derby that year was full of quality; indeed, the French trainer of *Gyr* thought so much of his horse that he had postponed his own retirement for a year in order to train him. *Gyr* was a great big American-bred chestnut colt, and as he set sail on the fast ground down the Epsom straight with two furlongs to go, Etienne Pollet must have been glad of his decision to continue training that year.

Then Lester Piggott simply shook the reigns up on *Nijinsky*; the colt swooped into overdrive — and the race was over. It was a truly brilliant performance, franked by *Gyr's* subsequent easy win in the Grand Prix de St Cloud. *Nijinsky* won by two and a half lengths from *Gyr*, with *Stintino*, no mean racehorse himself, third. The time was the fastest since electronic recording began, barely slower than the hand-held record of *Mahmoud* in 1936, who was the last horse before *Nijinsky* to win the Triple Crown.

Everyone went home happy after that Derby, with the possible exception of the bookmakers who stood to lose a great deal by *Nijinsky's* win.

When *Nijinsky* then won the Irish Derby in front of his understandably enthusiastic home crowd at The Curragh, he showed some of his old signs of boiling over, and sweated profusely. He won it all right, and then really underlined his superiority when, taking on older horses for the first time, he cruised to victory in the King George VI and Queen Elizabeth Diamond Stakes at Royal Ascot.

## TRIPLE CROWN AND RETIREMENT

It was his tenth successive victory; surely here was the Horse of the Century. He could take in the St. Leger, and with it the Triple Crown, on his way to the Prix de l'Arc de Triomphe and then retirement.

But the best laid plans . . . at home in Ireland, *Nijinsky* suffered a nasty bout of ringworm which sapped him of some of his vitality. he won the St. Leger all right, but the effort took much more out of him than any previous race.

Nevertheless, his jockey Lester Piggott would not hear of defeat in the Arc. It did not matter how far he lay out of his ground, *Nijinsky's* blistering acceleration would take him past any horse in the world. For ever afterwards, there were those who blamed Piggott for the great colt's defeat, by the shortest margin, by *Sassafras*. Never mind, instead of despatching him directly to stud, he could stay in training just a little longer to run in the Champion Stakes and give

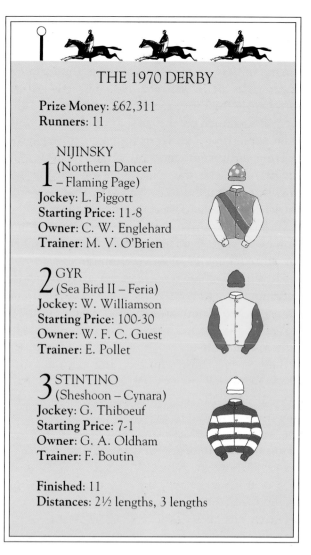

## THE 1970 DERBY

**Prize Money:** £62,311
**Runners:** 11

**1** NIJINSKY
(Northern Dancer
– Flaming Page)
**Jockey:** L. Piggott
**Starting Price:** 11-8
**Owner:** C. W. Englehard
**Trainer:** M. V. O'Brien

**2** GYR
(Sea Bird II – Feria)
**Jockey:** W. Williamson
**Starting Price:** 100-30
**Owner:** W. F. C. Guest
**Trainer:** E. Pollet

**3** STINTINO
(Sheshoon – Cynara)
**Jockey:** G. Thiboeuf
**Starting Price:** 7-1
**Owner:** G. A. Oldham
**Trainer:** F. Boutin

**Finished:** 11
**Distances:** 2½ lengths, 3 lengths

*Nijinsky leads the Derby followed by the French horses Gyr and Stintino. Gyr's trainer, Etienne Pollet, had postponed his retirement that year such was his optimism for Gyr's racing future.*

him a confidence-boosting win to retire on.

It was not to be. Upset by his milling, cheering fans and throng of Press photographers, he reverted to his yearling habits of rearing and being thoroughly overwrought and distressed. The lovely *Nijinsky* was beaten by all the way winner *Lorenzaccio*.

But that was not the end of the road for *Nijinsky*; he proved his true worth at stud, and already two of his sons, *Golden Fleece* and *Sharastani*, have also won the Derby.

## SHERGAR

For many the most memorable Derby came in 1981 as a magnificent horse with a broad white blaze and four white feet stormed up the Epsom straight alone and won by a record ten lengths pulling up: *Shergar*.

*Shergar* thus became the first of HH Aga Khan's three Derby winners during the 1980s, sending him on the path after his grandfather's five winners, *Blenheim*, *Bahram*, *Mahmoud*, *My Love* and *Tulyar*.

### A SURPRISING COLT

Bred by the Aga Khan and sent to Michael Stoute at Newmarket, *Shergar* seemed nothing out of the ordinary when he arrived there as a late-maturing colt; he did not start fast work until the autumn, by which time many precocious youngsters had run in and won a number of juvenile races.

But it was not long before he was impressing those around him, and when *Shergar* first saw a racecourse in a maiden at Newbury in late September, the dark bay colt beat his 22 rivals in course record time.

So his racing made an impact from the start, and for his next race he was sent straight into Group 1 company. He finished second to *Beldale Flutter*, and went off for his winter break.

### EARLY FAVOURITE

During that winter, *Shergar* made exceptional progress physically, and worked so well on the Newmarket gallops in the spring that his 33-1 price for the Derby did not remain so for very much longer. He won on his reappearance by no less than ten lengths, and his next race at Chester by 12 lengths — it did not take a great eye to see that here was an exceptional horse!

As Derby Day approached and no obvious market rivals appeared, his price became shorter and shorter — and as usual, the bookmakers were right. Even when it rained so hard that racing at Salisbury was abandoned through waterlogging the day before the Derby, it did not affect support for *Shergar*. Indeed, if anything it strengthened it, for he had proved himself on soft ground, and looking at the field what other horse was there in the race to seriously challenge him?

*A painting by G. E. Hoare of the Aga Khan's great horse Shergar. The painting shows quite clearly the famous white blaze and four white feet.*

Amazingly, there was only one other horse in the race whose price was below 10-1, and this was *Shotgun*, the mount of Lester Piggott who could even draw support riding a donkey.

### RUNAWAY WINNER

Although it was hardly a vintage Derby field, the manner of *Shergar's* victory was unforgettable. What's more, the colt had on his back a cherub-faced jockey who was only 19 years old, Walter Swinburn, but he had a wise head on his young shoulders, and never let the occasion get the

better of him. He was a credit to his proud father, Wally Swinburn, himself a top class jockey, and to trainer Michael Stoute who had had the confidence to appoint Walter his stable jockey.

Eighteen horses went to post — but 17 of them might just as well have stayed in their stables. Only second-placed *Glint of Gold* had a genuine hard luck story, as he was clipped into and nearly brought down by *Kalaglow* at the top of the hill,

*Shergar's Derby victory in 1981. His 10 lengths triumph was the biggest ever winning margin in this race.*

almost bringing him to a standstill; his was a brave recovery but since second place was the best he could realistically hope for, it did not make much difference.

Walter Swinburn always had *Shergar* well placed, not far behind leaders *Riberetto* and *Silver Season*. He came round Tattenham Corner on their outside simply cruising, and young Walter did not disappoint the horse for long, allowing him to coast into the lead and set sail for home as they entered the straight.

*Scintillating Air*, *Church Parade* and *Shotgun* did their best to go with him, but fully three furlongs from home the writing was on the wall. To the cheering crowds in the stands, on the lawn and lining the rails, as well as those who could see out on the Downs, there was this broad white face galloping effortlessly towards them, and the nearer it came, the more grass was put between the horse and its toiling rivals. Never before had a Derby winner so completely made the rest look like selling platers.

## A NEW RECORD

It is even said that the rider of the second, John Mathias, thought that he was winning as he came past the rest of the pack, so far out of sight was the winner! Exaggeration that may be, but it sums up the manner of the victory!

Walter Swinburn was easing *Shergar* long before the line, and even so the winning distance was a record ten lengths, recalling one of racing's best known sayings: '*Eclipse* first and the rest nowhere!'

Behind *Glint of Gold* came *Scintillating Air*, with Lester Piggott fourth on *Shotgun*, the Queen's colt *Church Parade* fifth, and *Sheer Grit* sixth ahead of the early pacemakers *Silver Season* and *Riberetto*.

The rest were well and truly 'out with the washing', — even though the race time, with the winner being eased up before the line, was the slowest since 1946. The previous longest winning margin recorded had been eight lengths by *Manna*, ridden by Steve Donoghue in 1925.

Less than three years had gone by since Walter Swinburn had ridden his first winner, and he modestly confessed he was 'just a passenger' this time, but that does not give credit to the sense and coolness with which he rode. Five years later, by now well established in his profession, he was to win again, on a horse of the same owner/breeder and trainer, *Sharastani*.

## FURTHER SUCCESSES

As for *Shergar*, he had a temperament to match his young rider's and came out of the race with flying colours, as fresh as paint. He was without his young pilot, through suspension, for his next race, the Irish Derby when Lester Piggott took his place — and won by an easy four lengths.

Walter Swinburn was back on board for *Shergar's* first attempt against older rivals in the King George VI and Queen Elizabeth Diamond Stakes at Royal Ascot.

By this time, of a significance only to become apparent a year and a half later, the Aga Khan had said he was willing for *Shergar* to stand at his Ballymany Stud in Ireland, so long as enough financial support could be found from British-based breeders. It was clear he could make much more money in America, but nevertheless, enough people came forward to invest £250,000 each to create a consortium ownership in the fabulous colt, and thereby keep his stud services available in Britain.

All this was in hand by the time of the King George, when *Shergar* set the seal on his two Derby victories. Only six turned out against him, and although for one awful moment it looked as if he might be trapped on the rails on the home turn, a gap appeared in time. *Shergar*, switching to overdrive, galloped through and, throwing off any challenges effortlessly, he beat the 40-1 shots *Madam Gay* and *Fingal's Cave* by another impressive four lengths.

## A TRAGIC FINALE

Sadly, *Shergar's* story takes a downward spiral from there. Like other bright summer flowers, he wilted somewhat in the autumn and was trounced by *Glint of Gold* in the St. Leger, finishing only fourth. It was the only really moderate race of his life, and it was his last, it then being decided to retire him to stud instead of going for the Prix de l'Arc de Triomphe.

There was every reason to suppose that *Shergar* would be a success at stud, but on the night of February 9, 1983, he was stolen from his stable. It is believed his kidnappers intended to demand a hefty ransom from the Aga Khan, without realising that the horse was no longer in his full ownership, but that of the consortium made before the King George.

*Shergar* was never seen again, but no-one who saw him will forget that broad white face blazing the Epsom trail.

# THE OAKS

IT WAS IN 1779 that Lord Derby, dining with Sir Charles Bunbury at The Oaks, his home near Epsom, devised a new race. It was to be for three-year-old fillies and run in one heat only of one and a half miles following the trend set by Anthony St. Leger at Doncaster. It was usual at that time for horses not to start racing until they were four or five years old and the distance was usually four miles, sometimes two, with two or three heats culminating in a final to determine the winner. By the time the winner had been decided the horses had sometimes raced up to 16 miles in the one day! The new race flouted this convention and was to be called The Oaks after Lord Derby's house.

There have been some great and popular winners of The Oaks. Nine of them have gone on to take the Fillies' Triple Crown, a feat which consists of winning the 1,000 Guineas, The Oaks and St. Leger. *Sceptre* was perhaps the greatest of these adding the 2,000 Guineas to her Triple Crown in 1902. In more recent times, *Oh So Sharp* owned by Sheikh Mohammed and ridden by Steve Cauthen lived up to her name by taking the Triple Crown during the 1985 season. However, there has been no more popular winner of this Classic than *Dunfermline* in 1977, for not only was she owned by the Queen, but this was also the Queen's Silver Jubilee year.

*Unite, pictured in the winner's enclosure after the 1987 Oaks. The race is run over the same course as the Derby.*

*Dunfermline edges ahead of Freeze the Secret to win the 1977 Oaks for the Queen by ¾ of a length.*

## DUNFERMLINE

The Queen is a fine judge of horse-flesh and finds the attraction of breeding and following the progress of her own stock on the Flat greater than National Hunt racing which she entered briefly in partnership with her mother during the 1949/50 season with *Monaveen*.

*Dunfermline* was a bright bay filly by the 1967 Derby winner *Royal Palace* out of the Queen's own mare *Strathcona* (by *St Paddy* the 1960 St. Leger winner), which she also bred out of a mare she selected herself, *Stroma*.

*Dunfermline*, quite tall with powerful hind-quarters was as lean as a greyhound when fit; she was a beautiful mover and, an invaluable quality in a racehorse, always tried her best.

*Dunfermline* made it a Royal Jubilee to remember by winning two Classics, the Oaks and the St. Leger. There were those who judged the Oaks victory as lucky, following the late withdrawal of the hot favourite *Durtal*, but she underlined her ability by beating the colts in the Leger.

### DAY OF DRAMA

Oaks day was full of drama. First, the ebullient royal jockey Willie Carson was involved in a car crash en route to Epsom. Luckily he was unhurt, but nevertheless he missed the first race and royal trainer Major Dick Hern had jockey Joe Mercer standing by.

Willie Carson made it in time, and, with prospects hopeful rather than high, nerves were not too taut. The filly, too, remained cool as she paraded in front of the Queen Mother and the crowd, the Queen being unable to be present.

There were 14 runners including the 1,000 Guineas winner and runner-up, *Mrs McArdy* and *Freeze the Secret*, and as they paraded in the June warmth, and prepared to canter to the start, *Dunfermline* sweated a little, but still seemed quite relaxed.

Suddenly it became apparent that it was the the favourite, *Durtal*, who was tense, and that

21

her jockey Lester Piggott was being 'carted'. A few strides later, she bumped into the rails, smashing a stirrup iron; this left Lester Piggott in real trouble, for without the iron, he could not use the strength in his legs to try and control her.

The filly panicked and headed straight for a solid rail; there was no way round it and, as she half tried to jump it, Lester was thrown, but his other foot was caught in the remaining stirrup iron. This is any rider's nightmare, for they can then be dragged, which in turn frightens the horse even more . . .

Mercifully his foot became free, and the filly galloped off, leaving Lester looking very shaken, but amazingly not seriously hurt. It had been a narrow squeak.

The start, of course, was delayed while *Durtal* was caught and withdrawn; inevitably, many felt that this affected the result, but Willie Carson himself always felt that the favourite's stamina was suspect and could have been tested.

*A jubilant Willie Carson pulls up having won the Oaks on Dunfermline. Later in the season he was to repeat his Epsom success in the longer distance St. Leger beating in the process the unbeaten colt, Alleged.*

**Above** *Brigadier Gerard crosses the line to win the epic 2000 Guineas confrontation with Mill Reef and the French colt, My Swallow.*

**Left** *A fine specimen at 16.2 hands, Brigadier Gerard, pictured here with Joe Mercer up, also had an ideal temperament taking most that life had to offer in his stride.*

bay with black points and small white star by *Queen's Hussar*.

They were looking at the start of a racing legend, *Brigadier Gerard*.

Owned by John and Jean Hislop, the colt was destined to win one of the highest class, most memorable 2,000 Guineas ever run, and was beaten only once in 18 races.

Without doubt he was blessed in possessing both astute owners and his trainer, Dick Hern. John Hislop was former champion amateur rider on the Flat for 13 consecutive seasons, an author and, with his wife, racehorse owner and breeder though without the backing of millions of pounds behind them. They had long harboured the dream of owning a brood mare tracing to their equine heroine *Pretty Polly*, which with the acquisition of *La Paiva's* dam for 400gns, they at last achieved.

## PREPARING A CHAMPION

Trainer Dick Hern, based not at Newmarket but on the undulations at East Ilsley, Berkshire, neither hurried the colt, gambled on him nor overworked him at home. In John Hislop's account of 'The Brigadier', he acclaims Dick Hern's training of him as 'a copy-book example of how a racehorse should be prepared for his engagements'.

The Brigadier had neither preferential treatment nor anything other than the most orthodox training. He had only one serious gallop before he ran in his first race, was joint-outsider when he first ran, and won by five lengths. Another bonus for *Brigadier Gerard*, apart from his own equable temperament and prodigious ability, was to have one top class jockey only throughout his career, Joe Mercer.

After *Brigadier Gerard's* second win, Joe dismounted and said, 'I don't know what this horse is; all I know is that when I ask him he just goes 'ping' and he's there'.

The policy of good breaks between races continued to the enormous benefit of the colt; he muscled up, strengthened and continued to gain in confidence.

## CLASSIC POTENTIAL

After three straight wins as a two-year-old, he headed for the more valuable Middle Park Stakes to assess whether he might be Classic material; he was only third favourite, but he dominated the paddock and the race, beating *Mummy's Pet* by three lengths with his ears pricked.

John Hislop writes in 'The Brigadier', 'It was a truly thrilling moment. To have won the Middle Park Stakes was a triumph in itself, but for the Brigadier to have slaughtered the opposition in this way was unbelievable. His right to contest the Two Thousand Guineas had been won with honours'.

Nevertheless, the Brigadier was not the talking horse for the 2,000 Guineas, far from it. For born in the same year as him was not one but two other outstanding colts, *Mill Reef* and *My Swallow*, and they were greatly preferred, finishing within 1lb of each other at the top of the Free Handicap, just 1lb ahead of *Brigadier Gerard*.

*My Swallow* won all seven of his two-year-old starts, most of them in France, while *Mill Reef* won six of his seven. That defeat came at the hands of *My Swallow*, but only by a short head. The only other defeat of his life was inflicted by *Brigadier Gerard*...

The Brigadier had not been as quick to mature as his two main rivals, but during the winter between his two and three year old seasons he

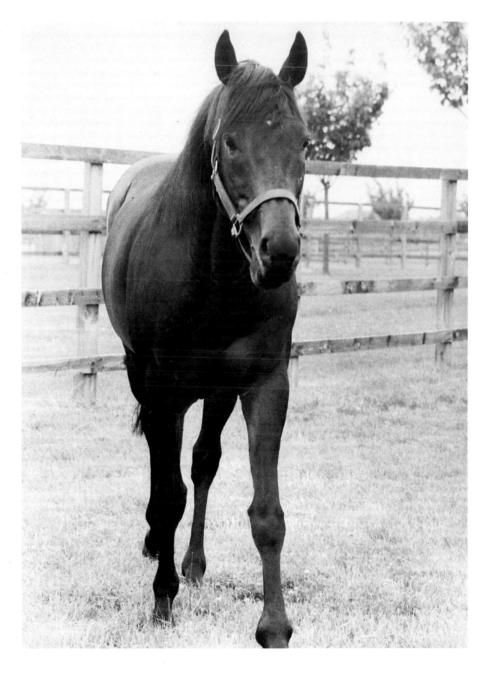

*The winner of six of his seven two-year-old starts, Mill Reef (pictured right) was the 6-4 favourite for the 1971 2000 Guineas.*

28

grew an inch, from 16.1 hands to 16.2 hands, which is big for a flat racer. He went from strength to strength and had an ideal temperament, taking most things that life had to offer in his stride. It was a tremendous advantage to him, for it meant he would not boil over, or throw away his races at home.

Perhaps the biggest credit of all to both horse and trainer is that he came to the 2,000 Guineas without a 'prep' race at all. Connections did not want a pre-Guineas clash with either *My Swallow* or *Mill Reef*, which could have expended too much energy in advance of the big one. It was well known in advance which race each of his rivals was to contest, and they both duly won them.

These were the two, then, who had been seen in public before the season's first Classic, and surrounding whom was all the Press build up and speculation. But horses like *Crepello* and *Royal Palace* had won the Guineas without a previous race, and John Hislop made no secret of the improvement he thought his horse had made.

## A CLASSIC ENCOUNTER
At last 2,000 Guineas day dawned, May 1, 1971, and a huge crowd came to Newmarket on a perfect spring day to watch the great race; the principal three were so far ahead of anything else that only another three took them on — one of those started at 100-1, and another, *Minsky*, was a full brother to Triple Crown winner *Nijinsky* — so it was the smallest field for over 80 years. It was *Minsky's* 'coltishness' that was in some corners used to explain the defeat of *Mill Reef* who was apparently upset by it, but one cannot help feeling this is an excuse.

The six runners came into the paddock and spectators craned their necks for their first view of *Brigadier Gerard* since the previous autumn. When he walked in, cool, calm and unruffled, they saw an exquisite racehorse, worthy to rival the market-leading pair both of whom were trained to the minute. All three cantered down to the start looking a picture of perfection; a real hum-dinger was in prospect.

They came under starter's orders and were off to a perfect break on the Rowley Mile's fast ground. As usual *My Swallow*, who had won all his previous races from in front, set off in the lead. He and *Mill Reef* were drawn on either side of the course but it was not long before they began to converge and race in earnest down the

centre of the course. Probably most of the crowds thought they were watching a two horse race; they were going a strong but not ridiculous gallop and made a great sight.

## A CLASSIC WINNER
*Mill Reef* moved up beside *My Swallow* at The Bushes, a clump beside the course that serves as a landmark three furlongs from home, and looked as if he might get the better of the duel, but at the same moment Joe Mercer decided to make his move. The rest were now effectively out of it, although *Minsky* had raced in third for some way.

With two furlongs to run, Joe gave *Brigadier Gerard* the order to go, and the response was instantaneous. Within a few strides, the colt had drawn level with and shot clear of the other pair — and there he stayed all the way to the line, to win by three clear lengths, one of the most impressive ever winners of the Guineas in what was already a vintage year!

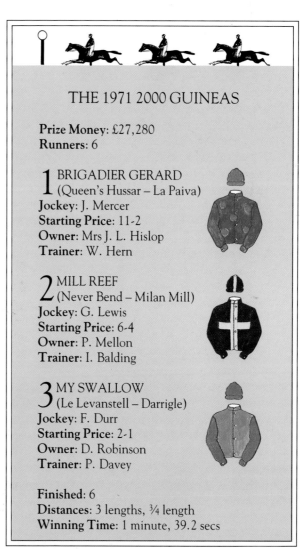

## THE 1971 2000 GUINEAS

**Prize Money:** £27,280
**Runners:** 6

**1 BRIGADIER GERARD**
(Queen's Hussar – La Paiva)
**Jockey:** J. Mercer
**Starting Price:** 11-2
**Owner:** Mrs J. L. Hislop
**Trainer:** W. Hern

**2 MILL REEF**
(Never Bend – Milan Mill)
**Jockey:** G. Lewis
**Starting Price:** 6-4
**Owner:** P. Mellon
**Trainer:** I. Balding

**3 MY SWALLOW**
(Le Levanstell – Darrigle)
**Jockey:** F. Durr
**Starting Price:** 2-1
**Owner:** D. Robinson
**Trainer:** P. Davey

**Finished:** 6
**Distances:** 3 lengths, ¾ length
**Winning Time:** 1 minute, 39.2 secs

# THE 1000 GUINEAS

THE 1,000 GUINEAS is for three-year-old fillies only, run over a straight mile at the Newmarket Spring meeting on the Rowley Mile course. It was founded five years after the 2,000 Guineas, making it the youngest Classic, its first winner in 1814 being a filly called *Charlotte*.

The Queen won the 1,000 Guineas in 1974 with *Highclere*, her father, King George VI, having won it in 1942 with *Sun Chariot* who, by also winning the Oaks and the St. Leger, held the fillies' Triple Crown.

*Sun Chariot* was by *Hyperion* and showed considerable 'temperament' but in the Guineas, although swishing her tail, she won easily by four lengths. At the same meeting, the King also won the 2,000 Guineas with *Big Game*, a wonderful Royal moment in the history of the Turf.

Two of the greatest fillies to grace the Turf won shortly after the turn of the century, *Sceptre* who came the closest ever to winning all five Classics in 1902, and *Pretty Polly* in 1904.

In 1892, *La Flèche*, who was bred by Queen Victoria, also won the fillies' Triple Crown and was second in the Derby. After winning all four of her races as a two year old, she was winter favourite for the Guineas, and won it 'in a canter'.

Two outstanding fillies won in 1955 and 1959 in *Meld* and *Petite Etoile* — *Meld* going on to win the fillies' Triple Crown.

*Pebbles, ridden by Philip Robinson, leads the 1984 1000 Guineas field.*

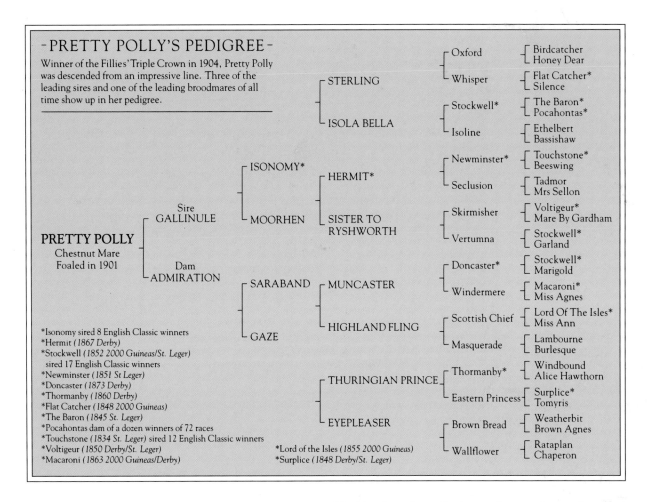

## -PRETTY POLLY'S PEDIGREE-

Winner of the Fillies' Triple Crown in 1904, Pretty Polly was descended from an impressive line. Three of the leading sires and one of the leading broodmares of all time show up in her pedigree.

**PRETTY POLLY**
Chestnut Mare
Foaled in 1901

Sire
GALLINULE

Dam
ADMIRATION

ISONOMY*

MOORHEN

SARABAND

GAZE

HERMIT*

SISTER TO RYSHWORTH

MUNCASTER

HIGHLAND FLING

THURINGIAN PRINCE

EYEPLEASER

STERLING

ISOLA BELLA

Oxford

Whisper

Stockwell*

Isoline

Newminster*

Seclusion

Skirmisher

Vertumna

Doncaster*

Windermere

Scottish Chief

Masquerade

Thormanby*

Eastern Princess

Brown Bread

Wallflower

Birdcatcher
Honey Dear

Flat Catcher*
Silence

The Baron*
Pocahontas*

Ethelbert
Bassishaw

Touchstone*
Beeswing

Tadmor
Mrs Sellon

Voltigeur*
Mare By Gardham

Stockwell*
Garland

Stockwell*
Marigold

Macaroni*
Miss Agnes

Lord Of The Isles*
Miss Ann

Lambourne
Burlesque

Windbound
Alice Hawthorn

Surplice*
Tomyris

Weatherbit
Brown Agnes

Rataplan
Chaperon

*Isonomy sired 8 English Classic winners
*Hermit (1867 Derby)
*Stockwell (1852 2000 Guineas/St. Leger)
sired 17 English Classic winners
*Newminster (1851 St Leger)
*Doncaster (1873 Derby)
*Thormanby (1860 Derby)
*Flat Catcher (1848 2000 Guineas)
*Pocahontas dam of a dozen winners of 72 races
*Touchstone (1834 St. Leger) sired 12 English Classic winners
*Voltigeur (1850 Derby/St. Leger)
*Macaroni (1863 2000 Guineas/Derby)

*Lord of the Isles (1855 2000 Guineas)
*Surplice (1848 Derby/St. Leger)

## ENSTONE SPARK

Every so often, the Press and public gets hold of a 'talking horse' and then, no matter what, they don't let go. Such was *Cherry Hinton*, a precocious two-year-old who was considered a 'certainty' for the 1,000 Guineas of 1978.

That she was well beaten in her seasonal début in the Fred Darling Stakes at Newbury did not stop her going to Newmarket as 85-40 favourite in a field of 16. She was ridden by the maestro, Lester Piggott, which added support for her, and she had an excellent trainer in Harry Wragg.

To the observant, however, there were ominous signs before the race as, on a perfect spring day, she sweated considerably in the preliminaries.

Second and third favourites were *Seraphima* at 5-1 and *Clear Picture*, 6-1. Right out at 35-1 was *Enstone Spark*, a bay filly by *Sparkler* who had cost a minuscule 3,400 guineas as a yearling.

## A TALENTED OUTSIDER

Nevertheless her victories as a two-year-old, when trained by Richard Hannon, had included York's Lowther Stakes. Since then she had changed hands and, by the Guineas, she was owned by Mr Richard Bonnycastle and trained by Barry Hills at Lambourn.

In the race, the lead was taken first by *Best Girl* and then *Seraphima* went on, with *Cherry Hinton* handily placed just in behind, giving her supporters plenty of encouragement.

## FALL OF THE FAVOURITE

But at the moment that mattered, when Lester Piggott asked her to quicken a furlong from home, there was not enough juice left in the tank, and *Cherry Hinton* was left toiling.

It was at about this moment that *Enstone Spark*, strongly ridden by Ernie Johnson, moved up to the head of affairs. It was her first run of the season, but she ran on most gamely as *Fair Salinia* launched a strong challenge.

The pair of them made a good race of it, with *Enstone Spark* holding on by a length, a victory that, on reflection, deserves all the more credit as *Fair Salinia* went on to dual Classic success, winning both the Oaks and Irish Oaks a few weeks later.

*Seraphima* finished two and a half lengths further back in third, with *Cherry Hinton* and *Clear Picture* not far behind in fourth and fifth.

Unplaced some ten lengths behind the winner was *Swiss Maid*, the Paul Kelleway-trained filly who was to beat Derby runner-up *Hawaiian Sound* in the Champion Stakes later that summer, and who was to fetch a record price for a horse in training at Newmarket's Tattersalls Sales.

So, although *Enstone Spark* did not win another race that year, her Guineas win was no mean performance, and it also gave Barry Hills, who now trains at the magical Manton establishment near Marlborough, his first ever Classic win.

## PEBBLES

What a super little horse *Pebbles* was, winner in 1984 of the 1,000 Guineas and in 1985 of the Breeders' Cup Turf in America.

Bright chestnut with a white blaze but no white on her legs, she was trained by Clive Brittain and bred by Captain Marcos Lemos being by *Sharpen Up* out of *La Dolce* by *Connaught*.

### A STEADY START

She proved a good but not outstanding two year old, when she won two of her six outings. She was also fourth in the Group II Lowther Stakes, and was second, beaten a neck by *Desirable*, in the Group 1 Cheveley Park Stakes. This was good enough to put her at the top of the two-year-old filly tree.

She became a very good but not brilliant three-year-old when her best claim to fame was in winning the 1,000 Guineas. Even before that, she had stamped herself as a filly with guts, when she produced a determined win first time out in the Nell Gwynn Stakes, beating *Leipzig* by a length, with *Meis El-Reem*, who had had the benefit of a previous outing, a further length and a half back in third.

### THE FIRST CLASSIC

She was installed second favourite for the first classic of the year, the 1,000 Guineas, on the strength of that race but *Mahogany*, who had headed the ante-post lists all winter, had become an even hotter favourite after an impressive win in the Fred Darling Stakes.

There were fifteen runners for the Guineas. *Mahogany* was the 6-5 favourite, and was followed in the betting by *Pebbles* and *Desirable*, who had

not run since beating *Pebbles* in the Cheveley Park Stakes the previous September, at 8-1. Luca Cumani's *Capricorn Belle*, also without an outing that season, was at 11-1, *Seattle Siren* at 14-1, then *Miss Beaulieu* and *Shoot Clear*, *Mahogany's* chief victim at Newbury, at 16-1.

As she had done before, *Pebbles* really sweated up and played up in the paddock beforehand, but she was got down to the post and installed without too much further worry.

*Meis El-Reem* tried to make every post a winning one and blazed a trail from *Miss Silca Key*, *Glowing with Pride* and *Capricorn Belle*, whilst *Pebbles* pulled hard, giving jockey Philip Robinson a testing time of it.

### A HARD WON VICTORY

At the two furlong pole *Meis El-Reem* was still in front, but *Pebbles, Desirable, Shoot Clear* and *Mahogany* were all making forward moves to challenge the leader.

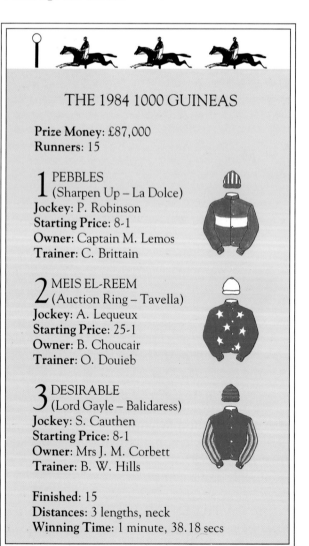

### THE 1984 1000 GUINEAS

**Prize Money:** £87,000
**Runners:** 15

1 PEBBLES
(Sharpen Up – La Dolce)
**Jockey:** P. Robinson
**Starting Price:** 8-1
**Owner:** Captain M. Lemos
**Trainer:** C. Brittain

2 MEIS EL-REEM
(Auction Ring – Tavella)
**Jockey:** A. Lequeux
**Starting Price:** 25-1
**Owner:** B. Choucair
**Trainer:** O. Douieb

3 DESIRABLE
(Lord Gayle – Balidaress)
**Jockey:** S. Cauthen
**Starting Price:** 8-1
**Owner:** Mrs J. M. Corbett
**Trainer:** B. W. Hills

**Finished:** 15
**Distances:** 3 lengths, neck
**Winning Time:** 1 minute, 38.18 secs

*Pebbles, in the colours of Sheikh Mohammed, wins the 1988 Champion Stakes during her victorious 4-year-old campaign. That year she also became the first filly ever to win the Eclipse Stakes and went on to win the Breeders' Cup Turf.*

*Shoot Clear* and *Pebbles* looked short of room but Robinson found a way through and pushed *Pebbles* Past *Meis El-Reem* inside the final furlong and once she had hit the front, the filly stormed clear to win by a convincing three lengths.

*Meis El-Reem* kept on to hold second place a neck in front of the fast finishing *Desirable* with *Shoot Clear* a further three-quarters of a length back in fourth.

After the Guineas she was sold by the Captain to Sheikh Mohammed, who switched her from the Oaks for which Clive Brittain had trained her, to Royal Ascot's Coronation Stakes in which she was beaten a length and a half by *Katies*, winner of the Irish 1,000 Guineas.

Trained for a rematch with *Meis El-Reem* in the Child Stakes, she stood on a stone just before the race and her only other outing that year was after a four month lay-off when she ran a very good second to *Palace Music* and was beaten by a neck.

## FOUR-YEAR-OLD TRIUMPH

At four she really reached the height of her powers, lending strong support to the argument in favour of keeping a horse in training beyond three; she won four of her five starts.

First she won the Trusthouse Forte Mile at Sandown easily, then went under by a head when slightly below par in the Prince of Wales's Stakes at Royal Ascot to shock 33-1 winner *Bob Back*.

She bounced back to become the first filly ever to win the Eclipse, beating *Rainbow Quest* who later won the Arc, no less. In the Champion Stakes she passed that year's Derby winner *Slip Anchor* as if he were standing.

She truly stamped herself world champion in America running in the Breeders' Cup Turf, held that year at Aqueduct Racecourse New York. There were 14 runners, and it was clear as the field turned out of the back straight and headed towards home that she was going the best. Although she had only a neck to spare on the line over the ex-Australian *Strawberry Road*, himself a good horse, she was truly the superior and stamped herself a world class turf champion.

# THE DEWHURST STAKES

THE DEWHURST STAKES was founded in 1875, and is one of the season's last major two-year-old tests, being run in October over seven furlongs at Newmarket.

It has been won by many future champions in its time, including such distinguished names as *Bayardo, Hyperion, Nijinsky, Mill Reef, Grundy, The Minstrel* and *El Gran Señor*. Robert Sangster and Vincent O'Brien were the winning owner/trainer combination five times in eight years from the mid 1970s.

## MILL REEF

When *Mill Reef* won in 1970 there were only three runners, but the neat colt by *Never Bend* out of *Milan Mill* had already established himself as top Classic material.

Bred in Virginia by his American owner Paul Mellon, he was trained at Kingsclere, Berkshire, by Ian Balding. He was a small, neat, athletic colt blessed with a perfect temperament and his race record was quite outstanding.

### CLASSIC QUALITIES

To jockey Geoff Lewis he was a rider's dream, 'easy to ride and easy to handle'. He adds, in My Greatest Race, 'He was a delightful little character. He was a kind horse with a marvellous temperament — especially on the big occasion.'

'Although full of quality, he always looked rather unpretentious in the paddock before a race. But the moment I was on his back and felt that flawless, magical action as he cantered to the post, I was filled with confidence.'

'He was brilliant in the stalls, totally relaxed, and yet always out like a rocket'.

*Mill Reef* confounded the punters on his racecourse début when he beat the Lester Piggott-ridden odds-on favourite at Salisbury by four lengths, making all the running. He won the Coventry Stakes by eight lengths, installing him

**Left** *Mill Reef in a formal pose photographed at Kingsclere.*

**Right** *Heading home the "King George" field as a champion three-year-old in 1971. After his 2000 Guineas disappointment he made amends by winning the Derby, the Eclipse and the Prix de l'Arc de Triomphe.*

as winter favourite for the 2,000 Guineas, but met with a gallant short-head defeat by *My Swallow* in France after a terrible journey over.

He redeemed himself by winning the Gimcrack Stakes by ten lengths, York's prestigious two-year-old race after which it is customary for the winning owner to make a speech at the Gimcrack Dinner later in the year, and followed that up with a narrower victory in the Imperial Stakes.

## TWO-YEAR-OLD FINALE

On October 16, 1970, looking as well at the end of a busy season as he had at the start, he travelled to Newmarket for the Dewhurst Stakes on good ground. With his number of wins, many of them by exceptionally wide margins especially for a juvenile, only two opponents faced him.

*Mill Reef* at 9-2 on was drawn in the centre between *Lombardo*, the second favourite ridden by Lester Piggott, and the outsider *Wenceslas*, ridden by Liam Ward.

*Wenceslas* set off in the lead and stayed there for the first five furlongs of the seven furlong straight course but then *Mill Reef* cruised through and never looked like being challenged to run out a comfortable four lengths winner. Behind him, outsider *Wenceslas* held off *Lombardo* to take second place by half a length.

## A BRILLIANT CAREER

*Mill Reef* was beaten only once more in his career, by *Brigadier Gerard* in the Guineas. He was a popular and deserving winner of the Derby, of the Eclipse by four lengths, of the King George VI and Queen Elizabeth Stakes by six lengths and of the Prix de l'Arc de Triomphe by three lengths, stamping him a truly great champion.

He stayed in training at four and won the Prix Ganay by ten lengths. Later that season he broke a leg on the gallops but happily his life was saved, and he stood at the National Stud until his death at the age of 18.

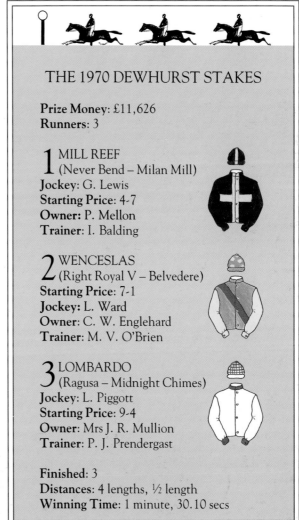

### THE 1970 DEWHURST STAKES

**Prize Money:** £11,626
**Runners:** 3

**1** MILL REEF
(Never Bend – Milan Mill)
**Jockey:** G. Lewis
**Starting Price:** 4-7
**Owner:** P. Mellon
**Trainer:** I. Balding

**2** WENCESLAS
(Right Royal V – Belvedere)
**Starting Price:** 7-1
**Jockey:** L. Ward
**Owner:** C. W. Englehard
**Trainer:** M. V. O'Brien

**3** LOMBARDO
(Ragusa – Midnight Chimes)
**Jockey:** L. Piggott
**Starting Price:** 9-4
**Owner:** Mrs J. R. Mullion
**Trainer:** P. J. Prendergast

**Finished:** 3
**Distances:** 4 lengths, ½ length
**Winning Time:** 1 minute, 30.10 secs

# DONCASTER

'SUNNY DONNY' is no idle name for Doncaster because it greets and is greeted with smiles and enthusiasm from all who come to it or work for it. Home of the oldest Classic in the calendar, the St. Leger, to northerners, is *the* race. They pour on to Town Moor on the city's edge in their thousands, resplendent in their finery and eager to witness and wager upon the final flat classic of the season.

The course at Doncaster is left-handed and has a hill on the far side. It has a straight mile, and a round course of two miles, inside which is the National Hunt course, revived and made a permanent feature of racing at Doncaster after the Second World War. The land was a common but is now looked after by the Doncaster Metropolitan Borough Council (formerly Doncaster Corporation) as Lords of the Manor by virtue of a charter granted by Henry VIII. The junction of the round and straight courses is known as Red House Farm and it is not far on from this point that many a Derby winner has begun to find the Leger's extra furlongs a burden not easily overcome.

It is known that racing took place here as far back as 1595, and in 1616 Doncaster Corporation was paying a man 1/6d for keeping the course clear during the races!

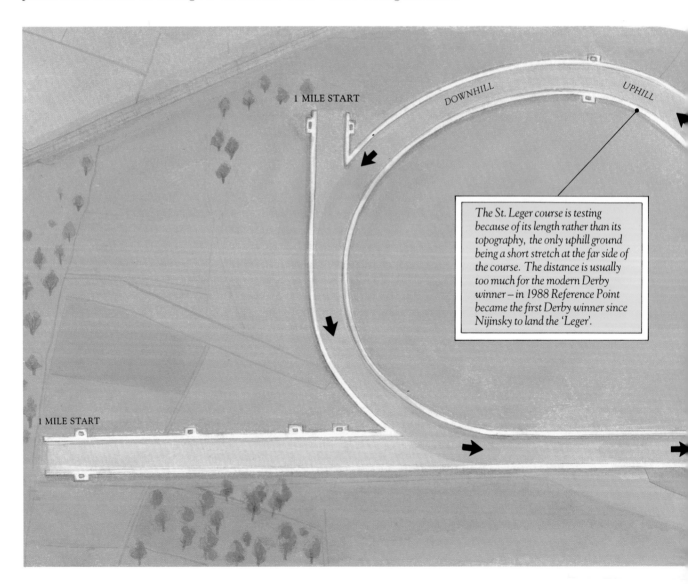

1 MILE START

DOWNHILL

UPHILL

1 MILE START

The St. Leger course is testing because of its length rather than its topography, the only uphill ground being a short stretch at the far side of the course. The distance is usually too much for the modern Derby winner – in 1988 Reference Point became the first Derby winner since Nijinsky to land the 'Leger'.

*Looking up the finishing straight at Doncaster close to the winning post. The parade ring and the old grandstand are in the centre of the picture.*

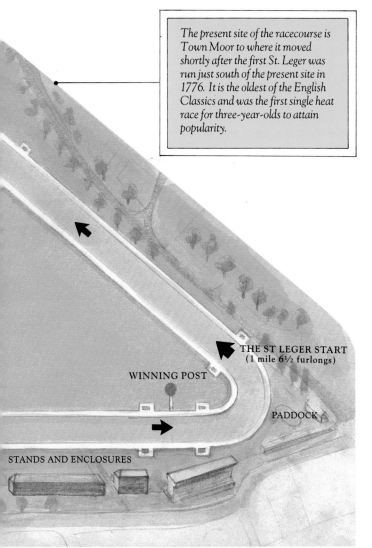

*The present site of the racecourse is Town Moor to where it moved shortly after the first St. Leger was run just south of the present site in 1776. It is the oldest of the English Classics and was the first single heat race for three-year-olds to attain popularity.*

THE ST LEGER START
(1 mile 6½ furlongs)

WINNING POST

PADDOCK

STANDS AND ENCLOSURES

Witnessing the good-humour and orderly nature of the modern Doncaster crowd, it is difficult to imagine that in 1617 the corporation ordered the grandstand to be pulled down and the races to cease because of brawls and riotous behaviour.

Luckily they had a change of heart and the next year paid twelve pence 'for making a way for the horse race at the water gapp'. In 1710 the corporation agreed to pay £5 for five years 'to encourage horse racing on Doncaster Moor'. By 1776, the year of the first Leger, racing was thriving to such an extent that the corporation went on to build a new grandstand and a new course as well.

The grand-stand, opened in 1969, is bedecked by colourful flowers for the Leger meeting in September and even the paddock attendants are decked out in bright red and yellow jackets.

# THE ST. LEGER

*A painting by Henry Alken showing the finish of the 1848 St. Leger. Note the rural background compared to today's urban scenery at Town Moor.*

YORKSHIREMEN claim that the fittest horse wins the Guineas, first of the year's Classics and run at Newmarket, the luckiest wins the Derby where perhaps survival is the name of the game — and the best wins the St. Leger.

Founded in 1776 by Colonel Anthony St. Leger, it was for three-year-olds only over two miles, going against the trend for longer races contested by older horses. The current length of just over one and three-quarter miles came in in 1813, still making it the longest Classic race.

## ENDURING TRADITION

When it became fashionable to breed ever faster and more precocious horses over shorter and shorter distances, the St. Leger looked doomed; no-one wanted an out and out stayer to breed from, so at one time it became almost a disadvantage to win this particular Classic. Matters have a habit of turning full circle, however, and although the proximity of a far more valuable race like the Prix de l'Arc de Triomphe can detract from it, some very good horses continue to win the Leger. Indeed, the triumph in 1970 of *Nijinsky* who became such an influential stallion, did much to restore its prestige.

The first winner of the St. Leger was on the old course at Cantley Common, just south of the Town Moor, and was a filly, Lord Rockingham's *Allabaculia*. Fillies continue to take on the colts in this Classic, the Queen's *Dunfermline* won in 1977, *Sun Princess* in 1983 and *Oh So Sharp* in 1985. *Diminuendo* was favourite in 1988, but hard though she tried, she could not catch *Minster Son*, ridden by his breeder Willie Carson.

It was a filly who won the third running in

1778, *Hollandaise*, and she was ridden by George Herring to whom went the honour of riding the winners of 19 successive races.

In 1822 the winner *Theodore* was so lame at the start that his owner sold all his betting tickets on him, and missed winning a fortune as a result, while in 1803, the jockey Benjamin Smith was kicked at the start and broke his leg, but still rode *Remembrancer* to victory. The first overseas winner was the mighty *Gladiateur* from France in 1865, who thus completed the Triple Crown.

## VOLTIGEUR

One of racing's old time greats is *Voltigeur*, who won both the Derby and St. Leger of 1850, and who contested a famous match, the 'race of the century' against *The Flying Dutchman* who had won the same two Classics the year before.

*Voltigeur* was a stocky, brown colt by *Voltaire*, bred in Yorkshire at the time when that county was pre-eminent in racing circles, both for breeding and training. Kindly natured, he allowed the stable cat to sleep on his back for hours on end. The whole of his pedigree on both sides traced to the Godolphin and Darley Arabians — two of the three great founders of the thoroughbred racehorse — while he became great grandsire of *St. Simon*, unbeaten in nine races and Champion Sire nine times.

*A stylized print of the great Voltigeur. Note the length of the stirrups compared to the modern racing position.*

### A BARGAIN BUY

He was sent to Tattersalls' Yearling Sales but failed to procure a bid, and was finally bought privately the following spring. He won his only race as a two-year-old and became a winter favourite for the Derby. This was his first race as a three-year-old and in a field of 24, he won nicely by a length, ridden by Job Marson.

By the time he went to the St. Leger, he was odds-on favourite, but this time things did not go smoothly. A horse called *Chatterbox* continually interfered with him, so that in the end Marson was forced to take the lead sooner than he really wanted to.

Consternation mounted in the stands when, with a furlong left to run, it was clear *Voltigeur* did not have much left in hand, and a horse called *Russborough*, a stable companion to the irksome *Chatterbox*, was challenging.

### FROM THE EDGE OF DEFEAT

To most eyes it looked as if the outsider passed *Voltigeur*, but the judge called a dead-heat. In those days, instead of sharing the prize, the two dead-heaters had to contest a run-off taking place two hours later.

This time, victory belonged to *Voltigeur*, but only after a hard fought contest. Just two days later, he beat *The Flying Dutchman* in the Doncaster Cup by half a length; a re-match for £1,000 a side was arranged for the following year at York, when the result was reversed by a 'short length' in front of a tremendous crowd.

## LIGHT CAVALRY

In 1980, the black jacket and red cap colours made famous by nearly one thousand winners of the Joel family stormed past the Doncaster winning post for *Light Cavalry* to add that year's St. Leger to the tally.

Nowhere can there be a man who is more the epitome of an old breed than nonagenarian Mr H. J. 'Jim' Joel, whose beautifully maintained Childwick Bury Stud near St. Alban's has been his life-time's hobby and a retreat from the demanding world of his South African diamond business.

### BREEDING LINES

The stud was founded in 1907 and became one of the show pieces of English private studs. Two cheap racing cast-offs, the colt *Sundridge* and tiny mare *Doris*, formed its foundation and they produced the 1911 Derby winner *Sunstar*.

One of the bravest Classic winners ever, followed in *Humorist*, who won the 2,000 Guineas and Derby of 1921 in spite of having only one lung working, a defect that was not discovered until later that year when he was found dead in his box from a massive haemorrhage.

Jim Joel inherited the stud in 1940 and upheld the tradition of its immaculate maintenance as well as its top class breeding policy. Of more than 800 flat race winners, over 500 of them have

### THE 1980 ST. LEGER

**Prize Money:** £71,256
**Runners:** 7

1 **LIGHT CAVALRY** (Brigadier Gerard – Glass Slipper)
**Jockey:** J. Mercer
**Starting Price:** 3-1
**Owner:** H. J. Joel
**Trainer:** H. Cecil

2 **WATER MILL** (Mill Reef – Heavenly Thought)
**Jockey:** W. Carson
**Starting Price:** 11-8
**Owner:** Lord Rotherwick
**Trainer:** W. Hern

3 **WORLD LEADER** (Bolkonski – Worlica)
**Jockey:** R. Guest
**Starting Price:** 25-1
**Owner:** C. D'Alessio
**Trainer:** L. Cumani

**Finished:** 7
**Distances:** 4 lengths, 4 lengths
**Winning Time:** 3 minutes, 11.48 secs

*Light Cavalry, pictured the year after his St. Leger success being cantered to the start at Ascot. Lester Piggott up.*

40

been home-bred, and he has had nearly 300 jumping winners, too, his *Maori Venture* having won the 1987 Grand National.

It is the continuation of heredity that is so fascinating to flat race breeders, as they watch the offspring over several generations mature, always hopeful, sometimes having dreams come true; a win with a home-bred horse holds an added dimension of pleasure to that of one bought as a yearling — although it must be said that to do well with a bargain basement purchase can give an added kick of its own.

Testing conditions and stamina doubts brought a field of only seven for the 1980 St. Leger, a race Jim Joel's father had won in 1908 with *Your Majesty* and in 1914 with *Black Jester*. Stable hopes were high, and trainer Henry Cecil was confident that *Light Cavalry* would stay. He had won the King Edward VII Stakes at Royal Ascot over one and a half miles, and had been beaten twice over that distance since, both times by a horse called *Prince Bee* whose stable companion, *Water Mill*, was himself favourite for the St. Leger.

*A worm's eye view of Minster Son as he heads the crack filly Diminuendo towards the finishing post in the 1988 St. Leger. The second favourite, Sheriff's Star has dropped out of contention by this stage.*

## VINDICATION OF BREEDING

Both horses were beautifully bred, *Light Cavalry* being by *Brigadier Gerard* out of a mare by *Relko*, and *Water Mill* by his old rival *Mill Reef* out of a mare by *St. Paddy*.

Joe Mercer, forever associated with *Brigadier Gerard*, rode his son now, and was quite confident that he would stay the extended one and three quarter miles.

How right he proved. *Light Cavalry* jumped off in front, as he usually did, and set out to try and make it all, doing it the hard way, the other runners content to sit in behind and wait their moment to challenge.

Only the favourite *Water Mill* was able to mount any sort of challenge. With three furlongs to run, he ranged up under the guidance of Willie Carson, but he could not sustain the effort.

*Light Cavalry* ran on the stronger in the final quarter mile to win by a decisive four lengths at 3-1. Outsider, *World Leader*, was a further four lengths back in third place. *Light Cavalry* stayed in training as a four-year-old and reverted to one and a half miles to win Newmarket's 1981 Princess of Wales's Stakes ridden by Lester Piggott.

## MINSTER SON

When *Minster Son* won the 1988 St. Leger, it was the first time a Classic winner had been ridden by its breeder. Before that, the most important English Flat race winner bred by a jockey was *By Jingo*, bred by Steve Donoghue who won the 1919 Ascot Gold Cup. The horse he beat was the odds-on favourite *Air Raid* and ironically he was ridden by none other than Steve Donoghue.

Willie Carson was faced with similar problems with several horses to choose from during *Minster Son*'s career. However, when it came to the crunch, he chose the horse he had bred on his stud near Cirencester, Gloucestershire, founded by him back in 1978.

*Minster Son* is a lovely strong chestnut by *Niniski* out of *Honey Bridge* by the 1957 2,000 Guineas and Derby winner *Crepello*. He was trained by Major Dick Hern at East Ilsley for the Dowager Lady Beaverbrook, who bought him as a yearling from Willie Carson.

## PROMISING BUILD-UP

As a two-year-old he beat his more fancied stable companion *Unfuwain* first time out at Newbury.

He was second on his next outing to *Carmelite House* and then in his final two-year-old outing he was fifth behind *Glacial Storm* in the Group III Horris Hill Stakes.

As a three-year-old, he again won first time out, beating *Red Glow*, who subsequently started favourite for the Derby, over ten furlongs in the Newmarket Stakes. A second win in the Listed Predominate Stakes, beating *Sheriff's Star* by a length and a half, with *Al Mufti* a neck back in third, put him well into the Derby reckoning, and Willie Carson, looking for a third win, finally plumped for him in that race.

### DISAPPOINTMENT

He started third favourite behind *Red Glow* and stable mate *Unfuwain*, but disappointed abysmally, trailing in eighth behind *Kahyasi*.

He was then given a two month lay-off before returning to Goodwood where he won the Group III Gordon Stakes from *Assatis*. The St. Leger was named as his autumn target after that success, but in the run up to the race, he was overlooked as media attention was centred on the crack filly *Diminuendo*, who earlier in the season had won the Oaks in sensational style, and the improving *Sheriff's Star* who was unbeaten after a decent sixth in the Derby.

A field of six lined up at the start, headed by the 4-7 favourite *Diminuendo*, owned by Sheikh Mohammed and trained by Henry Cecil. Chief opposition in the market was from the 7-2 shot *Sheriff's Star*, a half brother to the 1986 winner, *Moon Madness*, owned by Lavinia Duchess of Norfolk and trained by her daughter Lady Herries. *Minster Son* was third in the market at 15-2. The other three runners were very much there to make up the numbers, despite the fact that Clive Brittain's *Top Class*, 13-1, had won the Group Two Geoffrey Freer at Newmarket last time out. Michael Stoute's *Zaffaran* and Guy Harwood's *Mazzacano* were both lightly raced horses who were making a considerable step up in class.

*Minster Son takes the 1988 St. Leger by a length from Sheikh Mohammed's Diminuendo ridden by Walter Swinburn. This was the first ever Classic win in which a horse's breeder had ridden it to its success.*

*Willie Carson, wearing the St. Leger cap, joins the Dowager Lady Beaverbrook in a toast to Minster Son's success. The cap has been awarded to the winning jockey since the 200th running of the race in 1976.*

*Mazzacano* made all the early running from *Zaffaran* and *Top Class*, the big three being tucked in behind and waiting for the straight. Turning for home *Mazzacano* led from *Zaffaran*, *Minster Son* had been pushed up into third, the weakening *Top Class* was in four, whilst the two favourites continued to pursue their waiting policy in the rear.

## PRIDE REGAINED

As the field approached the three furlong post, Carson had taken *Minster Son* to the head of affairs, as *Sheriff's Star* and *Diminuendo* ranged up towards the front. The three were virtually in line as they passed the two furlong pole, with Walter Swinburn on *Diminuendo* seeming to be going best of all despite Carson and *Minster Son* still having the call.

*Sheriff's Star's* stamina ran out before the final furlong was reached and the race had become a two horse battle. Carson was urging his mount on as Swinburn still looked to be holding all the aces. But then Swinburn was riding and *Diminuendo*, who had not been beaten since the 1,000 Guineas back in May, was in trouble. Carson kept on the pressure and by the time the winning post was reached he had gone a length away from his rival.

*Minster Son* was the first Classic winner to be partnered by his breeder, and was the first Classic winner for his owner, the Dowager Lady Beaverbrook, since *Niniski*'s success in the Irish St. Leger at the Curragh in 1979.

## THE ST. LEGER CAP

At the prize giving afterwards, the rain that dogged the day having just about cleared up, Willie Carson was presented with the special St. Leger Cap, introduced with the 200th running of the Leger in 1976 when it was won by French Champion jockey Yves St Martin riding *Crow*. The cap, which is beautifully embroidered to an individual design each year, represents the International Cap that is presented to sportsmen in various fields such as rugby, cricket and football for appearances at international level.

# ASCOT

IT WAS Queen Anne, a keen follower of the Royal Buckhounds through Windsor Forest riding in a chaise, who, when she came upon Ascot Heath, thought what a good place it would make for a racecourse.

She bought it for £558.19s.5d in 1711, and in doing so, founded a truly royal meeting with its mixture of formality in the stands and informal picnics on the heath; the first race was the Queen's Plate that July. The Royal meeting today

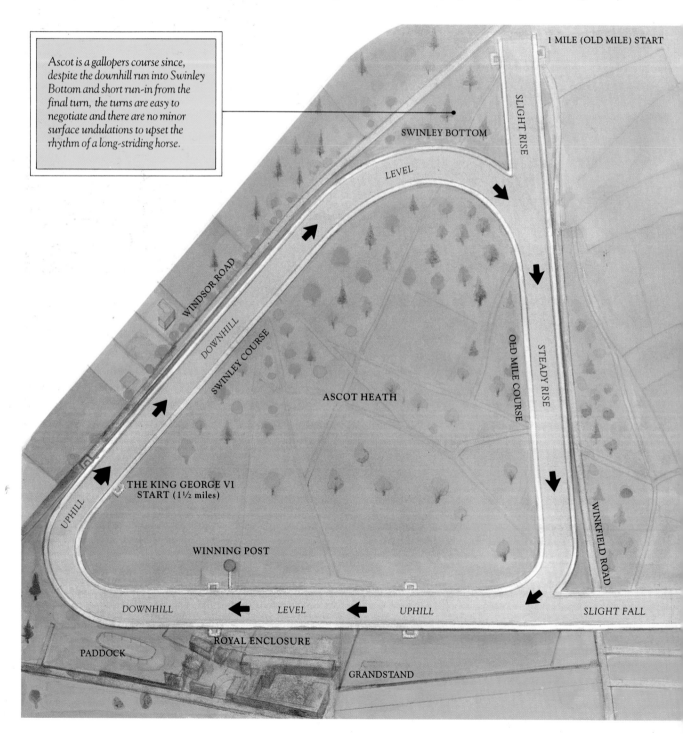

Ascot is a gallopers course since, despite the downhill run into Swinley Bottom and short run-in from the final turn, the turns are easy to negotiate and there are no minor surface undulations to upset the rhythm of a long-striding horse.

1 MILE (OLD MILE) START

SLIGHT RISE

SWINLEY BOTTOM

LEVEL

WINDSOR ROAD

DOWNHILL

SWINLEY COURSE

ASCOT HEATH

OLD MILE COURSE

STEADY RISE

WINKFIELD ROAD

THE KING GEORGE VI
START (1½ miles)

UPHILL

WINNING POST

DOWNHILL            LEVEL            UPHILL            SLIGHT FALL

ROYAL ENCLOSURE

PADDOCK

GRANDSTAND

stages four days of as consistently good, high class racing as can be found anywhere in the world.

## A GALLOPER'S COURSE

The Ascot round course is a right-handed triangular circuit of just over 1¾ miles with a run-in of 3 furlongs, with the attractive heath covering its centre. There is a straight mile course (down which the Royal procession proceeds), and the old mile course which joins the round course at Swinley Bottom. All races

*A milliner's dream. The Royal Ascot meet in July is one of the great events of the social as well as the sporting calendar. Morning dress is "de rigueur" in the paddock and in the royal enclosure.*

*The royal procession when members of the Royal Family ride in carriages down the course to the enclosure before the start of each day's racing of the June meet was initiated by George IV in 1820. The Royal meeting today provides four days of consistently good, high class racing.*

THE QUEEN ALEXANDRA
STAKES START (2¾ miles)

)URSE

ILL          SLIGHT FALL

THE GOLD CUP
START (2½ miles)

shorter than a mile are run on the straight course. For one and a half miles or longer, and National Hunt races (which were started in 1965), horses run downhill to the bend in Swinley Bottom where the ground levels out, before rising quite steeply for the run home until levelling out less than a furlong from the winning post.

The straight mile starts level, then rises to the 5-furlong post where it descends to the junction with the round course. There are few undulations to put off a long striding horse on either course, and it therefore suits gallopers; it also offers a test of stamina, especially when the ground is heavy.

# THE KING GEORGE VI AND QUEEN ELIZABETH DIAMOND STAKES

THE 'KING GEORGE' as it is popularly known, was first run at the July meeting of Ascot in 1951 in celebration of the Festival of Britain when it was known as the King George VI and Queen Elizabeth Festival of Britain Stakes. It was won by *Supreme Court*, a three-year-old owned by Mrs T. Lilley and ridden by E. C. Elliott from a field of 19 horses.

Run over one and a half miles, and open to any age, it has seen some epic contests between different generations.

The Queen's *Aureole*, by *Hyperion*, was the first four-year-old to win in 1954, and in 1960 Sir Harold Wernher's five-year-old *Aggressor* won.

Nearly every winner has been a great horse, many of whom have also won the Derby. One of the most popular fillies to win was *Dahlia*, who succeeded twice, in 1973 and 1974.

## GRUNDY v BUSTINO

From time to time a race gets billed as the Race of the Century; only very rarely does it live up to it.

For those who saw it, the King George VI and Queen Elizabeth Diamond Stakes at Royal Ascot in 1975 did just that; they enjoyed the privilege of witnessing the race of a lifetime, a once to be savoured, never to be forgotten spectacle.

*Grundy* and *Bustino*. *Grundy* is probably the better remembered of the two horses, not just because he was victor that day, but because he was also a Derby winner.

## A BARGAIN BUY

He nearly came out of the bottom drawer; a wishy washy chestnut, considered a bad colour for a horse, with flaxen mane and tail and three white feet, he fetched only 11,000 guineas as a yearling — and even that was 1000 guineas more than purchaser Dr Carlo Vittadini's intended limit!

It did not take connections long to discover he was a bargain, for he won all four of his races as a two-year-old, trained by Peter Walwyn. One was the Dewhurst Stakes when he beat *Steel Heart* by no less than six lengths, and that horse had won both the Gimcrack and Middle Park Stakes.

**Left** *Grundy, ridden by the 1975 Champion Jockey, Pat Eddery, canters up towards the start. Purchased by Dr Carlo Vittadini for 11,000 guineas he proved himself to be a great bargain.*

**Right** *Grundy's head just shows in front of Bustino during one of the best remembered finishes at Royal Ascot. Both horses gave totally of themselves and Grundy appeared to have little left for his next and final race, the Benson and Hedges at York.*

46

So he embarked on his three-year-old career with stable hopes high, only to receive a painful kick in the face by one of his stablemates while out on exercise. He recovered in time for the 2000 Guineas but did not seem back to his best, for he was beaten by an Italian horse *Bolkonski*, whose jockey took much less notice of the picketing stable lads at the start than did the English riders.

## DUAL DERBY WINNER

*Grundy* was back to his best to win the Irish 2000 Guineas, and then proved he could stay as well by winning both the Derby and the Irish Derby. He had established himself as the best of his age group, now the time had come for a test against older horses: his next goal would be the King George VI and Queen Elizabeth Diamond Stakes at Royal Ascot.

## ASCOT EPIC

The stage was set for an epic race, but nevertheless, *Grundy* was confidently expected to win, starting a shade odds on, with *Bustino* the 1974 St. Leger winner at 4-1 and *Dahlia*, winner for the previous two years, at 6-1.

Major Dick Hern, trainer of *Bustino*, however had a plan by which he hoped to run *Grundy* out of it: he was running not one but two pacemakers for his horse.

The ground was fast but even so, the pace at which the 1½ mile race started was more like a six-furlong sprint. Off shot the first pacemaker, *Highest,* and he lasted flat out until overtaken by the number two pacemaker, *Kinglet.* Already the rest were strung out behind in Indian file, with *Bustino* in fourth, then *Grundy* followed by *Dahlia,* and *Highest* dropped right out of it.

On swept *Kinglet*, now a National Hunt sire, until the final half mile, just before the course swings round into the straight. Here, he comple-

ted his task by moving off the rails and allowing the stable horse, *Bustino,* through. The pace was such that if there was any suspect stamina in *Grundy*, it would have to be found out.

For a few moments, that looked all too possible, for he was being run off his legs. He had certainly never had to gallop this fast in a middle distance race, yet still somehow he found another gear in which to go after the leader.

As they reached the straight, it was clear that a battle royal was in progress. *Bustino* was clear in front, but *Grundy* was coming. Could he make up the ground in time? Slowly but surely, *Grundy* and his rider Pat Eddery closed on *Bustino* and Joe Mercer. As they reached the final furlong, they galloped stride for stride, then *Grundy's* head just showed in front.

## GRANDSTAND FINISH

It was the moment to expect victor-elect to draw away from about-to-be vanquished, for it is rare that a long time leader rallies after losing the lead. *Bustino* was one of those rarities; showing tremendous courage, he fought his way back, and the pair galloped shoulder to shoulder towards that elusive winning post. It must have seemed like a mirage, the sort of experience more commonly encountered on that long run-in after the last fence in the Grand National than in a Flat race.

The crowds in the stands and lining the rails were roaring the horses on; then suddenly it was over. Yards from the line, *Bustino's* last reserves of strength were sapped; *Grundy* won the race by half a length, and it was no surprise to hear a new course record time had been set.

In many ways, both horses were losers, for neither was ever the same again. The flaxen *Grundy* was beaten into fourth place by *Dahlia*, who had been five and a half lengths behind him at Ascot, in the Benson and Hedges Gold Cup at York. He was retired to the National Stud, but Dr Vittadini's generosity in sending him there was ill-rewarded for *Grundy* was not very successful and was exported to Japan nine years later.

*Bustino*, too, saw the end of his career in this memorable race, but at least he proved himself as a successful sire of stayers, including the 1987 winner of the Ascot Gold Cup, *Paean*.

Two gallant horses had literally galloped their hearts out on that epic day at Royal Ascot; happily the brave sight they made has remained an inspiration to the many who saw it.

### THE 1975 KING GEORGE VI/QUEEN ELIZABETH DIAMOND STAKES

**Prize Money:** £81,910        **Runners:** 11

**1 GRUNDY**
(Great Nephew – Word From Lundy)
**Jockey:** P. Eddery
**Starting Price:** 4-5
**Owner:** Dr C. Vittadini
**Trainer:** P. Walwyn

**2 BUSTINO**
(Busted – Ship Yard)
**Jockey:** Joe Mercer
**Starting Price:** 4-1
**Owner:** Lady Beaverbrook
**Trainer:** W. Hern

**3 DAHLIA**
(Vaguely Noble – Charming Alibi)
**Jockey:** L. Piggott
**Starting Price:** 6-1
**Owner:** N. Bunker Hunt
**Trainer:** M. Zilber

**Finished:** 11
**Distances:** ½ length, 5 lengths
**Winning Time:** 2 minutes, 26.98 secs

*Troy, pictured here just after winning the 200th Epsom Derby, proved himself an outstanding middle distance horse by adding the 'King George' to his victory tally. He was partnered in both races by Major Dick Hern's stable jockey, Willie Carson.*

## TROY

By the time of the 1979 'King George', Sir Michael Sobell and Sir Arnold Weinstock's bay colt *Troy* had already won both the Derby and Irish Derby. Additionally, the horse he beat by seven decisive lengths in a memorable 200th running of the Derby, *Dickens Hill*, had gone on to win the Eclipse Stakes.

So it was no surprise to find *Troy*, trained by Major Dick Hern and ridden by Willie Carson, an odds on favourite.

Bred in Ireland at the Ballymacoll Stud in County Meath, he soon proved himself a top staying two-year-old, but he was not favourite to win the Derby at three, that distinction going to a colt who had already beaten him, the much fancied *Ela-Mana-Mou*.

Another fancied runner was *Troy's* stablemate *Milford* owned by the Queen, for whom victory in the bicentennial Derby would have been extremely popular. He ran prominently, but once *Troy* had extricated himself from a tricky position and set sail for home, nothing else could catch him.

Victory in the 'King George' against older horses would stamp *Troy* a top middle distance horse. On the day, only six horses lined up

against him, and one, *Road to Glory*, was a pacemaker from his own stable.

*Road to Glory* set off at a great rate performing his task admirably, and stayed in the lead until the field rounded the home turn.

### DANGER AVERTED

Here, there was nearly a disaster. The ground was firm and must have been a bit greasy, for three champion horses, *Troy*, *Swiss Maid* and *Gay Mecene*, all skidded.

Luckily all three regained their equilibrium, but it had allowed *Ela-Mana-Mou*, fourth in the Derby, to take up the running.

To the watching crowds, it looked for a few moments as if a shock result could be in prospect, but *Troy* was a determined, tough colt and as Willie Carson balanced him and set him off in pursuit, he responded gamely.

He caught and passed *Ela-Mana-Mou* with a furlong to run, pursued by the French four-year-old *Gay Mecene*. At the line, *Troy* had one and a half lengths to spare over him, with *Ela-Mana-Mou* three lengths back in third, just ahead of *M-Lolshan*.

*Troy*, by *Petingo*, had already been syndicated for stud at a valuation of £7.2 million, but sadly he died still a young horse in 1983.

# THE ASCOT GOLD CUP

FOUNDED IN 1807, the Ascot Gold Cup is run over two and a half miles on the third day of the Royal Ascot meeting in June. Originally it was worth 100 guineas with a sweepstake of ten guineas. In 1988 it was worth over £53,000 to the winner, but whereas in the old days it used to be a target for previous Derby winners when they were older, it rarely draws horses of Classic calibre now.

Nicholas 1 of Russia visited Ascot races in 1845 and gave a £500 plate which replaced the Gold Cup for a while but when the Crimean War broke out in 1854, it was deemed prudent to lapse the Emperor's Plate and re-instate the Gold Cup.

Twelve horses have won the Gold Cup twice. *Le Moss* and *Ardross* won it from 1979 to 1982 giving trainer Henry Cecil four consecutive victories, the last of which gave jockey Lester Piggott his eleventh success in the race, his first having been on *Zarathustra* in 1957.

Some of the greatest horses in racing's past won, such as Triple Crown winners *West Australian,* who set up a record time in 1854; *Gladiateur* who won by 40 lengths in 1866, and *Isinglass* in

1895 who set a record stakes earnings that was to last until 1952.

Greats such as *St. Simon* in 1884, *Persimmon* in 1897, and *Bayardo* in 1910, who won 22 of his 25 races, were all fine winners.

## SAGARO

Only one horse has won the Gold Cup three times, and that is *Sagaro,* from 1975 to 1977, ridden each time by Lester Piggot. *Sagaro* was a very international horse: he was owned by Mr Gerald Oldham a financier based in Geneva who bred *Sagaro* himself in Ireland, sired by a horse he also bought, *Expresso,* for only 1000 guineas. *Sagaro* was trained in France, by François Boutin and, of course, was ridden by an Englishman.

With stamina having gone out of fashion in preference to speed, *Sagaro* was able to show both, and it was his acceleration at the end of a long race that won the Gold Cup for him more than once.

As a three-year-old in 1974 he won the Grand Prix De Paris by two lengths from *Bustino,* but

**Left** *A painting by Lynwood Palmer of the great racehorse and prolific sire St. Simon. A Gold Cup winner in 1884, St. Simon went on to sire 17 English classic winners.*

**Right** *Two contrasting scenes. (Above) Ascot in 1834 and (below) Ascot in 1979. The buildings may have changed but the smart attire of the racegoers hardly has at all.*

*Sagaro, ridden by Lester Piggott, wins his second Gold Cup in 1976. Crash Course follows him in a length behind.*

when he contended France's equivalent of the Gold Cup, the Prix Du Cadran as a four-year-old, he was beaten by *Le Bavard*.

He was favourite that day and although *Le Bavard* was in the field for that year's Gold Cup, *Sagaro* was still the better backed. It turned out to be the correct assessment, as, starting at 7-4 in the eight runner field on firmer ground than there had been in France, he beat *Le Bavard*.

### AN ENDURING RACER

The next year, following good wins in France, *Sagaro* justified the odds laid on him, and beat *Crash Course* by an easy length with *Sea Anchor* third.

When his owner then offered him for sale as a stallion, one would have thought he would be snapped up, but not a bit of it, and it was actually more lucrative for Mr Oldham to keep him in training.

So, at six years old, he turned out for the Gold Cup again. This time there were six runners, and *Sagaro* started at 9-4 against. The race was a classic show-piece from horse and rider.

*Citoyen*, a confirmed front runner, set off at the head of affairs as usual, and stayed there for just over one and a half miles. Then, with seven

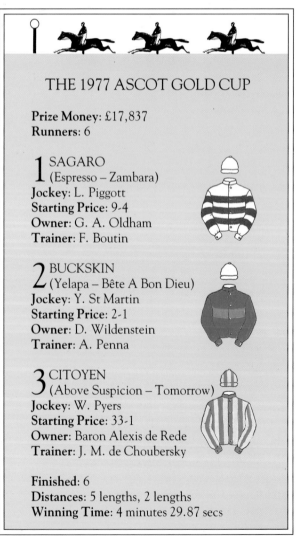

## THE 1977 ASCOT GOLD CUP

**Prize Money:** £17,837
**Runners:** 6

1 SAGARO
(Espresso – Zambara)
**Jockey:** L. Piggott
**Starting Price:** 9-4
**Owner:** G. A. Oldham
**Trainer:** F. Boutin

2 BUCKSKIN
(Yelapa – Bête A Bon Dieu)
**Jockey:** Y. St Martin
**Starting Price:** 2-1
**Owner:** D. Wildenstein
**Trainer:** A. Penna

3 CITOYEN
(Above Suspicion – Tomorrow)
**Jockey:** W. Pyers
**Starting Price:** 33-1
**Owner:** Baron Alexis de Rede
**Trainer:** J. M. de Choubersky

**Finished:** 6
**Distances:** 5 lengths, 2 lengths
**Winning Time:** 4 minutes 29.87 secs

*Sagaro clinches his hat-trick with a convincing five length win over Buckskin (far left) and Citoyen (centre).*

furlongs to run, *Buckskin* went on, followed by *Bright Finish*, with *Sagaro* nicely placed in third.

*Bruni*, the St. Leger winner of 1975, looked to be going smoothly as the field entered the straight, and to the casual observer it seemed like anyone's race. But Lester Piggott was riding with supreme confidence.

With only a furlong left to run, he let *Sagaro* go, and the good-looking bay responded with such an impressive turn of foot that within yards he was in front. Swiftly he extended his lead to five lengths at the post to win with his ears pricked from *Buckskin*.

He thoroughly deserved the ovation which the crowd gave the new record holder. Lester Piggott was reported as saying it was *Sagaro*'s finest and easiest performance.

Mr Oldham, who had won the St. Leger with *Intermezzo* in 1969, said simply, '*Sagaro* is the best I have owned'.

# THE QUEEN ALEXANDRA STAKES

THE QUEEN ALEXANDRA STAKES is the longest race in the Flat calendar, run on the final day of Royal Ascot each June over two and three quarter miles and 34 yards. Founded in 1865, it was known then as the Queen Alexandra Plate.

No winner is more fondly remembered than the horse who made it 'his' race, *Brown Jack* who won it for six successive years from 1929 to 1934.

There have been six other dual winners this century, the last of which was *John Cherry* who won in 1977 and 1979. *Trelawney* was a popular winner in 1962/3, and *Bitter Sweet* won in 1954-55. Just before *Brown Jack's* monopoly on the race, *Finglas* won for two years, and then it goes back to 1905 and 1908 when *Hammerkop* and *Torpoint* each won twice.

More significantly, perhaps, has been the top future National Hunt stallions that the race has turned up, where there is more emphasis on stamina and less on speed. Most famous of these is the 1948 winner *Vulgan* who was a stupendously successful National Hunt sire only challenged in recent years by *Deep Run*.

*Laurence O* who is a successful National Hunt sire standing in Ireland won in 1969, and in 1972 the race was won by *Celtic Cone*, sire of the 1988 Champion Hurdle winner *Celtic Shot*.

## BROWN JACK

In fact, it was as a jumper that *Brown Jack's* racing career began, and indeed, he won the second running of the Champion Hurdle in 1928 then, in a most unusual move, switched to running on the Flat on the advice of top jockey Steve Donoghue, who rode him with outstanding success in staying races.

### A SICKLY YEARLING

*Brown Jack* was bred in Ireland and was so backward that he failed to be purchased at the Sales and, having once come to England, suffered several illnesses, making him weak and certainly not a horse to be considered as having much of a racing future.

He had the good fortune to end up at Wroughton in the stable of the Honourable

Aubrey Hastings who was able to restore him to good health. In those days, the late 1920s, the village boasted seven stables, all of them long since swallowed up by the town of Swindon.

Aubrey Hastings trained four Grand National winners, one of them a wartime substitute at Gatwick (the old racecourse is now buried beneath the airport runways), *Ascetic's Silver* in 1906, *Ally Soper* in 1915, *Ballymacad* in 1917 and *Master Robert* in 1924.

When he died, midway through Brown Jack's career, his assistant, Ivor Anthony, took over, and he, too, won the Grand National of 1933 with *Kellsboro Jack* and in 1937 with *Royal Mail*.

Amongst the Wroughton stable lads there was

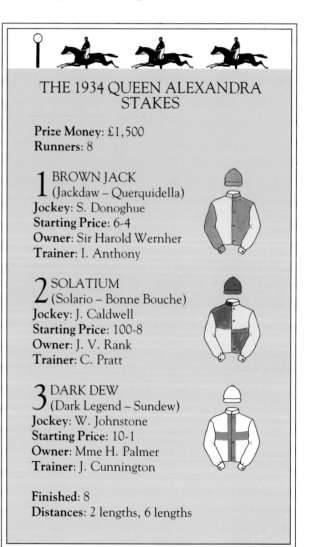

### THE 1934 QUEEN ALEXANDRA STAKES

**Prize Money:** £1,500
**Runners:** 8

**1 BROWN JACK**
(Jackdaw – Querquidella)
**Jockey:** S. Donoghue
**Starting Price:** 6-4
**Owner:** Sir Harold Wernher
**Trainer:** I. Anthony

**2 SOLATIUM**
(Solario – Bonne Bouche)
**Jockey:** J. Caldwell
**Starting Price:** 100-8
**Owner:** J. V. Rank
**Trainer:** C. Pratt

**3 DARK DEW**
(Dark Legend – Sundew)
**Jockey:** W. Johnstone
**Starting Price:** 10-1
**Owner:** Mme H. Palmer
**Trainer:** J. Cunnington

**Finished:** 8
**Distances:** 2 lengths, 6 lengths

hardly a rush to look after *Brown Jack*, but in the end it fell to the lot of Alfie Garrett, who is in his eighties and still lives in Swindon.

Alfie recalled, 'I was lumbered with him because I only had one horse to do at the time. He was very lazy at home, but once he reached the course, he couldn't wait to race'.

And every time he won, which was frequently, he earnt Alfie an extra £2, double his weekly wage!

### LIMITED AMBITIONS

All that remains of Wroughton's past today is a pub called the *Brown Jack*, filled with memorabilia of him. His stable was up a twitten by a stream a short walk from the pub, but it is now the site of a convent.

In the stable's early days, it had produced the Derby winner of 1874 called *George Frederick*. No such ambitious plans were laid out for *Brown Jack* but he ended up one of the most popular flat racers of all time, not least because the public could get to know him over so many more years than is usually the case.

He was also a real character which further endeared him to his fans. Only a few months after winning the Champion Hurdle, *Brown Jack* made his first of seven annual forays to Royal Ascot and won the Ascot Stakes.

He returned in 1929 and was beaten a short head in that race by a horse who was to become a long time rival, *Old Orkney*, then three days later ran in the Queen Alexandra Stakes for the first time and won.

### AN EXTRAORDINARY RUN

He kept repeating the process, often saving his best performance of the year for 'his' race, although he became so 'knowing' at home, that to get him to do any work at all he often had to be kidded into thinking he was going racing by being loaded into a horsebox and taken to another trainer's gallops!

At the advanced age, for a flat-racer, of ten, *Brown Jack* headed towards Ascot for the seventh and final time, intent upon his sixth victory in the Queen Alexandra Stakes before leading a life of honourable retirement.

It surely could not be done; he could not possibly be the horse he was; he must concede to age and a younger horse. The bookmakers thought so, too, and for the first time in four years allowed him to start at odds against for 'his'

*The legendary Brown Jack, six times winner of the Queen Alexandra Stakes, ridden by the great Steve Donoghue Champion Jockey for 10 successive years between 1914 and 1923. Brown Jack won his last Queen Alexandra at the age of 10 having been Champion Hurdler at 4.*

race. It was too much for trainer Ivor Anthony: he remained in the paddock unable to watch.

### THE FINAL CURTAIN

The field of nine was larger than usual, and included a former Cesarewitch winner and an Irish Derby winner as well as a French challenger, a country renowned for its stayers. Alfie Garrett led him round proudly, it being inconceivable in his mind that *Brown Jack* could be beaten.

An impromptu cheer broke out from the stands as the old horse cantered past on his way to the start. This was his day.

They were off, and the younger horses set off at a cracking pace, thinking to undo the old boy. They came past the stands on the first circuit having completed seven furlongs, with *Benskin* and *Mail Fist* sharing the lead, followed by *Solatium* and *Loosestrife*. A few lengths behind came *Nitsichin* and *Brown Jack*.

Going down to Swinley Bottom, *Loosestrife* went into the lead; *Brown Jack* moved up, attended by the French horse *Dark Dew*, but by the time they were approaching the straight, *Brown Jack* and *Solatium* came to the front, the pair drawing clear of the rest.

As they went neck and neck all the way up the straight, the suspense could be felt in the stands, the crowds willing the older horse to be the stronger — and so it proved. With the post almost reached, *Solatium* dropped back beaten and *Brown Jack* strode into the record book amidst the stupendous cheers of the crowd.

# SANDOWN PARK

W HEN SANDOWN PARK was opened amongst much fanfare and publicity in 1875, centuries of tradition were cast aside. It brought a new concept to racing: for the first time, the whole course was walled and enclosed and therefore every racegoer had to pay to go in, not just those wishing to use the grandstand or enclosure facilities. Until then, entry to other parts of a course had always been free.

## A SUPERIOR COURSE

It also heralded a superb course which has stood the test of time: now, as then, it offers superb viewing and, with the splendid line of fences down the far side, plenty of excitement. It has also always boasted facilities that leave many other courses wanting.

Hwfa Williams, chairman and clerk of the course for nearly fifty years, possessed flair and

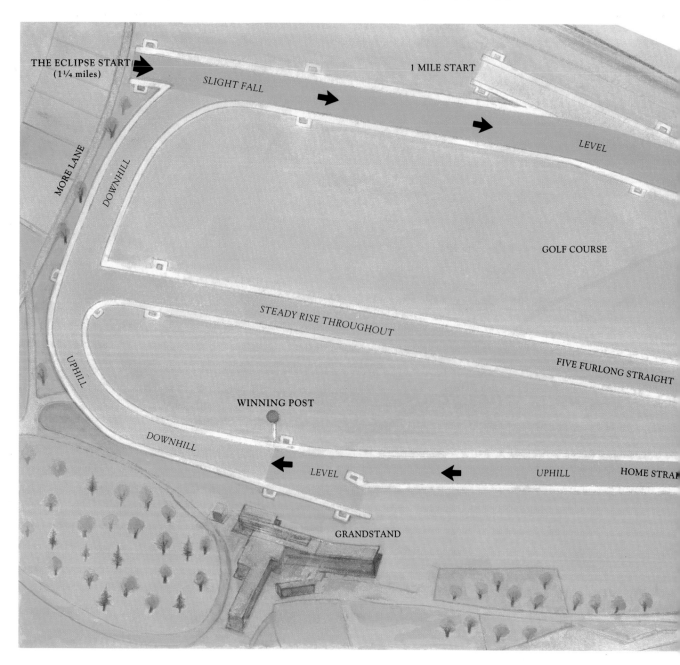

**Right** *The parade ring behind the stands at the modern Sandown Park complex.*

The first 'modern' enclosed course when opened in 1875, Sandown Park also became the first course in England to stage a £10,000 race with the Eclipse Stakes in 1886. 100 years later, in 1986, the year of Dancing Brave's victory, the prize money had increased to £134,000.

LOWER GREEN ROAD

UPHILL

PORTSMOUTH ROAD

invention and devised a mixed meeting of both flat and steeplechase races to inaugurate the course. The three-day meeting included a Grand National Master of Hounds Chase, the Household Brigade cup, a military steeplechase called the Grand International Chase, an Open Hunters and an Open Farmers Race, thus giving the course from the start a hunting and military flavour.

The new course was an immediate success, as it deserved to be for the amount of thought and planning put into it by the founders Hwfa Williams, his brother General Owen Williams, MP, and Sir Wilfred Brett. By its second meeting, the Prince of Wales, later King Edward VII, presented a cup to be ridden for by members of the Sandown Park or Bibury Clubs, and it was at Sandown that the prince won his first race on the flat, with a filly called *Counterpane*. He also won the 1887 Grand Military Gold Cup and two races at the next year's Household Brigade meeting, which was inaugurated during Sandown's second year of existence.

# THE ECLIPSE STAKES

SANDOWN WAS 11 years old when in 1886 the first £10,000 race ever to be staged in England was launched, with the backing of Leopold de Rothschild, and this, appropriately, was the Eclipse Stakes, in honour of one of racing's most illustrious ancestors.

The Eclipse Stakes takes its name from the great 18th century racehorse of that name, and down the years there have been many winners worthy of his memory.

*Eclipse* himself was bred by HRH William Duke of Cumberland, by a horse called *Markse* out of an unraced mare named *Spiletta*. The colt was born on the night of an eclipse, hence his name, but when the Duke died, there was a dispersal sale of the horses at his stud, among them the yearling *Eclipse*.

He was bought by a prosperous butcher for 75 guineas but proved such a handful that he was nearly gelded; luckily for the future of the thoroughbred racehorse he was not, for not only was *Eclipse* the unbeaten winner of 18 races, but he proved one of the best and most influential of early sires.

He was ridden day and night in an effort to subdue him, but nothing broke his spirit. By the time he first saw a racecourse, his reputation had gone far and wide before him, and he won at odds of 4-1 on at Epsom.

*Eclipse, painted in 1770 by the great 18th century equine artist, George Stubbs. Unbeaten in 18 races and a great success at stud, his early prospects looked less than hopeful after his purchase by a prosperous butcher for 75 guineas.*

## ECLIPSE FIRST — THE REST NOWHERE

He won next at Ascot, and before the season was out he was to win at odds of 70-1 ON — that was when any opponents could be found for him, for before long, he began to get walk-overs, such was his reputation. In all, he won 18 races, including 11 King's Plates, for seven of which he walked over. It should be borne in mind, however, that a race in those days was effectively several races, as they were run in three or four heats, usually of four miles each at half hour intervals followed by the final. *Eclipse* was renowned for his speed and eagerness, but he must have possessed abundant stamina, too.

*Eclipse* proved to be a great success at stud, comparable with *Herod, Matchem* and *Highflyer* of his time. He died from an attack of colic when he was 25 years old, and his skeleton can still be seen today in the National Horseracing Museum at Newmarket.

### A HUGE PURSE

Sandown was not in existence when *Eclipse* was alive and so perhaps it is odd that his commemorative race takes place there; but Sandown was 11 years old when its executive decided to stage a really valuable race and, with an eclipse coincidentally occurring that year, 1886, named it in honour of *Eclipse*.

The one and a quarter mile race was to have a then massive £10,000 purse, an idea that was ridiculed as financial suicide in some quarters, and could be likened to the 'Million' races of today. Entries closed two years in advance, and with a total of 263, it was clearly going to pay its way. There were still 40 left in at the four day declaration stage and on Friday July 23, 1886, 12 of the country's highest class runners filed out on to the track, justifying the organisers' initiative.

### BENDIGO

For this first ever running a record 30,000 crowd poured in by 35 special trains from London as well as by country trains and horse-drawn carriages, in spite of incessant rain making conditions most unpleasant.

They were not to be disappointed. Even without the hoped for 2,000 Guineas replay between *Ormonde* and *Minting*, as *Ormonde* did not run, there was a previous Derby winner in *St. Gatien* who had won 14 of his 15 races, and *Bendigo*, winner of the Cambridgeshire, Lincoln and Hardwicke Stakes.

There was drama on the morning of the race when *Minting* was found to be lame, possibly 'got at'. This left *Bendigo*, looking magnificent, as favourite; other good prospects in the line up were *Whitefriar*, at one time considered as good as *Ormonde*; *Candlemas*, ridden by the great Fred Archer; *Miss Jummy*, winner that year of the Oaks and 1,000 Guineas; and *Fra Diavolo*, a French winner.

### A FORTUNATE DELAY

The only good thing about *Whitefriar*'s fractious behaviour at the start was that it delayed the race for 20 minutes, by which time the rain had stopped. *St. Gatien* made the early pace until restrained and an outsider *Martine* went into the lead, staying there until the field turned into the straight.

But when they met the rising ground inside the final two furlongs, with *Fra Diavolo* showing briefly in front, it was *Bendigo* who was full of running. When Tom Cannon let him go, he swept by with contemptuous ease, and although *St. Gatien* did his best to go with him, it was *Candlemas* who followed *Bendigo* home a respectful three lengths in arrears, with *St. Gatien* half a length back in third place.

### DANCING BRAVE

The best colt in Europe in 1986, *Dancing Brave* won the 2,000 Guineas, the Eclipse, the King George VI and Queen Elizabeth and the Prix de l'Arc de Triomphe.

It is widely accepted that he was the best horse in the Derby field — and most people believe it was not his fault that he was beaten, for he was allowed to lay so far out of his ground that it was virtually impossible to make it up, even though he nearly succeeded.

Owned by Prince Khalid Abdullah, *Dancing Brave* was by *Lyphard* (by *Northern Dancer*) and was trained in West Sussex by Guy Harwood below the South Downs where Guy used to be a well known figure on the point-to-point circuit as is now his daughter, Amanda.

### UNBEATEN RUN

*Dancing Brave* was a neat bay with a little white snip above one nostril. He ran just twice in minor races as a two-year-old and won them both, then encountered soft ground on his reappearance as a three-year-old and won that as well, making him favourite for the Guineas.

In this, he showed the remarkable turn of foot that was to become his hallmark and shot to a three length victory. There were still those who felt that on breeding his ability to stay the 1½ miles of the Derby might be beyond him, and this could be why he was held up so far behind.

## DERBY DISAPPOINTMENT

Whatever the reason, once he got clear and launched his run, *Sharastani* was gone beyond recall . . . although *Dancing Brave*'s run was nothing short of sensational, covering the last two furlongs in record time and failing by only half a length.

Thus it was that when he went for the Eclipse Stakes, his unbeaten record gone, he needed to redeem himself. This time there was only a small field, so the likelihood of getting either boxed in

or too far behind looked remote.

Crowds flocked to Sandown and craned their necks around the paddock, to be treated to only a brief glimpse of 'the Brave'. What they saw in one quick turn of the paddock was a colt looking in the bloom of good health (he won the best turned out prize), and off he cantered to the start on ground eased by overnight rain.

## REPUTATION REDEEMED

With two pacemakers in the field, the pace was sure to be a good one, and so it was as *Grand Harbour* and *Come On The Blues* set about their tasks. They were followed by Willie Carson on *Bedtime* and close up behind them came *Dancing Brave*, ridden as usual by Greville Starkey, and the consistent French four-year-old mare *Triptych*.

*Bedtime* took over with three furlongs to run as the pacemakers dropped back, but his lead was brief, for *Triptych* quickly took over. She had run in five Classics the year before and won the Irish 2,000 Guineas, the first filly to do so.

For a moment it looked as if she might win the Eclipse, but this time *Dancing Brave* was poised — and then he pounced.

Once he got into top gear, his acceleration was again electrifying, and the excited crowds roared encouragement; in one furlong, he caught *Triptych* and drew away for a decisive, impressive four lengths win, with Greville Starkey punching the air in salute with his whip, relieved to put Epsom behind him.

*Teleprompter*, who had won the 1985 Arlington Million, was 1½ lengths behind *Triptych* in third. Only twice in the previous 20 years had the winning distance been as much, by *Mill Reef* and *Kalaglow* who was another Hardwood/Starkey combination, in 1982.

## DERBY REVENGE

Although this fine performance against older horses answered a lot of questions as far as *Dancing Brave* was concerned, *Sharastani* had nevertheless followed up his Derby win with an impressive eight length victory in the Irish Derby, effectively quashing those who threw doubts upon his Epsom win.

So the prospect of the pair having a re-match was a tantalising, mouth watering one to say the least. And the possibility looked a live one, for both were intended starters for the King George VI and Queen Elizabeth Stakes at Royal Ascot.

*Sharastani* was a rich chestnut by *Nijinsky* (also

---

### THE 1986 ECLIPSE STAKES

**Prize Money**: £134,460
**Runners**: 8

**1 DANCING BRAVE**
(Lyphard – Navajo Princess)
**Jockey**: G. Starkey
**Starting Price**: 4-9
**Owner**: Prince K. Abdullah
**Trainer**: G. Harwood

**2 TRIPTYCH**
(Riverman – Trillion)
**Jockey**: E. Legrix
**Starting Price**: 9-1
**Owner**: A. Clore
**Trainer**: P. Biancone

**3 TELEPROMPTER**
(Welsh Pageant – Ouija)
**Jockey**: T. Ives
**Starting Price**: 9-1
**Owner**: Lord Derby
**Trainer**: J. Watts

**Finished**: 8
**Distances**: 4 lengths, 1½ lengths
**Winning Time**: 2 minutes, 6.18 secs

*Dancing Brave hugs the rails during his victory in the 1986 Eclipse Stakes. His four lengths win over Triptych put him back on course after a disappointing second in the Derby when a late run had left him ½ a length short.*

by *Northern Dancer*), owned by the Aga Khan, and had done everything asked of him, so the scene was set for Ascot.

Greville Starkey had been hurt, so Pat Eddery took his place in *Dancing Brave*'s saddle. He rode a peach of a race, and beat *Sharastani*'s stable companion *Shardari* by three-quarters of a length, with *Sharastani* a lack-lustre fourth.

## CROWNING ACHIEVEMENT

Pat Eddery was on board again for an above average Prix de l'Arc de Triomphe in October. En route, he had taken in a 1¼ mile race at Goodwood, intended as a warm up for Longchamp, but he promptly beat the course record! Clearly, he was in great form.

So it proved in Paris. Although left for an agonising late run again, his triumph over *Bering* was simply brilliant, his acceleration blistering, and he could bow out of racing and go off to stud in a blaze of glory.

*Dancing Brave* stands at the Dalham Hall Stud in Newmarket, having been syndicated for £350,000 per share in a $20 million valuation.

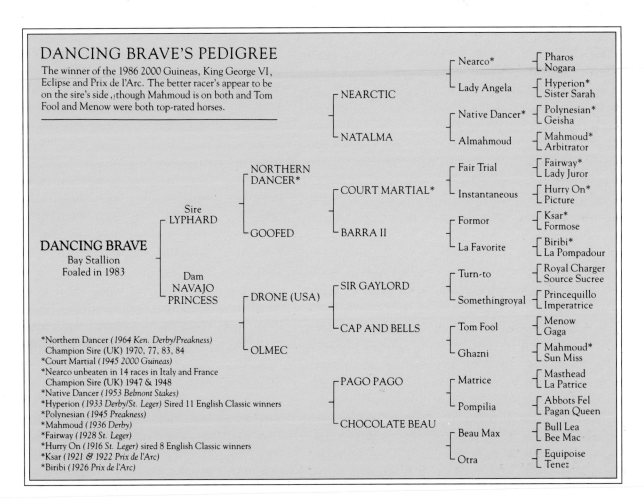

## DANCING BRAVE'S PEDIGREE

The winner of the 1986 2000 Guineas, King George VI, Eclipse and Prix de l'Arc. The better racer's appear to be on the sire's side, though Mahmoud is on both and Tom Fool and Menow were both top-rated horses.

**DANCING BRAVE**
Bay Stallion
Foaled in 1983

Sire
LYPHARD

NORTHERN DANCER*

NEARCTIC
- Nearco*
  - Pharos
  - Nogara
- Lady Angela
  - Hyperion*
  - Sister Sarah

NATALMA
- Native Dancer*
  - Polynesian*
  - Geisha
- Almahmoud
  - Mahmoud*
  - Arbitrator

GOOFED

COURT MARTIAL*
- Fair Trial
  - Fairway*
  - Lady Juror
- Instantaneous
  - Hurry On*
  - Picture

BARRA II
- Formor
  - Ksar*
  - Formose
- La Favorite
  - Biribi*
  - La Pompadour

Dam
NAVAJO PRINCESS

DRONE (USA)

SIR GAYLORD
- Turn-to
  - Royal Charger
  - Source Sucree
- Somethingroyal
  - Princequillo
  - Imperatrice

CAP AND BELLS
- Tom Fool
  - Menow
  - Gaga
- Ghazni
  - Mahmoud*
  - Sun Miss

OLMEC

PAGO PAGO
- Matrice
  - Masthead
  - La Patrice
- Pompilia
  - Abbots Fel
  - Pagan Queen

CHOCOLATE BEAU
- Beau Max
  - Bull Lea
  - Bee Mac
- Otra
  - Equipoise
  - Tenez

*Northern Dancer (1964 Ken. Derby/Preakness) Champion Sire (UK) 1970, 77, 83, 84
*Court Martial (1945 2000 Guineas)
*Nearco unbeaten in 14 races in Italy and France Champion Sire (UK) 1947 & 1948
*Native Dancer (1953 Belmont Stakes)
*Hyperion (1933 Derby/St. Leger) Sired 11 English Classic winners
*Polynesian (1945 Preakness)
*Mahmoud (1936 Derby)
*Fairway (1928 St. Leger)
*Hurry On (1916 St. Leger) sired 8 English Classic winners
*Ksar (1921 & 1922 Prix de l'Arc)
*Biribi (1926 Prix de l'Arc)

# THE CURRAGH

RACING ON THIS lovely expanse of heath near Kildare, south of Dublin, has gone on since time immemorial; even the word Curragh is derived from the Irish 'Cuirrach', meaning racecourse. Ancient laws regarding horse racing were handed down from the native Irish by the Brehons, or judges, who decreed that foster children should be provided with horses and taught riding, and that a foster son should be given a horse at the time of the races. The Curragh was known as the King's racecourse, and only young nobles were allowed to race on it.

### THE 'CLASSIC' TEST
In Ireland, all the Classics are decided on the Curragh, and have been so ever since they were founded, the Irish Derby in 1864, the Irish Oaks in 1895, Irish St. Leger in 1915, and the Irish

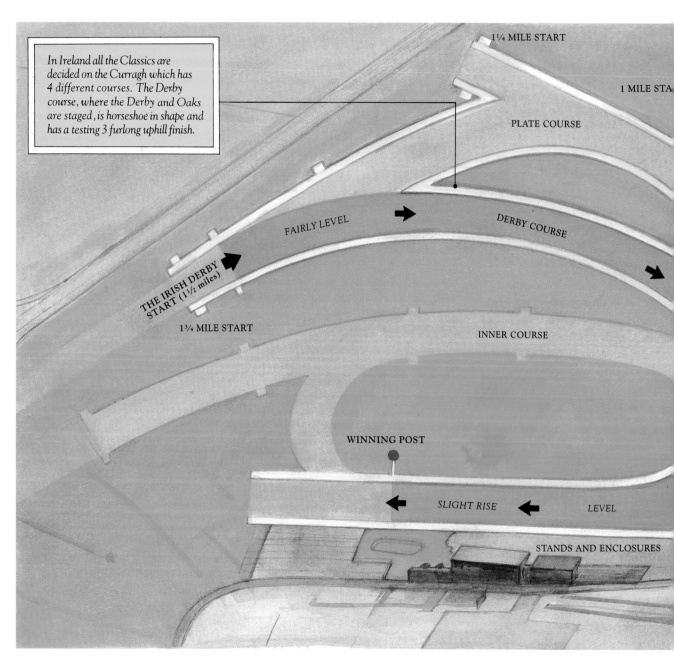

In Ireland all the Classics are decided on the Curragh which has 4 different courses. The Derby course, where the Derby and Oaks are staged, is horseshoe in shape and has a testing 3 furlong uphill finish.

1¼ MILE START

1 MILE STA

PLATE COURSE

FAIRLY LEVEL

DERBY COURSE

THE IRISH DERBY START (1½ miles)

1¾ MILE START

INNER COURSE

WINNING POST

SLIGHT RISE    LEVEL

STANDS AND ENCLOSURES

**Right** *Looking down the finishing straight at the Curragh, Co. Kildare.*

**Right** *Looking down the finishing straight at the Curragh, Co. Kildare.*

*Racing has taken place on this site from the very earliest days of Irish history. 'Curragh' is derived from the Gaelic word 'Cuirrach' meaning race-course. The first Irish Derby took place here in 1864 the winner picking up £400. By 1988 the prize money had risen to £330,000.*

2000 and 1000 Guineas in 1921. The country has come to the forefront of innovation here, too, for with the popularity of the Irish St. Leger waning, the authorities opened it up to horses older than three years old.

The galloping horseshoe track on fine old springy turf with no sharp bends offers an ideal Classic test. The view from the stands is superb across the Curragh, crossed on the far side of the course by the main Dublin to Kildare road, the Curragh itself dotted with gorse bushes and grazing sheep, training gallops and schooling fences.

The two-mile course has a 3-furlong uphill finish, and there is also a straight mile, with sprint races being run on both courses. A new inner course with 1-mile and 7-furlong starts is expected to be used only occasionally, and in 1988 a separate two-mile-long National Hunt course was constructed, returning hurdle racing to the Curragh after many years absence.

1 MILE START

STRAIGHT COURSE

SLIGHT RISE

GHT FALL

# THE IRISH DERBY

IN 1817, 37 years after the first Epsom Derby, an Irish counterpart christened the O'Darby Stakes and run over the longer distance of 1¾ miles, first took place at the Curragh. It was a flop, and by 1824 was abandoned; a second attempt to establish it was made in 1848, entitled The Curragh Derby, but this, too, was soon forgotten, as racing went into something of a decline.

Then, in 1864, Lord Howth, the Marquis of Drogheda and the Earl of Charlemont, decided to inaugurate the Irish Derby. Although thirty eight entries were received, and there was much pre-race publicity and extra trains put on to convey racegoers, only three horses stood their ground, victory going to the favourite, *Selim*. Two years later, it was worse, with only two runners and the outsider *Madeira* beating the hot favourite, *Bee Quick*.

At last matters turned for the better, as in 1907 greater credence and acceptance was given to the race when the winner of the Epsom Derby, *Orby*, travelled over and won the Irish equivalent. This victory drew English trainers' attention to the race, and before long they dominated it.

Then in 1962, the Irish had the enterprise to introduce sponsorship into the Classic, forming an association with the Irish Hospitals Sweeps which brought with it an extra £30,000 shot in the arm that year. Sponsorship for the Classics had been resisted in England, but they eventually followed suit, just as in 1988 the Irish jumped on the 'Million' bandwagon, started in Australia, but rejected so far by England's Jockey Club.

*Kahyasi stretches out to win the 1988 Irish Derby by a short head from Insan. In the last twenty years 7 horses have won both the Epsom and Irish Derbys, Kahyasi amongst them.*

The American firm, Anheuser-Busch, who brew Budweiser beer, began their sponsorship of the race in 1986, and have contracted to do so until 1991.

## KAHYASI

One of the bravest winners ever seen of the Irish Derby was *Kahyasi* in 1988, for he came back with such a deep cut it was a wonder he even finished the race, let alone won.

*Kahyasi* is the epitome of the modern day racehorse: small, neat, and beautifully proportioned. He follows the trend towards American blood, although he was bred by his owner, and Aga Khan, within a mile of the Curragh racecourse at his Ballymany Stud. His sire was *Ile de Bourbon* who won the King George VI and Queen Elizabeth Diamond Stakes in 1978, but is now standing in Japan.

*Kahyasi* was not hurried and ran once as a two-year-old, winning in the Autumn at Newmarket from Luca Cumani's Newmarket stable. The stable lad who looked after him during his two-year-old season left the following year to be an assistant trainer at another yard so missing the greatest pay day of his life when *Kahyasi* won the Derby.

### SIGNS OF PROMISE

*Kahyasi* ran twice in the spring of 1988 when it became clear he was a useful colt — but there were still many who did not see him as a dual Derby winner. He won at Sandown in April and then the Lingfield Derby Trial, which is usually a useful pointer to the Derby as it is one of the few racecourses in the country with both a sharp bend and steep gradient, as is found on the Epsom Derby course.

Significantly as it turned out, the horse he beat at Lingfield was *Insan*, who was giving 5lb to *Kahyasi*, and was beaten by two lengths. *Insan* was then unable to run in the Derby due to a bruised foot and did not run again until the pair clashed in the Irish Derby.

The Epsom Derby, meanwhile, looked the most open for years, with a number of market leaders, *Red Glow* finally setting off favourite. After half a mile, as they turned at the top of the hill, he was running in last place and when they came down Tattenham Hill it was *Unfuwain* making the best of his way home.

*Kefaah* looked to be going better than his stable companion *Kahyasi* at this stage, but then the

### THE 1988 IRISH DERBY

**Prize Money:** IR £329,250
**Runners:** 11

**1 KAHYASI**
(Ile de Bourbon – Kadissya)
**Jockey:** R. Cochrane
**Starting Price:** 4-5
**Owner:** HH The Aga Khan
**Trainer:** L. Cumani

**2 INSAN**
(Our Native – Artania)
**Jockey:** T. Quinn
**Starting Price:** 10-1
**Owner:** F. Salman
**Trainer:** P. F. Cole

**3 GLACIAL STORM**
(Arctic Tern – Hortensia)
**Jockey:** S. Cauthen
**Starting Price:** 3-1
**Owner:** R. Sangster
**Trainer:** B. W. Hills

**Finished:** 11
**Distances:** Short Head, 2½ lengths
**Winning Time:** 2 minutes, 32.5 secs.

picture changed dramatically: there were two furlongs left to cover, with *Unfuwain* still leading; *Glacial Storm* set up his challenge, and hot on his heels were *Kahyasi*, ridden by former hurdle race jockey Ray Cochrane, and *Doyoun*.

But it was *Kahyasi* who produced the finishing spurt to sweep him to a thoroughly deserved victory in the fastest time since electrical timing began at the Derby.

### DOUBLE ATTEMPT

So *Kahyasi* came to the Irish Derby the only unbeaten runner and not surprisingly this time was a hot favourite. Barry Hills's stable was hoping that their relaxed colt *Glacial Storm* could reverse the Epsom placings, when he was runner up beaten one and a half lengths, but this time there was to be two and a half lengths, and another horse, between them.

Crowds flocked to the Curragh for the rich Budweiser sponsored event with eleven runners.

65

Pacemaker, *Wagon Load*, by *Bustino*, set off in front but when he dropped out with half a mile to go it was *Insan* who took over the lead, closely followed by *Glacial Storm*.

### AN INDOMITABLE SPIRIT

As they turned into the straight, *Insan* had set up what looked to be an unassailable lead, with *Glacial Storm* appearing one-paced. *Kahyasi* seemed to be making surprisingly heavy weather of catching up, and although he was slowly but surely gaining ground, his task with only a furlong left to run looked hopeless. What was not known to the spectators then was that half a mile before he had been struck into and gashed below the knee.

It was with the greatest courage that he came after the leader. Fifty yards from the line they were locked together and Richard Quinn dropped his whip on *Insan*; it might or might not have made all the difference: the pair passed the post seemingly as one, then, after a nerve sapping wait, came the photographic verdict — *Kahyasi*, the winner by a short head!

It was the third time the English had white-washed the result filling the first three places, and it was the Aga Khan's third horse to complete the Epsom-Irish Derby double in the one decade, following *Shergar* in 1981 and *Sharastani* in 1986.

*Kahyasi* will be remembered as a very brave winner of the Irish Derby.

*Kahyasi, ridden by Ray Cochrane, wearing the familiar colours of the Aga Khan. All the present Aga Khan's Derby winners have gone on to win the Irish Derby.*

## BALLYMOSS

The transition period when Vincent O'Brien turned from National Hunt training to the Flat came in the early 1950s, and one of the first horses to show the racing world that the young man from Tipperary was just as good at preparing flat racers as jumpers was *Ballymoss*.

By the then unfashionable *Mossborough*, *Ballymoss* was a horse who kept improving with age, and a fine example of one who, kept in training at four, was able to prove himself even better than had been thought.

*Ballymoss* did not immediately show his ability. He was beaten on his first two outings as a two-year-old, the second at humble Mallow in Co. Cork, and the horse who beat him, *Bell Bird*, became the great grand-dam of the dual Ascot Gold Cup winner *Ardross*.

He did win one race at two, but then was beaten again over heavy ground, on which he never ran his best. But the stable knew he stayed, and felt that, given good physical progress in the winter, he could even make a Classic horse.

### A SURPRISING THREE-YEAR-OLD

It did not augur well when he was beaten out of sight on his reappearance, on heavy ground, and then suffered a training set-back with a bruised foot but then, on the fast ground he needed, he beat his stable companion *Gladness* at 20-1.

*Ballymoss winning the 1958 Eclipse Stakes ridden by 4 times Champion Jockey, Scobie Breasley. He won the Irish Derby and St Leger as a three-year-old and at four added the 'King George' and 'Prix de l'Arc'.*

His next race was the Derby itself, and he was still a rank outsider, at 33-1, although at home it was clear he had finally begun to come good and galloped really well, so the stable was happy for him to take his chance.

In the Derby only one horse finished ahead of him, the great *Crepello*. Vincent O'Brien was sure that the race would have brought him on further, and that by the Irish Derby three weeks later the horse would be even better.

So it proved. The Curragh, Ireland's answer to Newmarket Heath, was swelled by crowds to see their country's premier Classic. This time *Bally-moss*, the neat bay with attractive white star, far from being a rank outsider, was an odds-on favourite. Buoyed up by the cheers of the crowd he galloped his way to an easy victory, ridden as usual by Australian Scobie Breasley.

### FOUR-YEAR-OLD SENSATION

He added the St. Leger that year, and at four won the 'King George', the Eclipse Stakes, the Coronation Cup and, in final crowning glory, the Prix de l'Arc de Triomphe. Retiring to stud on a wave of victories few could remember that two-year-old defeated at Mallow!

67

# PHOENIX PARK

PHOENIX PARK claimed to be the only race-course in the world to have every race fully sponsored, this for some seventeen race meetings a year, including two on Sundays.

It boasted both left and right-handed courses on level ground. Its left-hand course had 1 mile, 1 mile 1 furlong, 1 mile 2 furlong, and 1 mile 3 furlong starts and, like the right-hand course, had a three furlong straight.

The right-hand course had two five furlong courses, a straight six furlongs, a dog-legged seven furlong course, and starts for 1 mile, 1 mile 1 furlong and 1 mile 2 furlongs. There was a course watering system used when the going appeared to be too hard and the state of the going was measured by Penetrometer.

The racecourse was built in 1901 in late Victorian style. It was refurbished in 1983 but had retained much of its charm. The new management team brought in at that time put in an enormous amount of money and effort to transform and revitalise racing in Ireland, not least being the introduction in 1988 of the Cartier Million.

Situated in a huge park close to the centre of Dublin it was an ideal venue for townspeople to come and enjoy flat racing. This was made easier by

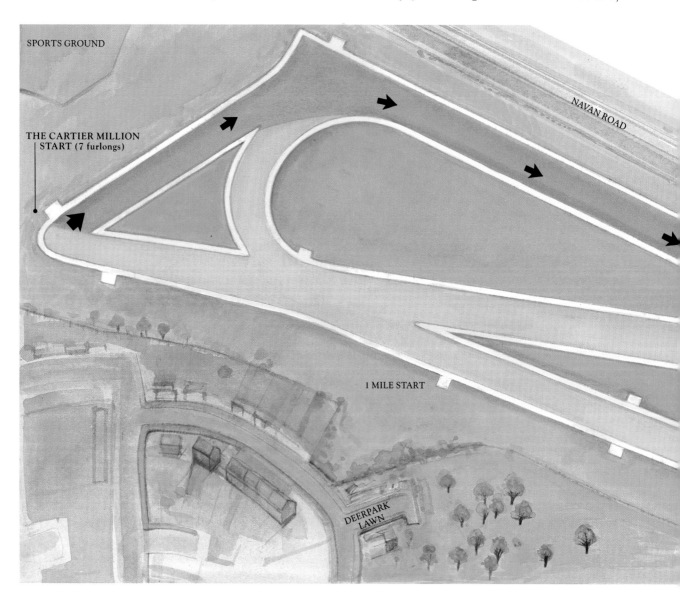

SPORTS GROUND

THE CARTIER MILLION
START (7 furlongs)

NAVAN ROAD

1 MILE START

DEERPARK
LAWN

**Right** *The parade ring at Phoenix Park.*

*Phoenix Park racecourse was built in 1903 but was recently refurbished to provide the most up-to-date racing facilities. There were right and left-handed courses both on level ground — the Cartier Million was run on the right-handed dog-legged 7 furlong track.*

having adjacent free car parking and a supervised children's playground complete with entertainers.

Dubliners flocked to the course on race days attracted by the possibility of observing top class racing whilst enjoying ultra-modern facilities. The many bars and restaurants were all served by closed circuit television and the food had a high reputation for its variety and quality.

Sadly the 1990 running of the Million was the last day's racing at Phoenix Park, which its owners hope to redevelop for housing and hotels. Only a last-ditch stand will allow the phoenix to rise from the ashes.

1¼ MILE START

WINNING POST

STANDS AND ENCLOSURES

1½ MILE START

# THE CARTIER MILLION

CONTROVERSY CONTINUES to surround the concept of races like Ireland's Cartier Million, with the English Jockey Club firmly putting its foot down against them. It says they are restrictive races, as they are open only to horses bought at one particular yearling sale, and that unless such big prize money is made open to all possible competitors stallion statistics may be distorted.

The idea originated in Australia, when Queensland first introduced a 'million dollar race' for horses bred in the state. It caught on among the other states, was followed in America by the Breeders' Cup concept, and arrived in Ireland in 1988. In the Irish version the race is funded by the vendors of the Goff's Cartier Million yearling sale paying an entry fee of IR

£2,500 plus 2½ per cent commission.

But while detractors claim it as being bad for the future of the bloodstock breeding industry, bringing lower prices overall with just the few in the 'million' sale making big profits, those for it say it is a great way for small time owners and breeders to receive a slice of the big prizes that normally go year in year out to the rich and well-established owners.

## OPPORTUNITY FOR THE SYNDICATES

This has certainly proved to be the case in Ireland. The first three horses home in the 1988 race were all owned by syndicates, making lots of

people winners. The race, open to two-year-olds bought at the previous October's 'million' sale, was won by *Corwyn Bay*, trained by Tommy Stack, better known to the English racing public as *Red Rum's* winning rider in the 1977 Grand National than as a top flat-race trainer.

In fact, it was only his first full season as a flat-race trainer, having concentrated more on building up and establishing his Thomastown Castle Stud since retiring from the saddle ten years before. He had the added satisfaction of having bred the colt himself, making it a very popular victory with the Irish.

*Corwyn Bay*, a good-looking iron grey by *Caerleon*, cost IR £60,000. His owners, many of them American, shared half a million *punts* (Irish pounds) from the victory.

### 1988 RACE

The race attracted 20 runners, and in the early stages the lead was disputed by *Cartier Bijoux* and *Gaijin*. The runners remained well bunched until inside two furlongs when *Corwyn Bay*, his run well timed by jockey Stephen Craine, surged clear. Willie Carson sent the favourite *Miss Demure* after him but he was gone beyond recall.

*Corwyn Bay* won by a length. *French Pretender* stayed on well after interference but failed by a short-head to deprive *Miss Demure* of second. Only five lengths separated the first 11 horses home, making it a keenly fought contest.

Both second and third were owned by the British syndicate Kennett Valley Thoroughbreds Ltd and together earned £300,000 for their members, headed by Lord Caernarvon's second son Harry Herbert, another of their part shareholders being Sir Ian Trethowan, chairman of the Horserace Betting Levy Board.

The winner returned to an ecstatic hero's welcome and clearly the race was a great success in Ireland. It was the brainchild of Jonathan Irwin, managing director of the promoting Goffs Sales and also chief executive of Phoenix Park, who was understandably delighted. 'It's just like Cheltenham — there is a real buzz', he said; 'The race is everything I wanted it to be. I haven't seen jockeys going for the line like that in a long time'.

*Corwyn Bay ridden by Stephen Craine wins the 1988 Cartier Million. An Irish-bred colt, he was trained by Tommy Stack and owned by a syndicate who received half a million punts as a result of his victory.*

# LONGCHAMPS

IN 1854 the Société D'Encouragement, the governing body of French racing, gave its permission for the construction of a racecourse in the Bois De Boulogne, a large park to the west of Paris. Lacking the funds to complete the grand-stand, the Société had to borrow money from its own members to complete its ambitious project.

The first meeting was held on April 27th, 1857.

The Emperor Louis-Napoleon, who arrived by boat, was amongst the crowd of almost 100,000. Five races were held, the second of which was won by *Miss Gladiateur* who was to become famous as the dam of the great *Gladiateur*.

Facilities at Longchamps are good. The original stands were completely rebuilt in 1903 and since then there has been continual improvement to

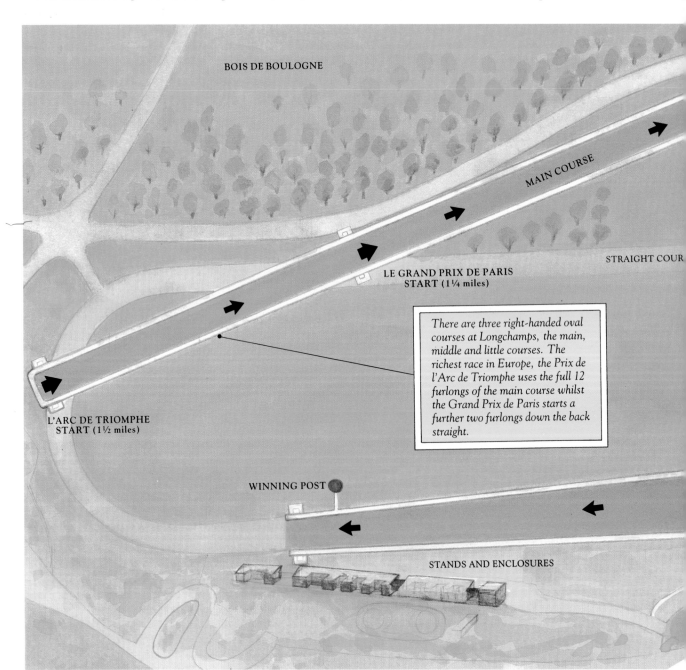

BOIS DE BOULOGNE

MAIN COURSE

STRAIGHT COUR

LE GRAND PRIX DE PARIS
START (1¼ miles)

L'ARC DE TRIOMPHE
START (1½ miles)

*There are three right-handed oval courses at Longchamps, the main, middle and little courses. The richest race in Europe, the Prix de l'Arc de Triomphe uses the full 12 furlongs of the main course whilst the Grand Prix de Paris starts a further two furlongs down the back straight.*

WINNING POST

STANDS AND ENCLOSURES

**Left** *The parade ring at Longchamps. Along with Chantilly it is the major flat racing course in France and stages a succession of meets from April to October.*

the viewing facilities. In 1962 a fantastic new stand was built around the old rococo one. That was destroyed once the old one had been moved into place — an architectural operation of bewildering complexity.

The course itself is a right-handed oval with three separate tracks, the largest of which allows races of eleven furlongs to be run in one circuit of the course.

The straight five-furlong course bisects the oval one on the far side making viewing of some races particularly difficult. Problems are also caused by the two finishing posts in the straight which have been known to confuse some foreign jockeys, an occurrence that is, of course, thoroughly enjoyed by the local riders.

Yves Saint Martin who ruled the French jockeys' roost for 20-odd years between 1962 and 1987 was a master at Longchamps and a great favourite with the crowd. His course record of 4 Arcs, 12 Guineas' and 4 Grand Prix's compare favourably with that of Lester Piggott — the English maestro of the same era.

### THE LONGCHAMPS SEASONS

The first part of the season at Longchamps runs from April to the end of May during which time it stages not only the first two French Classics (Poule D'Essai Des Poulains, Poule D'Essai Des Pouliches) but also the major trials for the Prix Du Jockey Club and the Prix De Diane.

After the Chantilly interlude at the start of June, Longchamps stages just one more Sunday meeting — that of the Grand Prix De Paris — before the mid-summer break.

When racing returns to the course in September, the eight week meeting is, if anything, of an even higher quality with races such as the Prix Du Moulin (named after the famous windmill that stands in the centre of the track) the Prix Vermeille (The Fillies' Arc) the Prix De La Salamandre and the Grand Criterium.

However, it is the first weekend in October that produces the highlight. With ten group races on the two day card, all presently sponsored by the Aga Khan-owned Ciga Hotel Group, the weekend is a veritable feast for the European racing enthusiast and at around 4.20 on the Sunday they line up for the Prix De L'Arc De Triomphe — the biggest one of all.

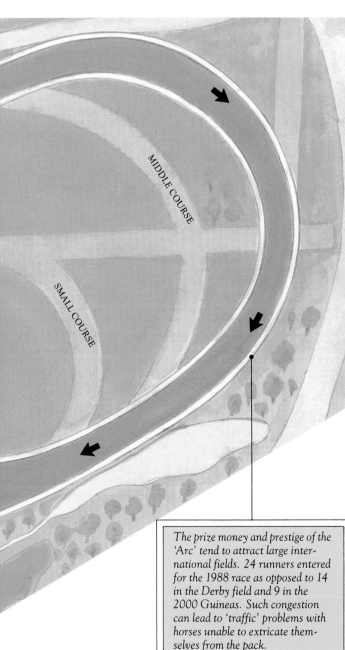

MIDDLE COURSE

SMALL COURSE

*The prize money and prestige of the 'Arc' tend to attract large international fields. 24 runners entered for the 1988 race as opposed to 14 in the Derby field and 9 in the 2000 Guineas. Such congestion can lead to 'traffic' problems with horses unable to extricate themselves from the pack.*

# LE PRIX DE L'ARC DE TRIOMPHE

TRADITIONALLY RUN on the first Sunday in October, the Arc is now accepted as the official all-aged middle distance championship of Europe. The Derby winners, the older champions and the other pretenders will line up for Longchamps's exacting 12-furlong trip. The prestige attached to winning it is unparalleled.

It was in 1920 that the Société D'Encouragement held the inaugural running of the Prix De L'Arc De Triomphe. The idea was to hold a race of comparable status to the Grand Prix in the middle of the Autumn season which would attract the best of all Europe to Longchamps for an end of season championship. The idea worked immediately with the first running seeing horses from both Italy and England competing against the best of the French.

The winner proved to be a wonderful international combination with Evremond De Saint-Alary, one of France's leading owner/breeders of the time winning the race with *Comrade* who was trained in England by Peter Gilpin and ridden by the Australian jockey Frank Bullock. The honour of the best ever Arc winner must lie between three great colts. *Ribot*, the Italian Champion won the race in 1955 and 1956, the astonishing *Sea Bird II* who left his field for dead in 1965 and the brilliant *Dancing Brave* who won the memorable Arc of 1986 in record time to put his Derby débâcle behind him.

## RIBOT

*Ribot* won the Prix de L'Arc de Triomphe twice and the King George VI and Queen Elizabeth Diamond Stakes as well as a whole string of top races in Italy. He also became one of the most influential sires this century — and yet had the reputation for a bit of 'temperament' that was likely to be bred on.

*Alleged, ridden by Lester Piggott. Twice winner of the Prix de l'Arc de Triomphe in 1977 and 1978 and yet another successful horse from the O'Brien stables.*

*The Italian Champion Ribot shown winning his first 'Arc' in 1955. The following year he travelled to England to win the King George VI and Queen Elizabeth Diamond Stakes before adding another 'Arc' to his tally.*

Even if this was so, his racing credentials were so high that the odd idiosyncracy could be forgiven; he sired such well-known Classic winners as *Ribocco, Ribero, Ribofilio, Ragusa, Long Look, Boucher* and *Romulus*.

He sired two more Arc winners in *Molvedo* and *Prince Royal II*, while in America, where he stood at stud in Kentucky, he was responsible for some of their top horses including *Tom Rolfe, Graustart* and *Art and Letters*.

It was in the mid 1950s that *Ribot* burst on to the European racing scene. He ran in 16 races and retired unbeaten, one of the greatest racehorses of all time.

## SMALL EXPECTATIONS

Signor Federico Tesio, who was responsible for breeding *Nearco* nearly 20 years earlier in his life, owned *Ribot*'s sire, *Tenerani*, a good stayer, out of a mare whose mother, like *Nearco*'s grand-dam, he bought cheaply at Newmarket Sales.

The resulting small colt was named *Ribot* and ran in the name of Signor Tesio's partner, the Marchesa Incisa della Rochetta and was trained by Ugo Penco and ridden by Enrico Camici.

Nothing much was expected of the colt, and so he was not entered for the Classics, but he soon showed himself as useful, if somewhat with a mind of his own, when racing. He was fine when allowed to bowl along in front, but if restrained he resented it and showed it.

Luckily, these tactics were only tried once nearly ending in defeat and so in 1955, having won a string of non-Classic Italian races, the three-year-old travelled to Paris for the Arc on Sunday October 9, 1955. It was chucking him in at the deep end, but nevertheless he came out with flying colours, winning impressively by three lengths, the field strung out behind him on the soft ground, *Beau Prince* and *Picounda* following him home.

## A NAME TO BE CONJURED WITH

By the following year, all of European racing was taking notice of the neat, bay Italian colt who was still unbeaten, and, what's more, winning his races by wide margins.

Before a second crack at the Arc he was brought over to England to contest the King George at Ascot, and started at odds-on. At first he found it hard to cope with the heavy ground, and defeat looked a real possibility, but a true sign of greatness is a horse who can cope with any ground and difficulties.

In overcoming the soft going, lengthening his stride once he reached the straight, and drawing away to win by five lengths, he stamped himself among the truly greats.

His finest hour was still to come, in his second Arc. He held his condition well through to the October date, and again was confronted with heavy ground. He also faced a strong challenge,

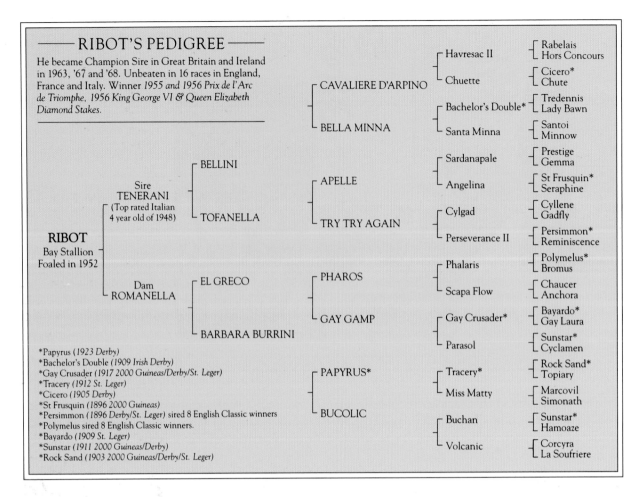

## RIBOT'S PEDIGREE

He became Champion Sire in Great Britain and Ireland in 1963, '67 and '68. Unbeaten in 16 races in England, France and Italy. Winner 1955 and 1956 Prix de l'Arc de Triomphe, 1956 King George VI & Queen Elizabeth Diamond Stakes.

**RIBOT**
Bay Stallion
Foaled in 1952

Sire TENERANI (Top rated Italian 4 year old of 1948)
- BELLINI
- TOFANELLA
  - APELLE
    - Sardanapale — Prestige / Gemma
    - Angelina — St Frusquin* / Seraphine
  - TRY TRY AGAIN
    - Cylgad — Cyllene / Gadfly
    - Perseverance II — Persimmon* / Reminiscence

CAVALIERE D'ARPINO
- Havresac II — Rabelais / Hors Concours
- Chuette — Cicero* / Chute

BELLA MINNA
- Bachelor's Double* — Tredennis / Lady Bawn
- Santa Minna — Santoi / Minnow

Dam ROMANELLA
- EL GRECO
  - PHAROS
    - Phalaris — Polymelus* / Bromus
    - Scapa Flow — Chaucer / Anchora
  - GAY GAMP
    - Gay Crusader* — Bayardo* / Gay Laura
    - Parasol — Sunstar* / Cyclamen
- BARBARA BURRINI
  - PAPYRUS*
    - Tracery* — Rock Sand* / Topiary
    - Miss Matty — Marcovil / Simonath
  - BUCOLIC
    - Buchan — Sunstar* / Hamoaze
    - Volcanic — Corcyra / La Soufriere

*Papyrus (1923 Derby)
*Bachelor's Double (1909 Irish Derby)
*Gay Crusader (1917 2000 Guineas/Derby/St. Leger)
*Tracery (1912 St. Leger)
*Cicero (1905 Derby)
*St Frusquin (1896 2000 Guineas)
*Persimmon (1896 Derby/St. Leger) sired 8 English Classic winners
*Polymelus sired 8 English Classic winners.
*Bayardo (1909 St. Leger)
*Sunstar (1911 2000 Guineas/Derby)
*Rock Sand (1903 2000 Guineas/Derby/St. Leger)

---

including two runners from America for the first time in 20 years.

This time, though, he left his supporters in no doubt as to his ability to cope with both the ground and the opposition. Top class they might be, but he had the race sewn up fully half a mile from home, galloping effortlessly behind *Fisherman*.

From the stands, he could be seen moving smoothly into the lead on a tight rein as they turned into the straight; then he simply quickened and left his rivals struggling with fully two furlongs still to run. As he reached the post to the enthusiastic roar of the crowd, he was at least six lengths clear of his nearest rival, *Talgo*, with *Tanerbo*, *Career Boy* and *Master Boing* fighting for the minor honours.

It was, perhaps, his finest win.

## TONY BIN v MTOTO

In 1988 there was an older horse who had not even run in the Classics but who had improved so much with age that the English racing public had taken him to their hearts.

This was the five-year-old, British-trained *Mtoto*, who had won the Eclipse and Prince of Wales's Stakes twice each, and the King George VI and Queen Elizabeth Stakes, and who became a firm favourite for the Prix de l'Arc de Triomphe. He travelled over in the same aeroplane as that year's Derby winner, *Kahyasi*, the pair needing so many extra security guards that there was no room for any other horses on board. Even *Kahyasi*'s two pacemakers, *Roushayd* and *Taboushkhan*, had to travel by separate 'plane.

### AN INTERNATIONAL CLASH

The Arc is a true test between generations and between countries, and 1988 proved no exception. There were eight runners from Britain, a handful from Ireland, and representing Italy was the previous year's runner up, *Tony Bin*.

The home side included the great mare *Triptych*, third in both the last two runnings of the race, and among the Classic horses in a strong field, apart from *Kahyasi*, were *Emmson* from France, Britain's smashing little filly *Diminuendo* who won both the Oaks and 1000 Guineas and *Dark Lomond* who won the Irish St. Leger.

So the scene was set for a classic confrontation and the massive crowds, for many of whom the Arc is the social highlight of the year, were not to be disappointed.

*Mtoto*, ridden by former South African champion jockey Michael Roberts, started favourite. Pat Eddery opted to ride *Indian Rose* in preference to *Tony Bin* who was ridden instead by John Reid, based with Vincent O'Brien in Ireland.

### A HARD AND FAST RACE

With the ground riding fast, and with the presence of three pacemakers in the race, the pace was a cracking one. *Taboushkhan* made the early running pressed by *Roushayd*, the pair undertaking their allotted task, with *Mtoto*, *Tony Bin*, *Indian Rose* who was slowly away, and the French mare *Triptych*, hating the firm ground, near the back of the field.

As they swept round the long turn for home,

*Tony Bin shown as a four-year-old in 1987. He improved from runner-up to winner of the 'Arc' in 1988.*

*Unfuwain's* pacemaker *Polemos* took over, with *Emmson* close behind and *Diminuendo* looking the best placed of all, on the rails behind them.

*Unfuwain* and *Boyatino* moved up to challenge and took over the lead from *Emmson*, while behind them *Mtoto* was keeping close to *Tony Bin* as the Italian horse swept down the hill towards home still full of running, poised behind *Kahyasi*.

### HOT PURSUIT

*Tony Bin* then strode past the Derby winner and, *Mtoto*, momentarily held in his place by *Village Star* on his outside, set off in hot pursuit. The pair got into top gear but *Tony Bin* had 'first run' and his acceleration proved decisive.

*Mtoto* was gaining ground but the post came in time for the sporting Italian contingent, and *Tony Bin* held on by a neck. *Boyatino* was a length behind to take third and *Unfuwain*, the best of the three-year-olds, a respectable fourth.

*Village Star* and *Kahyasi* were also close up in fifth and sixth. Next came *Fijar Tango* and *Emmson*, followed by *Light the Lights* and *Dimi-*

## THE 1988 PRIX DE L'ARC DE TRIOMPHE

**Prize Money:** £497,512
**Runners:** 24

**1** TONY BIN
(Kampala – Severn Bridge)
**Jockey:** J. Reid
**Owner:** Mrs V. Gaucci del Bono
**Trainer:** L. Camici

**2** MTOTO
(Busted – Amazer)
**Jockey:** M. Roberts
**Owner:** Sheik A. Al Maktoum
**Trainer:** A. C. Stewart

**3** BOYATINO
(Concertino – Boyarina)
**Jockey:** M. Philliperon
**Owner:** J. Lesbordes
**Trainer:** G. Blizniansky

**Finished:** 24
**Distances:** Neck, 1 length
**Winning Time:** 2 minutes, 27.3 secs

nuendo who faded into tenth place, ahead of the struggling *Dark Lomond*.

It was a great triumph for the Italian colt in the second fastest time ever, richly deserved after his second berth the previous year, and worthy of his illustrious compatriot, the mighty *Ribot* who won in 1955 and '56.

*Tony Bin's* was a bargain basement story. By *Kampala* out of *Severn Bridge*, he was bought by Señor and Señora Gaucci del Bono for just 3,000 guineas at Goff's Irish National Foal Sale in 1983. After the 1988 Arc, he had won 15 races and earnt over £1 million in prize money. He was trained in Italy by Luigi Camici and named after an artist Antonio Bin.

*Mtoto* was far from disgraced, even less so when he was found to be lame on a front joint on his return to his stables at Newmarket. He retired to Aston Upthorpe Stud in Oxfordshire where he replaced his own sire, *Busted* (also sire of Bustino), who had died.

## SEA BIRD II

For many racing enthusiasts, the greatest Arc winner was *Sea Bird II* in 1965. He completely outclassed a field of 20, having earlier treated a good class Derby field with similar contempt.

However, as a two-year-old the tall, rangy colt had not seemed anything special and was very much the second string in his French stable. In fact, having needed time to develop, he had not been raced until the autumn of his two-year-old year. He was then beaten for the only time in his career by a stable companion *Grey Dawn II*.

*Sea Bird's* breeding was unexceptional to say the least; he was by an undistinguished stallion called *Dan Cupid* (although *he* was by the great American horse *Native Dancer*), but on his dam's side, not one of his five female forebears had won a race of any description.

### A GENETIC MIRACLE

That *Sea Bird* should have become a Classic contender, let alone a winner, was therefore one of those miracles that keeps dreams alive in the bloodstock business.

Hardly a handsome colt, he nevertheless possessed the long and graceful stride of a greyhound, and it was this, in the end, that determined his greatness.

He was owned and bred by M. Jean Ternynck, trained by Etienne Pollet, and ridden to victory in both the Derby and Arc by the Australian jockey Pat Glennon.

### A TOP QUALITY RACE

The Arc once more lived up to its reputation as top all-age, international contest. Lined up alongside *Sea Bird* were such doughty competitors as the unbeaten *Reliance II* and *Diatome*, winner and runner up of that year's French Derby. The Russian champion *Anilin* was also present along with *Sea Bird's* Derby runner up and subsequent Irish Derby and King George winner *Meadow Court*, and from America, the Preakness winner *Tom Rolfe*.

The three French horses, *Sea Bird*, *Reliance* and *Diatome* headed the betting, but there were one or two anxious punters as the chestnut favourite dripped sweat in the early October sunshine.

If anything, it only improved him, for there was nothing that could live with *Sea Bird* that day. As they turned into the straight, *Anilin*, putting up a valiant fight, got his head in front, but then Pat Glennon just let out a notch of rein and *Sea Bird* swept by.

For a brief moment it looked as if *Reliance* would make a race of it, but Glennon, sensing his presence, simply shifted *Sea Bird* into overdrive to leave his rivals toiling.

He stormed into a decisive five-length lead, which he increased to six on the line in spite of suddenly swerving into the centre of the course. *Diatome*, who went on to win the Washington DC International in America, was a further five lengths back in third.

*Sea Bird II ridden by Pat Glennon. He won the 1965 Derby and 'Arc' with almost contemptuous ease.*

## A SUCCESSFUL SIRE

*Sea Bird* was an extremely popular as well as impressive winner of the Arc. He was retired to stud after it, standing in America for five years before returning to France where, unfortunately, he died soon afterwards.

His daughter *Allez France* herself won the Prix de l'Arc de Triomphe of 1974 and many other top French races; his son *Gyr*, like him trained by Etienne Pollet, was considered invincible, but in *Nijinsky* met an even better horse at Epsom; Another son was *Sea Pigeon*, a great dual purpose horse who mixed Flat racing and hurdling with equal ease. During his career he won several flat races before going on to win both the Champion Hurdle and Scottish Champion Hurdle.

# LE GRAND PRIX DE PARIS

THE GRAND PRIX DE PARIS was inaugurated in 1863. For many years this race was to be one of the highlights of the Parisian social calendar and the grand procession of carriages from the centre of Paris out to the Bois De Boulogne excited almost as much interest as the race itself.

In the 20th century the two-mile Grand Prix De Paris became something of a racing enigma with its emphasis on stamina-sapping battles. Eventually, in a belated bid to arrest its decline, the Société D'Encouragement agreed, in 1986, to cut the distance of the race to ten furlongs. Time, alone, will tell whether they have succeeded.

## NEARCO

*Nearco* was an Italian horse who became one of the all time international greats both on the racecourse and at stud and whose influence on the thoroughbred is still felt.

Bred by an Italian ex-Cavalry officer, Federico Tesio, *Nearco* was by *Pharos*, who stood in France, out of *Nogara*, whose dam Signor Tesio had bought for just 75 guineas at Newmarket Sales in 1915. She was by the Derby winner *Spearmint* out of a 1000 Guineas winner so although she had only won one small race herself she was beautifully bred.

In her grandson, *Nearco*, there was the near perfect racehorse, full of quality with perfect conformation and a solid temperament that thrived on hard work.

As a foal he showed himself a natural leader as he cavorted with the other youngsters around his paddocks near Rome, a far cry from the prime breeding grounds of Newmarket, Kentucky or France!

Tesio trained *Nearco* himself, with outstanding results, for the bay colt was unbeaten in no fewer than seven races as a two-year-old in 1937.

## KING OF ITALY

At three, he won the Italian equivalent of the 2000 Guineas, the Premio Parioli, easily. Then, the Italian Derby by a huge distance!

More Italian victories followed, then it was time to see if he could take on the best in Europe. He was sent to France for the Grand Prix De Paris at Longchamps over one mile seven furlongs.

This was a truly international contest, which brought together the Derby winners of France (*Cillas*), England (*Bois Roussel*) and Italy.

*Nearco, fifteen times in the top ten sires list — his descendants include Sir Ivor, Nijinsky, Mill Reef, Roberto and the Minstrel.*

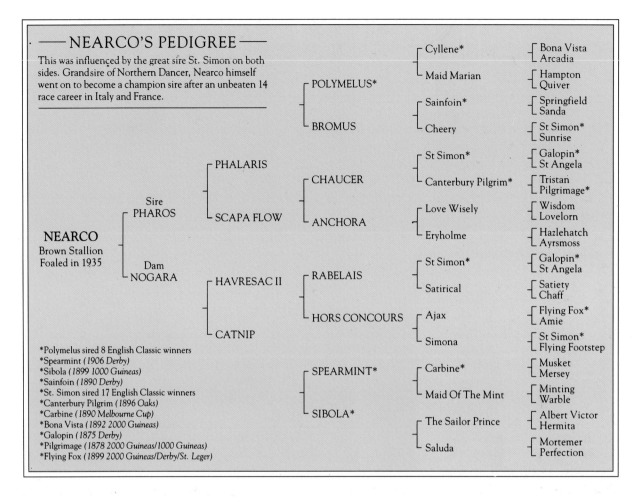

## NEARCO'S PEDIGREE

This was influenced by the great sire St. Simon on both sides. Grandsire of Northern Dancer, Nearco himself went on to become a champion sire after an unbeaten 14 race career in Italy and France.

**NEARCO**
Brown Stallion
Foaled in 1935

- Sire **PHAROS**
  - **PHALARIS**
  - **SCAPA FLOW**
    - **CHAUCER**
      - St Simon*
        - Galopin*
        - St Angela
      - Canterbury Pilgrim*
        - Tristan
        - Pilgrimage*
    - **ANCHORA**
      - Love Wisely
        - Wisdom
        - Lovelorn
      - Eryholme
        - Hazlehatch
        - Ayrsmoss
- Dam **NOGARA**
  - **HAVRESAC II**
    - **RABELAIS**
      - St Simon*
        - Galopin*
        - St Angela
      - Satirical
        - Satiety
        - Chaff
    - **HORS CONCOURS**
      - Ajax
        - Flying Fox*
        - Amie
      - Simona
        - St Simon*
        - Flying Footstep
  - **CATNIP**

- **POLYMELUS***
  - Cyllene*
    - Bona Vista
    - Arcadia
  - Maid Marian
    - Hampton
    - Quiver
- **BROMUS**
  - Sainfoin*
    - Springfield
    - Sanda
  - Cheery
    - St Simon*
    - Sunrise

- **SPEARMINT***
  - Carbine*
    - Musket
    - Mersey
  - Maid Of The Mint
    - Minting
    - Warble
- **SIBOLA***
  - The Sailor Prince
    - Albert Victor
    - Hermita
  - Saluda
    - Mortemer
    - Perfection

*Polymelus sired 8 English Classic winners
*Spearmint (1906 Derby)
*Sibola (1899 1000 Guineas)
*Sainfoin (1890 Derby)
*St. Simon sired 17 English Classic winners
*Canterbury Pilgrim (1896 Oaks)
*Carbine (1890 Melbourne Cup)
*Bona Vista (1892 2000 Guineas)
*Galopin (1875 Derby)
*Pilgrimage (1878 2000 Guineas/1000 Guineas)
*Flying Fox (1899 2000 Guineas/Derby/St. Leger)

In the event, *Nearco* was never in any danger. He took up the running soon after entering the straight and thereafter drew away to win by an easy one and a half lengths from the stayer *Canot* with *Bois Roussel* third.

### ARISTOCRATIC BREEDING

*Nearco* was sold to England for a record price to stand at stud in Newmarket. There, he consolidated his reputation as top European racehorse of his generation by becoming a truly great sire, 15 times in the top ten list.

His sons included *Dante* (winner of a war-time Derby), *Nimbus* (Derby), *Sayajirao* (St. Leger), *Nasrullah*, *Mossborough* and *Royal Charger*. Descendants of his include *Sir Ivor*, *Nijinsky*, *Mill Reef*, *Roberto*, *The Minstrel* and *Shirley Heights* — Derby winners all of them.

## GLADIATEUR

In 1865, a colt called *Gladiateur* became the first French horse to win the English Triple Crown of 2000 Guineas, Derby and St. Leger, dubbing him the 'avenger of Waterloo' — and a life-size statue of him graces the entrance to Longchamps where before an enthusiastic, partisan crowd, he also won the Grand Prix De Paris.

Although French bred and owned, it was to Newmarket that he was despatched to be trained. At the time England reigned supreme in the world of racing, and it came as something of a jolt to her ego when first France and then, nearer the turn of the century, America began to emulate and even beat her bloodstock.

*Gladiateur* won both the Guineas and Derby with ease from very big fields and for his next race re-crossed the Channel to his native country to line up for the Grand Prix De Paris.

A stupendous crowd of some 150,000 flocked to Longchamps to hail their hero, and when he won their cheers rose to a crescendo that jubilantly filled the air — truly here was the avenger of Waterloo!

*Gladiateur* also won the Prix Royal Oak that year as well as the St. Leger, and stayed in training as a four-year-old when he made more successful forays into France to win the Grand Prix De l'Impératrice, Grand Prix De l'Empereur and La Coupe as well as the Ascot Gold Cup.

# CHURCHILL DOWNS

CHURCHILL DOWNS, in Louisville, Kentucky, is a showpiece racecourse with its splendid, capacious stands adorned by their world famous twin spires. The current head of Churchill Downs Inc. is Thomas H. Meeker who in the 1980s set in motion a huge modernisation and improvement programme, including building a turf course and renovating the restaurants and offices to the tune of over $13 million.

The course has not always been so prosperous.

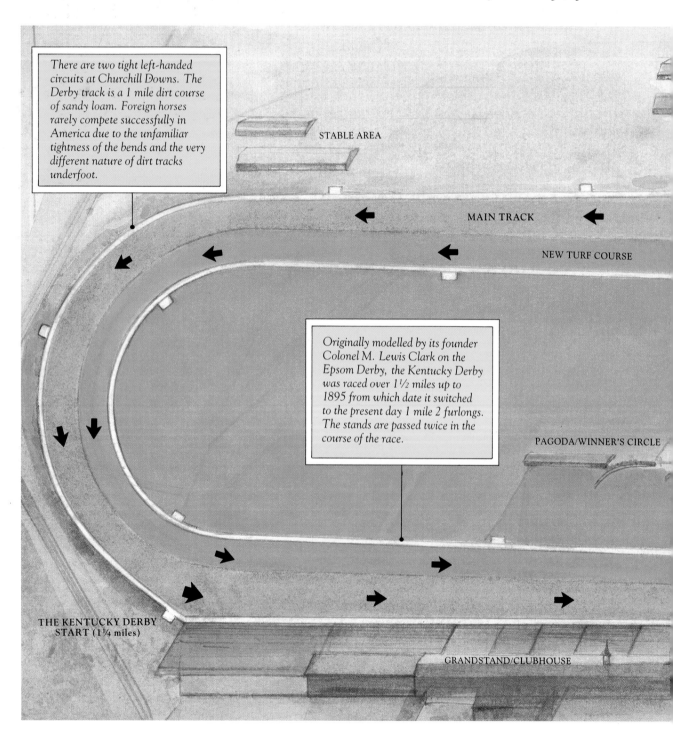

*There are two tight left-handed circuits at Churchill Downs. The Derby track is a 1 mile dirt course of sandy loam. Foreign horses rarely compete successfully in America due to the unfamiliar tightness of the bends and the very different nature of dirt tracks underfoot.*

STABLE AREA

MAIN TRACK

NEW TURF COURSE

*Originally modelled by its founder Colonel M. Lewis Clark on the Epsom Derby, the Kentucky Derby was raced over 1½ miles up to 1895 from which date it switched to the present day 1 mile 2 furlongs. The stands are passed twice in the course of the race.*

PAGODA/WINNER'S CIRCLE

THE KENTUCKY DERBY
START (1¼ miles)

GRANDSTAND/CLUBHOUSE

Towards the end of the last century it was in decline and had passed through several hands before becoming the property of one Matt. J. Winn. A wealthy tailor, he was also a born promoter and within ten years of taking over the beleaguered racetrack had marketed the Kentucky Derby into America's most prestigious horse race.

Much of American racing is on dirt tracks, and even where there is grass it is, like the dirt, on a tight, oval, left-handed track. This makes for little variety, apart from physical setting, and

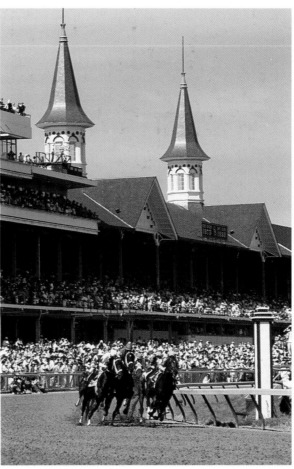

**Above** *The famous twin spires of the old Churchill Downs grandstand provide a striking and elegant backdrop to racing on the dirt track.*

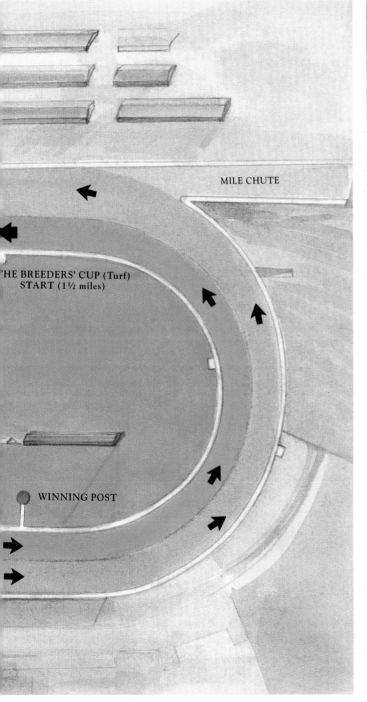

MILE CHUTE

'HE BREEDERS' CUP (Turf) START (1½ miles)

WINNING POST

there is not nearly as much room for 'horses for courses' as in Great Britain. As a result, although racing is wealthy, it is also stereotyped. Also, as in Australia, much more emphasis is put 'on the clock', both in training and in running, with the time of every furlong recorded, and sometimes even displayed on a huge digital board during the running of a race.

# THE KENTUCKY DERBY

IT WAS IN 1875 that one Colonel M. Lewis Clark inaugurated the Kentucky Derby and Oaks following a visit to England where he had watched the Epsom Classics. The American thoroughbred industry was in something of a decline at the time, and he resolved to pattern new races on the English ones in an effort to bring fresh life to it.

On returning home he founded the Louisville Jockey Club in his Kentucky state home, then set about staging the new American Classic.

He would have been pleased to see the result of his initiative one hundred years later when 163,675 people crowded on to Churchill Downs to watch the race live, with millions more world wide watching it on television. The race, held on the first Saturday in May, has become more than just a Classic: it is now a National Event.

The Kentucky Derby, the Preakness and Belmont Stakes have since 1919 made up the American Triple Crown. That was the year when *Sir Barton* won all three Classics. Since then,

*Kentucky Derby Day — like the day at Epsom it never fails to draw the crowds — though not in double decker buses!*

there have been 11 more, including such greats as *Secretariat* in 1973 (still the only sub two minute winner), *Seattle Slew* in 1977 and *Affirmed* the year after that.

### SPEND A BUCK

Big money is the name of the game, but the 1985 winner was a real 'rags to riches' colt, *Spend A Buck*. He was bred in an unfashionable area of Kentucky, in the coal and oil area near the River Ohio in the west of the state, far away from the Blue Grass region of Kentucky famed for its bluebloods.

Bred by Rowe Harper on his Irish Hill Farm, he was sent to a bankruptcy sale at Lexington where he was bought by Dennis Diaz, a Tampa businessman, for a paltry $12,500. Two years later, he had earned over $4 million.

American racing tends to be centralised, and the 'circuit' chosen for *Spend A Buck's* early career was New Jersey; he won the valuable Cherry Hill and Garden State races by wide margins, and so he was directed towards the Kentucky Derby, no less. On May 4, 1985, he travelled to Churchill Downs for the 111th running of the great race.

### DERBY DAY

The favourite was *Chief's Crown*, and it was thought that *Spend A Buck* and *Eternal Prince* would cut out the early running. But the anticipated duel never developed. Angel Cordero Jun., a top American jockey who is both skilful and 'racewise', jumped *Spend A Buck* so smartly out of the gate that he gained a one and a half lengths lead within the first 'quarter'.

Racing down the 'backstretch', the lead was increased to nine lengths, and at the finish he breezed in to win as he liked by five and a quarter lengths (distances are measured much more precisely in America than in England).

It was a stupendous victory. The winning margin was the widest for 39 years, since that of *Assault* in 1946, and was the third-fastest ever.

The victory brought a gold trophy valued at $45,000 for Dennis Diaz as well as prize money of $406,800, but that was only the start: by the end of the season, *Spend A Buck* had also won the Jersey Derby and a bonus of $3 million, bringing his total to $4,220,689.

### NORTHERN DANCER

Perhaps even more remarkable was the victory in 1964 of *Northern Dancer*. Today, everyone in the world of racing has heard of him, for he became a phenomenally successful sire, the most influential of modern times. But no-one would rank Canada, where *Northern Dancer* was bred, as one of the world's leading racing countries.

What's more, as a newly-broken yearling, *Northern Dancer* was virtually unrideable. He did everything within his powers to unseat his rider, and usually succeeded.

*Spend a Buck, chalking up the widest winning margin for 39 years in the 1985 Kentucky Derby.*

Northern Dancer, in front by a neck, heads Willie Shoemaker and Hill Rise at the line in the 1964 Kentucky Derby.

Northern Dancer did have the advantage of beginning life on a large stud farm, that of E. P. Taylor at Oshawa on the outskirts of Ontario, and was well bred, by *Nearctic* who was by *Nearco*. *Nearco* was himself reputed to be something of a bully as a yearling, and in later years, *Northern Dancer's* most famous son, *Nijinsky*, was very highly strung.

*Northern Dancer* was so little thought of as a yearling that he failed to reach his reserve of $25,000 at the Sales, and so he stayed in Mr. Taylor's ownership, moving to his farm at Willowdale, Ontario, to go into training.

The climate in a Canadian winter is not conducive to outdoor work, and so the yearlings did their exercise in a large indoor barn. Whoever drew the 'short straw' had to try and ride *Northern Dancer* who would invariably career through the rest of the string like a cavalry charger, and thought nothing of bumping headlong into the wooden walls.

### EARLY CAREER

Once racing began and a purpose in his life was apparent, he became more tractable, and was given a busy time, winning five of his seven races as a two-year-old. This included the Coronation Futurity and Carleton Stakes which were import-

ant enough for it to be decided to give the colt a chance against the best in the USA.

First, he travelled to Aqueduct where he proceeded to give a good horse, *Bupers*, an eight length thrashing over one mile, and soon followed it up with another win at 4-1 on. But, just as he had begun to look a great prospect, he developed what is known as a hairline quarter crack on a front hoof. Without treatment, the hoof would split to the coronet, a bit like a human nail cracking to the quick, and would make him lame and unraceable. His trainer Horatio Luro called in a specialist blacksmith all the way from California who successfully fused the hoofwall with heat treatment.

At the beginning of his three-year-old season, *Northern Dancer* flew to Florida where he lost his first race and the jockey was sacked for making too much use of the whip. With his suspect temperament, trainer Luro was convinced *Northern Dancer* did not want too much stick. Instead, Willie 'The Shoe' Shoemaker, the world's all time rider of most winners, was engaged, and he won the colt's next two races, including the Florida Derby.

86

## THE BIG RACE

Now the moment had come to take on the big time. He would go for the Kentucky Derby. Willie Shoemaker was booked to ride, but two days later changed his mind. Instead, with admitted uncertainty in his own mind, he opted for a Californian colt called *Hill Rise*.

The build up to the Kentucky Derby is big every year, and this time there was the added interest of the little colt with his distinctive white blaze representing Canada. Across the USA enthusiastic Americans entertained each other to Kentucky Derby Parties in their homes, taverns, bars and on the beach.

On the day of the race, Churchill Downs had a carnival atmosphere but *Northern Dancer* did not let the heightened tension affect his nerves. Ridden now by Bill Hartack, the race turned into a close-fought battle between him and Willie Shoemaker's mount. Together they raced stride for stride, and Hartack turned to the whip all the way down the straight but instead of resenting it, *Northern Dancer* showed great guts and held off his rival by a neck.

He had set a new record time of two minutes exactly, which stood until *Secretariat* surpassed it nine years later. He went on to beat *Hill Rise* again in the Preakness Stakes, this time by two-and-a-quarter lengths but failed in his bid for the Triple Crown when his stamina found him out in the Belmont over the longer distance of one-and-a-half miles.

He made a triumphant return to his native Canada, where he won the Queen's Plate, but then injured a tendon at exercise and was retired to stud, standing at Windfield Farm, Kentucky, until he was 26 years old. He became a Champion Sire in both Europe and North America and with such as *Nijinsky*, *Lyphard*, *The Minstrel*, *Shareef Dancer*, *Storm Bird*, *Nureyev*, *El Gran Senõr*, *Try My Best* and *Sadlers Wells* — between them the winners of several Classics — among his offspring his place in the history of horse racing has been immortalised.

*The 1988 Kentucky Derby was won by Winning Colors (no. 8) who became only the third filly to triumph in the race when she beat Forty Niner.*

# THE BREEDERS' CUP

IT WAS IN 1982 that one of America's leading bloodstock breeders conceived the idea of staging a global 'Thoroughbred Olympics'.

John R. Gaines, owner of Gainesway Farm, in Lexington, Kentucky, announced at the Kentucky Derby Festival luncheon in April of that year a bold plan for a multimillion-dollar programme of championship calibre races that would provide an international focal point at the end of each racing season.

He envisaged a single day card of seven races for all age, sex and distance divisions. To make it a success, he needed support from thoughout the industry, not only in the States, but also in Canada and Europe, from whose ranks a Breeders' Cup board of directors was drawn.

The funding of the prize money was to come through the breeding industry itself, generated by annual nomination payments for stallions and one-time nomination fees for those stallions' offspring. These nomination funds are retained solely to provide purses and awards for owners and nominators.

The inaugural Breeders' Cup series was run in 1984. There were $1 million purses for sprint, juvenile fillies, distaff, mile and juvenile races, plus $2 million for the Breeders' Cup Turf, and a further $3 million for the Breeders' Cup Classic run on dirt.

By 1988, there was a year long series of 56 events culminating in the $10 million Breeders' Cup Day at Churchill Downs, the single richest day in racing.

## THE BREEDERS' CUP TURF

The 1988 Breeders' Cup Turf prize stayed in America, but not without a spirited try by the best in Europe. One big difference between European and American racing, apart from the type of courses, is that America allows horses to run on drugs, whereas the English Jockey Club strictly does not. It takes the rational view that the use of drugs can disguise a horse's true merits and, particularly in breeding terms, can pass on unpublicised faults detrimental to the breed.

Henry Cecil, trainer of the super English filly *Indian Skimmer*, fearing firm ground, decided he would take the Americans on at their own game, and announced he would run his horse on the pain killing drug Phenylbutazone (Bute), which would have been quite legitimate. The Jockey Club let it be known, however, that they thoroughly disapproved of such an action and, while not obliged to do so, Cecil reversed his decision. He added that, if he felt the ground was too firm, he would not run at all, despite the distance travelled and the expense involved in getting to Churchill Downs.

Of the 75 horses running that day, 61 were indicated on the racecard as being under medication, either the anti-inflammatory pain killer Bute or the anti-haemorrhageing agent Lasix. It is indeed an indictment of the sport in America that without the permitted use of these drugs, there probably wouldn't be enough sound horses left to fill the racecards.

## HEAVY GOING

Torrential overnight rain turned the ground first from an official 'SLOPPY' to 'MUDDY'; all the dirt track races were run on appalling ground, and the runners and riders returned after each event unrecognizable.

With the tight tracks in America — and the turf track at Churchill Downs is laid out inside the dirt track making it more like a greyhound circuit to British horses — horses are obliged to pop out of the stalls like champagne corks, get straight into top gear, and to stay there, taking sharp bends and incredible mud in their stride all the way to the 'wire'. In the event, *Indian Skimmer* went to post and, although she took her time to settle on the strange track, she looked poised for a winning challenge at the crucial moment in the hands of 11-times South African champion jockey Michael Roberts, now successfully based in England.

*Triptych* also looked a danger until a furlong out, but up front it was *Great Communicator* and *Sunshine Forever* battling it out.

At the line, *Great Communicator* held on by half a length, with *Indian Skimmer* just three-quarters of a length behind, and *Triptych* a further nine lengths back in fourth place.

The brilliant French filly *Miesque* won the Breeders' Cup Mile for the second successive year and then retired to stud, while the world's richest single race, the Breeders' Cup Classic, was won by the previous year's Kentucky Derby winner *Alysheba*, bringing his career earnings to some $6.6 million, surpassing the record of *John Henry*.

# PIMLICO

P IMLICO IS the home of the Maryland Jockey Club which proudly boasts that it is older than the Republic of the USA itself. It is also the second oldest racecourse in the States having been founded in 1870, and its attractive Maryland setting has seen some titanic struggles. Most famous of all, Pimlico is the venue of the Preakness Stakes, the second and shortest leg of the American Triple Crown, which is normally held a fortnight after the Kentucky Derby.

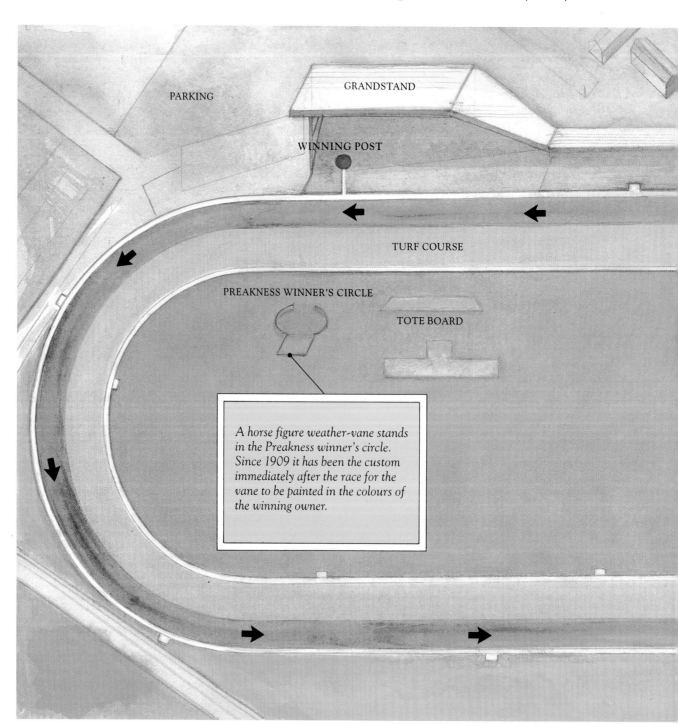

PARKING
GRANDSTAND
WINNING POST
TURF COURSE
PREAKNESS WINNER'S CIRCLE
TOTE BOARD

*A horse figure weather-vane stands in the Preakness winner's circle. Since 1909 it has been the custom immediately after the race for the vane to be painted in the colours of the winning owner.*

*The field about to turn into the final straight at Pimlico racecourse. The glass-enclosed grandstand is pictured in the background.*

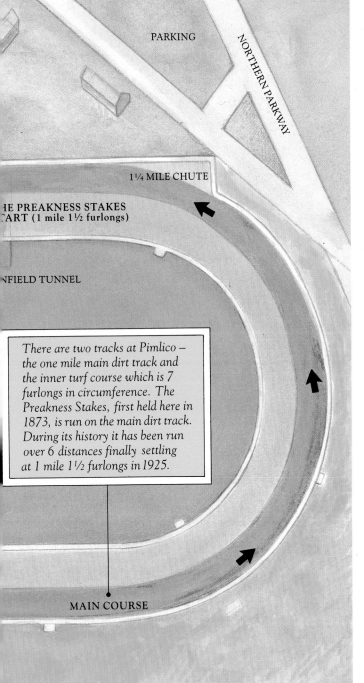

PARKING

NORTHERN PARKWAY

1¼ MILE CHUTE

HE PREAKNESS STAKES
ART (1 mile 1½ furlongs)

NFIELD TUNNEL

There are two tracks at Pimlico –
the one mile main dirt track and
the inner turf course which is 7
furlongs in circumference. The
Preakness Stakes, first held here in
1873, is run on the main dirt track.
During its history it has been run
over 6 distances finally settling
at 1 mile 1½ furlongs in 1925.

MAIN COURSE

## A THREE SEASON RACETRACK

Unusually for an American track Pimlico has three separate seasons. Starting in February they race through until the third Saturday in May (the traditional date of the Preakness). In July/August the track has a high summer meeting (when the glass enclosed grandstand and clubhouse offers welcome protection from the blistering mid-summer heat). The autumn meeting that closes in mid-October completes one of the busiest seasons for any track in the USA.

Surprisingly then, Pimlico only has stable facilities for 1,000 horses, a small number by American standards, where horses are mostly trained in the vicinity of one track and race predominantly around the same track. So, for its run of the mill races, Pimlico needs to attract runners from Laurel Park and Bowie whilst raiders from the rich New York circuit will only appear for Pimlico's most prestigious events which include the Dixie Handicap, the exotically named Black Eyed Susan Stakes and, of course, the Preakness Stakes.

Close to Washington DC, Lyndon Johnson and Richard Nixon are both presidents who have been seen on the track, whilst back in 1877, exactly seven years after Pimlico was founded, Congress adjourned so that its members could journey en masse to witness 'The Great Sweepstake'.

The race, which matched the best horses from the east and west coasts of the USA, drew national attention and lived up to its billing when *Parole* just got home in a thrilling finish.

# THE PREAKNESS STAKES

I F 'THE GREAT SWEEPSTAKE' was a one off, the Preakness Stakes — first run in 1873 — has become an annual spring celebration in Baltimore and regularly draws crowds of over 80,000. It has been run at seven different distances, starting at 1½ miles and finally settling at 1 mile 1½ furlongs in 1925.

For the first seventeen years the Preakness star seemed to be in its ascendancy as field after field of outstanding thoroughbreds contested the race. But the upward curve was to receive a severe jolt when in 1889 political wranglings within the Maryland Jockey Club led to the cancellation not only of the Preakness but also of all flat racing at Pimlico.

But the Preakness had become too big to keep down and, after a brief adoption by the Brooklyn Jockey Club in New York, it returned to the Pimlico course in 1909 when it began its ascent to its present eminence as one of the big three Triple Crown races contested each year.

## A PREAKNESS TRADITION

One of the oldest traditions at Pimlico centres around the weathervane which stands in the Preakness winners' circle. Since 1909 it has been the custom to paint the horse-figured weathervane in the colours of the Preakness winner. Immediately after the race a workman may be seen, bucket and brush in hand, ready to immortalise another outstanding thoroughbred. Tommy Ennis, a semi-retired sign writer has been doing the job since 1960. It takes him about four minutes to complete the painting. One of the few times he has felt the Preakness excitement, he says, was in 1973 when *Secretariat* won the second leg of the Triple Crown. 'I never saw so much excitement in my life', he says, 'the infield went crazy'.

A few weeks later, at Belmont Park in New York, *Secretariat* went on to become only the ninth horse in history to complete the elusive American Triple Crown.

*The awesome power of Secretariat captured as he makes his move in the 1973 Preakness Stakes. This photo became the model for John Skeaping's bronze statue of Secretariat which stands in the paddock at Belmont Park.*

*Tommy Ennis about to go to work emblazoning the colours of the 1981 Preakness winner, Pleasant Colony, on the weathervane.*

## SEATTLE SLEW

*Seattle Slew* cost only $17,000 as a yearling at the summer sales in Kentucky in 1975. In February 1978, a half share in him was sold for $6 million.

As a yearling, the dark brown colt by *Bold Reasoning* out of *My Charmer* by *Poker* was bought by a young couple, Mickey and Karen Taylor, in partnership with vet Dr James Hill and his wife Sally. It was Dr Hill who suggested the purchase of the colt, bred by Ben S. Castleman in Kentucky, and he ran in Karen Taylor's name.

He was trained by Billy Turner a former steeplechase rider from Maryland and ridden by French-born Jean Cruguet, who between them became known as 'the Slew Crew'.

As a two-year-old he was not raced until September, but soon made up for lost time, and showed himself to be something rather special in spite of his unfashionable breeding and low purchase price. He won the prestigious Champagne Stakes, which made a good many people sit up and take notice, and resulted in him being nominated two-year-old Champion.

### TRIPLE CROWN WINNER

When the *Slew* reappeared as a three-year-old, he quickly showed his juvenile form was no fluke by winning three spring races. He soon demonstrated that he was as good as anything America had to offer, then or at any time.

By the time he completed the Triple Crown, he was still unbeaten. His victory in the Kentucky

93

Derby by 1¾ lengths was followed by a 1½ length victory in the Preakness, and by four lengths in the Belmont.

Nine horses lined up for the Preakness Stakes on May 21, 1977, with *Seattle Slew* short odds-on favourite. Next in the betting came *Cormorant*, followed by *J. O. Tobin* and *Run Dusty Run*, but the writing was on the wall soon after the race had started.

*Run Dusty Run* broke fast at an angle, slightly interfering with the *Slew*, and it was *Cormorant* who took the early lead. Cruguet had the *Slew* held hard but even so he was trying to take the

lead at the first turn, where *Run Dusty Run* was forced to run wide.

The *Slew* stayed in second down the back stretch where, just given a notch of rein, he simply took command and never looked like being headed. On the home stretch he drew clear readily until eased near the line for an easy one and a half lengths win over *Iron Constitution*.

*Iron Constitution* had started slowly but moved up well along the backstretch, moving out to make his run, and was best of the rest. He had 2 lengths to spare over *Run Dusty Run* who passed *Cormorant*, *J. O. Tobin* finished fifth, while *Regal*

*Seattle Slew pictured going for the line in the 1978 Marlboro Cup. As a three-year-old during the previous year he had won the American Triple Crown. In the Marlboro Cup he beat Affirmed who had just repeated his feat.*

94

*Sir*, who was close up early, suffered a bump at the half mile pole which stopped him in his tracks, and finished last.

## FOUR-YEAR-OLD CAREER

After the *Slew* had completed the Triple Crown he was hot property and all the hype may have gone to his young owners' heads. Ultimately it led to a parting with their trainer, and later still the new trainer parted with their jockey.

The *Slew* suffered various ailments at home and some defeats on the track, yet some of his finest performances were still to come. First, as a four-

*The 'Slew' pictured after another four-year-old victory. By this time his trainer and jockey of the previous year had been replaced.*

year-old, he beat the current Classic three-year-old *Affirmed* in a marvellous clash in the Marlboro Gold Cup, and then he beat *Kelso* in a memorable race for the Woodward Stakes.

But greatest of all was his run in the 1½ mile Jockey Club Gold Cup, when all three horses met again. After only one furlong, the saddle slipped on *Affirmed*, effectively putting him out of it. Up front, the pace was so hot that *Exceller*, ridden by the great Willie 'the Shoe' Shoemaker, was more than 20 lengths behind after half a mile.

Slowly, very slowly, he began to make ground, until in the straight he went by the *Slew* on the inside. Few spectators could believe it as he went half a length up.

But the *Slew* would have none of that, and now a battle royal between two great horses ensued. The *Slew* had run extremely fast from the start, and yet, somehow, he mustered up some reserves, and started pulling back the lost ground.

Inch by inch, stride by hard fought stride, the pair fought their way towards the winning post; the *Slew* looked as if he might make it — but the post came just too soon for him and he went under in gallant defeat.

It was good to see him racing as a four-year-old, after the $6 million half share purchase had been completed and just reward for his owners when he made a great success at stud, standing at Spendthrift Farm, Kentucky.

95

# BELMONT PARK

BELMONT PARK offers both the charisma and the prize money that attracts from coast to coast the best horses in the USA, and any jockey who is riding regularly round the mile and a half oval circuit at Belmont Park, can rest assured he's close to the top of his professional ladder.

Situated some 20 miles outside the centre of New York City in the bustling Jamaican district, Belmont Park came into existence on May 4th, 1905. It seemed to herald a new dawn for racing

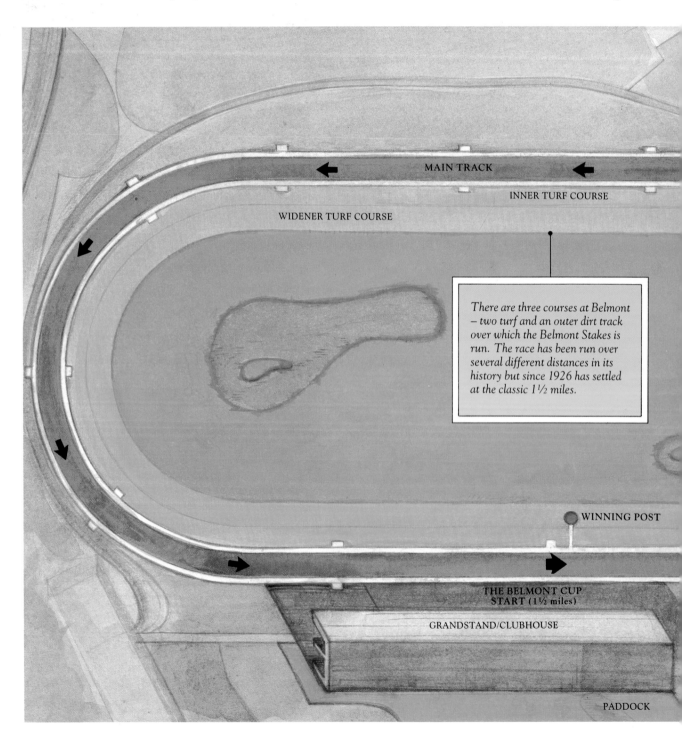

MAIN TRACK

INNER TURF COURSE

WIDENER TURF COURSE

There are three courses at Belmont – two turf and an outer dirt track over which the Belmont Stakes is run. The race has been run over several different distances in its history but since 1926 has settled at the classic 1½ miles.

WINNING POST

THE BELMONT CUP
START (1½ miles)

GRANDSTAND/CLUBHOUSE

PADDOCK

in the state following the demise of the New York Jockey Club in 1895 and the sudden disappearance of local tracks such as Morris Park and Coney Island.

This, however, proved to be an illusion as a bitter debate in the state senate some three years later resulted in the notorious Hart-Agnew bill outlawing all forms of betting in New York.

Belmont Park racetrack closed, though it did continue to stay in the news for different reasons. The pioneering Wright Brothers — Wilbur and

*Horses erupt out of the starting gate and onto the well-manicured dirt track at Belmont Park, the largest racecourse in the USA.*

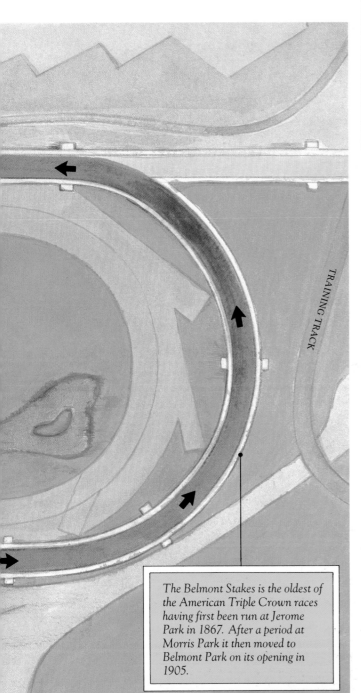

TRAINING TRACK

*The Belmont Stakes is the oldest of the American Triple Crown races having first been run at Jerome Park in 1867. After a period at Morris Park it then moved to Belmont Park on its opening in 1905.*

Orville — ran an international aerial tournament at the track in 1911 attracting 150,000 visitors.

Anticipating correctly the re-legalization of betting, Belmont Park reopened in 1913 but faced further traumas in 1917 when a series of fires almost destroyed the grandstands.

Of the many notable horses who have raced at Belmont over the years few have had a bigger impact than *Kelso*, a handicap specialist who made the track his own in the early '60s. His reign was cut short, however, when serious structural defects were discovered in the grandstand, making the course a potential deathtrap.

To avoid such a calamity the course was closed while rebuilding work took place and its fixtures were shared between Acqueduct and Saratoga.

Belmont came back with a bang in 1968 when the centennial of the Belmont Stakes was witnessed by a massive crowd. Unfortunately, *Forward Pass* just failed on that day to take the Triple Crown but this was not the case in 1973 when one of the largest crowds in the course's history turned out in anticipation of *Secretariat's* Triple Crown victory.

# THE BELMONT STAKES

THE AMERICAN JOCKEY CLUB was founded in 1865 and efforts were made to establish a three year old sweepstake race that would attract the best and build a prestige for American racing comparable to the Derby in England. The resultant race was the Belmont Stakes.

The race was first run in 1867 at Jerome Park, which venue is no longer in use. From 1890 it was run at Morris Park until Belmont Park opened in 1905. Over the years the race has also been run at various distances between 1 mile 5 furlongs and 1 mile 1 furlong. The present distance of 1½ miles was finally established from 1926.

There were 11 nominations at $200 each and $1500 added for the first running on June 19, 1867. The second horse was to receive $300 out of the stakes and "a beautiful saddle made by Merry of London, England." Four went to post,

*A restful Seattle Slew pictured as a three-year-old in the year he won the Belmont Stakes.*

and although the day was fine, the ground was heavy. The race was won cleverly by a head by a filly called *Ruthless*, one of only two fillies ever to win. The other was *Tanya* in 1905, although in 1980 *Genuine Risk* finished second.

## MAN O'WAR

The 1970s saw America produce two of its best ever racehorses in *Secretariat* and *Seattle Slew*, half a century after its long time most popular horse, *Man O'War*.

*Secretariat*, who like *Man O'War* was known as 'Big Red', and *Seattle Slew*, known as 'the Slew', both won America's Triple Crown of Kentucky

98

Derby, Preakness Stakes and Belmont Stakes. *Man O'War* was never entered for the Derby but easily won the other legs.

*Man O'War* was a deep, rich chestnut and a fine, big, upstanding individual, powerfully muscled with a strong character, who was only once beaten in 21 races. Foaled in 1917, he was by *Mahuba* out of *Fair Play*.

He was owned originally by Major August Belmont II, chairman of the American Jockey Club, who although he was 64 years old, joined up as a commissioned officer in 1917 to help Europe in the Great War.

This led to the sale at Saratoga in 1918 of all his yearlings, among them the chestnut named *Man O'War* who went for $5,000 to Samuel D. Riddle, a textile magnate. Strangely, it was at Saratoga that *Man O'War* met his only defeat in life, half way through his two-year-old career — beaten by a horse called *Upset!*

### A HUNDRED LENGTHS WINNER

His career began, however, at Belmont Park, scene later of one his greatest triumphs. His ability was clear from the start, for on that début

as a two-year-old, he won with little apparent effort by six lengths. From then on, with the exception of that one defeat when he was left at the start and only just beaten, his career was a procession of victories and on no fewer than three occasions he won at odds of 100-1 ON! Once, in the Lawrence Realization at Belmont Park, he was even judged to have won by one hundred lengths! He started at odds-on for every race he ever ran in.

### AN ENDURING RECORD

He also set no fewer than five course records over different distances, including his brilliant Belmont Stakes victory in 1920 when his time of 2 minutes 14.2 seconds was not beaten for nearly 50 years. He was the last winner on the right-handed course, for the following year the Belmont Park executive reluctantly accepted that it would have to fall in line with the rest of America and changed the direction of its races to anti-clockwise.

*The original 'Big Red', Man 'O' War, pictured with his jockey, Clarence Kummer, his rider in the 1920 Belmont Stakes.*

A record 23,500 spectators thronged into Pimlico for the Preakness Stakes on Tuesday May 18, 1920. Reporting on the race afterwards, the Baltimore Sun correspondent said, '. . . . it was not a race, only a performance. Those who saw it will not forget it'.

Among the runners was *Upset*, the horse who beat him the previous year when he was Champion two-year-old, but *Man O'War* still started at 4-5. There was a delay at the start, then they were off and running.

*Man O'War* burst straight into the lead and set a terrific pace, so fast that a horse called *Blazes*, who was meant to be the speed horse, was soon out of the reckoning.

One by one, as his rivals tried to take him on, *Man O'War* saw them off disdainfully. *Upset*, who had been running handily in third, gamely attempted to make a challenge going into the home straight and got within one and a half lengths of 'Big Red', but by that time his jockey, Clarence Kummer, knew he had the race won and barely bothered to extend him to beat his pursuer. The rest were strung out between five and 35 lengths behind.

### RETIREMENT TO STUD

*Man O'War* did not race at four but retired instead to a stud which had been built specially for him, where his owner restricted him to only a few mares per year. As his groom, Will Harbutt, said, 'He broke all the records and he broke down all the horses, so there wasn't nothing for him to do but retire'.

He was without doubt a truly great racehorse, one of the outstanding Champions of the American Turf who did much to boost American blood internationally.

Apart from siring Belmont Stakes winners such as *American Flag* and *Crusader*, he also sired *Battleship*, the little horse who made history by winning the 1938 Grand National ridden by the youngest ever victorious jockey, 17-year-old Bruce Hobbs, later a top Newmarket trainer.

He also sired *American Flag, Crusader, Mars, Blockade, Edith Cavell, Scapa Flow* and, probably the best, *War Admiral*.

*War Admiral*, like *Battleship*, stood only 15.2 hands but became the fourth winner of the American Triple Crown in 1937, in spite of stumbling at the start of the Belmont Stakes. He won 21 of his 26 races and was unplaced only once in his career.

### ZEV

*Man O'War's* blood directly descends to such greats as *Never Say Die, Relko* and *Sir Ivor*, all Derby winners, and to top American horses *Damascus, Buckpasser* and *Arts and Letters*.

His place as darling of the New York crowds was taken by *Zev*, who in 1923 supplemented his wins in the Kentucky Derby and the Belmont Stakes by winning a match with *Papyrus*, that year's Epsom Derby winner.

The English colt was rushed across the Atlantic after getting beaten in the St. Leger, but there were still plenty of people betting on him.

A crowd of 45,000 flocked to Belmont to watch the two fight it out for a $110,000 prize. Wall Street virtually came to a standstill that afternoon as brokers waged over 3 million dollars on the outcome. But on a track that was a muddy quagmire, the American champion, who was sent off the 4-5 favourite in the betting, was always going the better in the race, winning by an easy five lengths.

### CITATION

The next hero of New York achieved what not even *Man O'War* or *Zev* had managed and that was the elusive Triple Crown of the Kentucky Derby, the Preakness stakes and the Belmont Stakes. His name was *Citation* who, unbeaten on the track in 10 races in 1948, not only won the

*Secretariat demonstrates how to lead a field by 31 lengths in the 1973 Belmont Stakes.*

Belmont but also the Sysonby Mile, the Jockey Club Gold Cup and the Belmont Gold Cup — and all in the space of little more than two weeks.

## SECRETARIAT

Like *Man O'War, Secretariat* was another slashing big chestnut, with three white stockings and a star (usually covered up by blue and white checked blinkers when he was racing). He stood 16.2 hands and had a huge girth and massive heart room, and appropriately, one of the races he won as a three-year-old was the Man O'War Stakes.

He was beautifully bred by *Bold Ruler* out of *Something Royal,* and was born at Meadow Stud in Virginia, home of his owner Mrs Penny Tweedy. He was trained at the New York centre of Belmont Park by French Canadian Lucien Laurin and ridden in every race except for his final one by Ron Turcotte.

He was the first Triple Crown winner since the great *Citation,* who some say was the greatest of all, 25 years before. However, it is for his sensational victory in the Belmont Stakes of 1973 that 'Big Red' is best remembered.

### RACE FOR THE CROWN

He had already won the first two legs of the Triple Crown, setting a new course record in both and lowering *Northern Dancer's* time in the Kentucky Derby by 0.6 seconds. Also in both races he had beaten the same horses, *Sham* and *Our Native.*

Bravely, *Sham* faced *Secretariat* again in the Belmont, along with just three others, and he set out to make a race of it. *Sham* and *Secretariat* shot straight into their stride and raced neck and neck for the first six furlongs; once or twice, *Sham* got his head in front as the pair clocked record sprinting speed even though they were running in a one and a half mile race. Enthralled by this magnificent sight the huge crowd cheered the two horses to the echo.

Suddenly, it was all over. Gallant *Sham* dropped away beaten, but instead of slowing up, as could be expected, *Secretariat* was drawing ever further away, his huge, magnificent stride devouring the ground.

On he galloped until he passed the post an incredible 31 lengths clear in a world record time for the distance of 2 minutes 24 seconds. In the winner's enclosure he was garlanded with the traditional blanket of 400 fresh carnations. The thousands privileged to have witnessed such a super equine performance went home quite overwhelmed and totally elated.

Over 41,000 spectators then watched him win the Arlington Park International, and he ended his career with victory in the Canadian International Champion Stakes.

*Secretariat* was not unbeaten in his career; once or twice he failed quite inexplicably. He retired to stud at Claiborne Farm, Kentucky, at the age of three, the winner of 16 races, but was not an immediate success as a sire. He will be remembered more for his feats on the track than off it.

# FLEMINGTON

ALMOST THE WHOLE population of Melbourne turned out, it seemed, to come to the inaugural race meeting at Flemington on March 3, 1840. Its popularity soon established Melbourne as Australia's racing capital, a position it still holds.

The influx of population and wealth that came with the gold rush transformed Flemington on raceday to something resembling an English fair with canvas tents lining the river bank selling food and alcohol and a variety of amusements. Wandering minstrels entertained the racing crowds and picnicking on the already famous lawns was the order of the day.

The man who played the most vital role in the development of the racecourse was R. C. Bagot

the Victoria Racing Club's first Secretary. 'Indefatigable Bagot' as he was known built the first Hill Stand, introduced training facilities and continually upgraded public and administration facilities. His ideals and ambitions are still pursued at Flemington today.

Flemington is located six kilometres from the centre of Melbourne on the banks of the Maribyrnong, formerly known as the Saltwater River. It is Australia's big occasion racecourse with a massive capacity in excess of 100,000 people and a total area of about 120 hectares, all of which is Crown Land.

To accommodate the huge crowds, there is extensive car parking at the western end of the racecourse, in the centre, and at the rear of

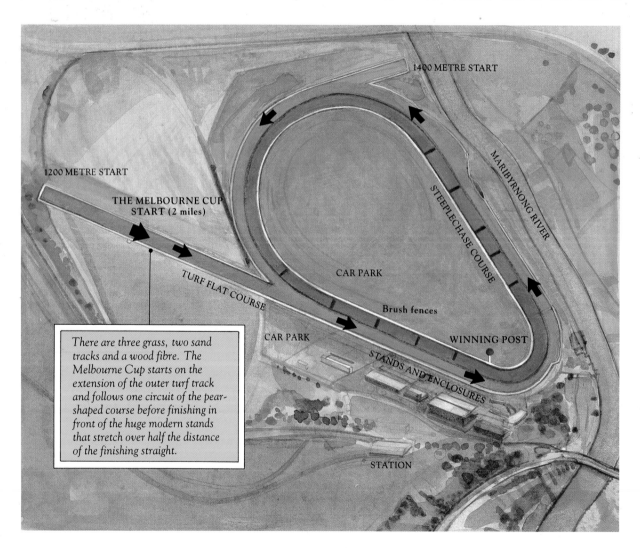

*There are three grass, two sand tracks and a wood fibre. The Melbourne Cup starts on the extension of the outer turf track and follows one circuit of the pear-shaped course before finishing in front of the huge modern stands that stretch over half the distance of the finishing straight.*

*The customary huge crowd witnesses the 1988 Melbourne Cup race won by the filly Empire Rose.*

the hill. Buses park at the Elms or River end of the course, and those travelling by train are provided with a free bus service linking to the course. One further mode of transport has remained unaltered since the first running of the Melbourne Cup, and that is the train which carries passengers right up to the track.

The Flemington Track is pear-shaped, and its most recent improvement has been the widening of the straight, making it a uniform thirty three metres across. Training is carried out on all six tracks. There are three grass, two sand tracks and a wood fibre which was laid in 1981 and has proved very popular with trainers. Another essential modern aid is an automatic sprinkler system which helps with the daunting job of keeping all the tracks watered. At the height of the spring racing season the training facilities at Flemington support 550 horses of which 250 are stabled at the racecourse.

The huge grandstands offer the ultimate in racing facilities with bars, restaurants, private boxes and tote betting facilities. They offer a superb view of the course and from them the whole race can be seen without obstruction.

A total of 29 meetings a year are held at Flemington, and others of note, besides the Melbourne Cup Carnival, are a two-day autumn festival in March, and a two-day Grand National meeting in July.

# THE MELBOURNE CUP

ON THE FIRST Tuesday of every November, commerce and business throughout Australia closes down. School children have the day off. It is a national holiday. And in Melbourne itself there is a carnival atmosphere and only one topic of conversation: the Cup.

It is strange for a country's premier horse race to be a long distance handicap, instead of a middle distance Classic, but that is Australia's own tradition, and the Melbourne Cup has its own distinct flavour; the height of fashion and famous for its socialising, up to 100,000 pour into Flemington to watch the Melbourne Cup which was founded in 1861.

Some four thousand people watched a horse called *Archer* win the first Melbourne Cup race for a prize of £710, a feat he repeated the following year. By 1879, less than 20 years later, 100,000 racegoers were attending. The biggest

*Empire Rose's jockey, T. Allen, is congratulated by the crowd as he makes his way past a packed grandstand during the victory parade.*

crowd of all was in 1926, when a staggering 118,877 people watched *Spearfelt* win.

Over the years, a highly respectable 80-90,000 has been the more usual attendance figure, but it topped six figures again in 1980, the year international owner Robert Sangster's *Beldale Ball* won. Prize money increased rapidly from the 1970s, due mainly to sponsorship by Fosters Lager and is now worth some £300,000.

## A REMARKABLE DUO

Two remarkable horses dominate Australian racing lore separated by 40 years, *Carbine* and *Phar Lap*. Both were bred in New Zealand, and both became living legends.

In appearance, they could hardly have been more different; *Carbine* was a compact, stocky individual, with a sensible head. *Phar Lap* was enormous for a racehorse, standing over 17 hands high, and had a heart that weighed nearly twice as much as a normal one.

## CARBINE

Carbine was unbeaten as a two year old in New Zealand in 1887 even though he was left 50 metres behind at the start on his début race, so it was no surprise that richer pickings were sought for him in Australia thereafter.

After an initial failure following a bad sea crossing and possibly poor jockeyship, resulting in his being scratched from the Melbourne Cup, he went from strength to strength in staying races, and soon earnt a popular following and the affectionate nick-name 'Old Jack'.

He was exceptionally robust, as his record shows, for at one meeting, he won three of the four races he was entered for and as a four year old, he won all five races he contested at a four day meeting!

When he contested the Melbourne Cup for the first time he was allotted 14lbs over weight for age, and went under by a length. By the time he was five, *Carbine*, who was by the ex-English horse *Musket*, had matured even more, which was just as well, as he was set to carry 10st 5lb in the Melbourne Cup of 1890.

What followed was memorable beyond the wildest dreams. Eighty-five thousand people swarmed into Flemington to see a record 39 horses line up for the Cup. *Carbine* not only beat the other 38 under his burden, but did so in record time, giving an unbelievable 53lbs to the runner up, *Highborn*.

### A CONTEMPORARY REPORT

Describing the race in 'On and Off the Turf in Australia', Nat Gould wrote: 'When the saddling bell rang there was intense excitement and *Carbine* held his position as favourite firm as a rock; and *Highborn* was 33-1. 'Old Jack' was fairly nobbled as he was saddled, but as usual he took

*Carbine pictured on his retirement to stud in England. His most notable progeny was Derby winner, Spearmint.*

no notice of the crowd. When he came on to the track there was a terrific burst of cheering. *Carbine* stood still and looked around, and then declined to go to the post. Mr. Hickenbotham gave him a push behind, and *Carbine* moved a few paces. This was a slow process. At last Ramage threw the reins over the horse's head, and Mr. Hickenbotham fairly dragged him up the course. I never saw a more sluggish horse until he commenced to race, and then there was a different tale to tell.

'*Carbine* held a good position throughout, but did not get well to the front until they were in the straight. At the home turn *Highborn* looked to have a chance second to none, and the hopes of his backers were high. No sooner, however, did *Carbine* see an opening than he shot through, and after that it was a case of hare and hounds. On came 'Old Jack' with his 10st 5lb, and at the Distance he had the race won. Cheer after cheer rent the air, and people went almost frantic with excitement. It was a wild scene. For months *Carbine* had been backed by the public, and at last the suspense was over. It was a glorious victory, and everyone knew it, but none better than Mr. Forrester, whose crack *Highborn* finished a couple of lengths behind him. Not only did *Carbine* carry 10st 5lb, but he ran the two miles in 3 min 28¼ sec., the fastest time on record for that distance in the Colonies'.

## GLORIOUS RETIREMENT
*Carbine* retired to stud at the end of the season, the winner of 33 of his 43 races, with six seconds, three thirds and only once unplaced. Eventually he was bought by the Duke of Portland and travelled to England where he sired *Spearmint* winner of the 1906 Derby. Five years had passed since *Carbine's* memorable Cup win, yet even so 2,000 fans lined the docks to wave him farewell.

## PHAR LAP
*Phar Lap* also won the Melbourne Cup just once, but added to this wins in most of Australia's other important races and ended his career with 37 wins from 51 competitive races.

## EARLY DISAPPOINTMENT
At first it looked long odds against him living up to his name, which is Sinhalese for 'lightning', for he was unimpressive at two, finally managing to win a maiden but without showing much

potential for prestige staying races. At three, he began to place in good races and then at last came his breakthrough: he won the Rosehill Stakes in a canter, followed by slashing wins in the AJC and VRC Derbys.

This resulted in him becoming the shortest priced favourite ever for the Melbourne Cup, carrying 7st 6lbs at odds-on, but, fighting his jockey for his head all the way, he only managed to finished third.

He was a big horse who was bound to need time to fill out, and this he achieved during a break, with startling results; he was beaten on his post-holiday début, but thereafter was a catalogue of continuing success.

## ON THE VERGE OF SUCCESS
At the Victorian Racing Club's autumn carnival he won the St. Leger, the Governor's Plate and the King's Plate, all at the same meeting.

It was the same story in Sydney, where he added the AJC St. Leger, the Chipping Norton Stakes, and the Cumberland Stakes and Plate.

Next it was the turn of the people of Adelaide to see the star. There, the Elder Stakes and King's Cup were his without so much as sweating a hair.

At four, he was again beaten first time out after a rest, but from then the mixture was as before. He won a string of races in Sydney, and then in Melbourne during the build up to the Cup. Naturally there was no end of money being wagered on him for the Cup race itself and the bookies stood to lose thousands.

## NERVOUS BUILD UP
It was on the morning of the Melbourne Stakes, one of the earlier races of the meeting, that as *Phar Lap* was being led back to his stable after light work, a shot rang out. It came from a nearby parked car but fortunately the attacker missed. Instead of tragedy, *Phar Lap* strolled to success in that afternoon's Melbourne Stakes.

There were now three days left before the 1930 Melbourne Cup and suddenly security was paramount. A committee member of the Victoria Racing Club arranged for *Phar Lap* to be stabled in secret at the St. Alban's Stud, Geelong while the Press and public set up a hue and cry about his disappearance.

Cup day arrived, with *Phar Lap's* groom and the Victoria Racing Club committee man having spent the night with him at his hideaway. He was

*Phar Lap, ridden by Jimmy Pike, wins the 1930 Melbourne Cup. When he died in California shortly after beginning a new racing career there were rumours of Mafia involvement.*

in sparkling form in his five furlong 'pipe-opener' on the morning of the race and at noon he was loaded ready for the trip to the racecourse at Flemington.

The engine would not start. Mechanics were brought in in a frantic bid to get it under way. At last they succeeded — and *Phar Lap* arrived with just 40 minutes to spare!

### THE GREAT DAY

Strangely, the attendance was smaller that year than in many but *Phar Lap*, carrying 9st 12lbs (nearly a stone more than weight for age), started at 11-8 on. He did not disappoint his supporters; other jockeys did their best to slow down the pace, but neither *Phar Lap* nor his rider Jimmy Pike were in the least concerned; Jimmy gave his mount the signal to go rounding the turn, and from then on, all the others saw were his disappearing heels.

The following year, after a string of eight successes, *Phar Lap* lined up for the Melbourne Cup again, but this time he had to carry the enormous weight of 10st 10lbs (five pounds more than *Carbine* carried). For once he had not been as impressive as usual when beaten by a neck earlier at the meeting, although the conditions had been altered in favour of the winner who in previous years would have run at level weights and this time was in receipt of no less than 21lbs.

*Phar Lap* should not then have run in the Cup, but connections, against their better judgement, were implored by the race officials to run him. When, with a furlong to go, it became clear that he could not win, Jimmy Pike to his credit eased the great horse.

### A TRAGIC END

It was the last time Australians saw their fine champion. He enjoyed a holiday in his native New Zealand and then travelled to America where he made mincemeat of his rivals in a rich handicap across the border in Mexico.

His performance stunned this new set of spectators: his jockey Bill Elliott dropped him out last of the ten runners as a blistering pace was set. Then at halfway, Elliott nonchalantly pulled *Phar Lap* out on to the wide outside and passed all the runners so effortlessly that he was in front fully three furlongs from home — winning as he liked in record time!

In less than a month he was found dead where he was stabled in California. Rumours were rife that it was the work of the Mafia; it seems more likely that he picked up a poison spray.

He was the subject of a full length feature film; his great heart is at the Institute of Anatomy in Canberra; his stuffed hide is in Melbourne Museum; his skeleton is in new Zealand; and his memory is in the minds of all those racing enthusiasts fortunate enough to have seen and admired him.

# TOKYO

THE TOKYO COURSE is situated 25 kilometres west of Tokyo. The race track is left-handed and has a turf steeplechase course on the inside of the dirt course with the main turf course, on which the Japan Cup is run, on the outside.

Founded in 1933 it has since become firmly established as Japan's number one racecourse, monopolizing the featured events in the calendar including the Japanese Derby and Oaks, The Emperors Cup and Yasuda Kinen.

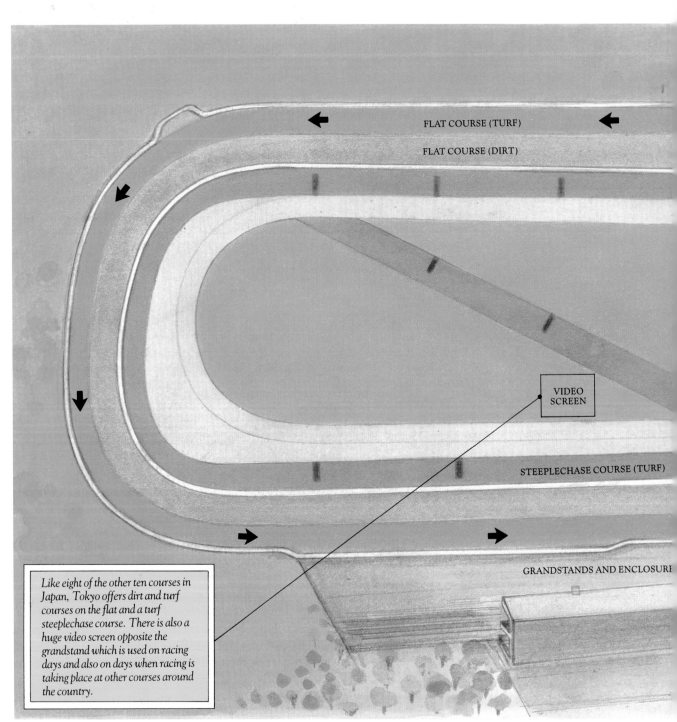

FLAT COURSE (TURF)

FLAT COURSE (DIRT)

VIDEO SCREEN

STEEPLECHASE COURSE (TURF)

GRANDSTANDS AND ENCLOSURE

*Like eight of the other ten courses in Japan, Tokyo offers dirt and turf courses on the flat and a turf steeplechase course. There is also a huge video screen opposite the grandstand which is used on racing days and also on days when racing is taking place at other courses around the country.*

A throughly sophisticated operation, a day's racing at Tokyo Racecourse is a far cry from the 'Ceremonial' horse racing whose history goes back twelve centuries and which indeed still exists in certain parts of the country.

Modern horse racing in Japan, involving public betting, began in 1861, introduced principally by British and American residents. The Japanese Government gave tacit approval in 1906. The Horse Racing Law of 1923 officially approved the sale of betting tickets, and under

**Above** *Racing on the dirt track at Tokyo. To the left of the 4 furlong marker is the outer turf track used for the Japan Cup. The brown colour of the grass makes it difficult to distinguish the two tracks.*

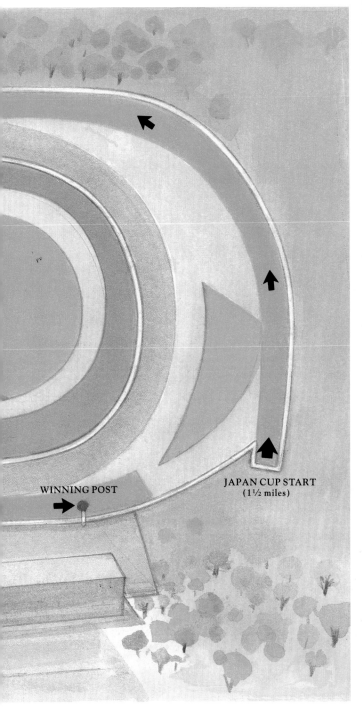

WINNING POST

JAPAN CUP START
(1½ miles)

this law a total of eleven race clubs were established in various areas. In 1936, they were amalgamated into the Japan Racing Society, who took over all the administration. The Classic race system for three-year-olds, created around the Japanese Derby, was established, ushering in a golden era until the Second World War.

Nowadays, like Japan's ten other official race-courses Tokyo is run by the Japanese Racing Association, an all powerful government-controlled agency which, under law, has the right to allocate the race days between the various courses. It also regulates both on and off track betting, and takes rigorous action at any whiff of corruption.

# THE JAPAN CUP

CONSIDERING THAT Tokyo racecourse regularly attracts crowds in excess of 100,000 and stages some of the world's richest races, it took its time to gain a reputation on the international stage. This situation changed in 1981 when the Japanese racing authority instigated the Japan Cup, an international race based on invitation.

Usually staged on the last Sunday in November, the race is planned with the meticulous detail that characterizes the Japanese mentality. Even the annual booklet produced by Tokyo racecourse to coincide with the Japan Cup provides mind-boggling detail, including, for example, the precise quantity of cement that was required to build the grandstand.

*Lady Tavistock's Jupiter Island contests the lead in the 1986 Japan Cup. The 7 year old bay, ridden by Pat Eddery provided Britain's first ever success in this race and in doing so broke the course record.*

### JUPITER ISLAND

On November 24th, 1986, *Jupiter Island*, the 'Old Man' of the field and running his final race, broke the course record to win the sixth running of the Japan Cup, not only that but his time of 2 minutes 25 seconds was the fastest ever recorded time by a British-trained horse over a mile and a half.

*Jupiter Island* had always been just below top class in his own country, and will never be classified as a 'great' horse. Nonetheless his trainer Clive Brittain was surely not just expressing post-race euphoria when he described the imposing seven-year-old bay as 'one of the toughest and bravest horses ever bred in England'.

For his owner, Lady Tavistock, who had bred *Jupiter Island*, the race was to vindicate her

decision to keep him in training long after many of his contemporaries had been packed off to stud. It also provided her with what she describes unashamedly as 'the happiest day of my life'.

Of the aftermath of the race she recalls how 'the Japanese flag was lowered, the Union Jack raised, a brass band played "God Save The Queen", and, standing on the dais in front of 150,000 Japanese, we felt like Olympic athletes must when winning for their country. It was unbelievable'.

### A SOLID PERFORMER

The son of *St. Paddy*, out of *Mrs Moss*, *Jupiter Island* was not bred to excel over a yard less than a mile and a half. Indeed in 1983 Lester Piggott had ridden him to a brilliant success in the Ebor Handicap at York over a mile and three quarters, a performance that was to ensure that *Jupiter Island* was to be set a stiff task in future handicaps.

Whilst that did not prevent him winning them (he notched up three in a row in the last months of that season), the imposing bay horse was destined for better things, and in subsequent years won races of the quality of Royal Ascot's Hardwicke Stakes, Longchamp's Prix du Conseil de Paris and, in the autumn of 1985, he enhanced his globetrotting and had put up an outstanding performance against strong opposition to finish second in the Washington DC International at Laurel Park.

### A LONG LAY OFF

The 1986 season, which was to be *Jupiter Island*'s last, began disastrously after he had returned to the USA to run in the San Juan Capistrano Handicap at San Anita. That he was able to finish third in that race says much for the courage of the horse who it was later discovered had sustained a deep quarter-crack in his near fore during the race. It was to keep him off the racecourse for six months.

Indeed, when he reappeared in the St. Simon Stakes at Newbury in late October, it seemed to have been forgotten that *Jupiter Island* was still in training, not least by the Japanese.

### JAPANESE INVITATION

However, the scratching of *Moon Madness* from the big race and *Jupiter Island*'s devastating return to the racecourse in the St. Simon Stakes, precipitated the much sought after telex invitation from the Japanese Racing Association. On its receipt Pat Eddery, Champion Jockey that year, was immediately booked for the ride.

The field he was to meet there was to be truly international, and it included perhaps the most talked about horse in the world at the time. That horse was *Bonecrusher*, an ugly four-year-old chestnut by an unfashionable sire who had carried all before him in Australia and New Zealand. Tragically, *Bonecrusher* was infected by a mystery illness the day before the race, with one news agency actually reporting that he was dead. Thankfully, *Bonecrusher* did recover to race again though the spark had departed and he was never to recapture his former glory.

The great racemare *Triptych* was sent from France and seemed to many observers to have the best chance of giving the Europeans their first success in the race, although there was also some backing for *Allez Milord*, *Jupiter Island*'s fellow countryman who was trained by Guy Harwood at Pulborough in Sussex.

America, who had won the first two runnings, were represented by *Flying Pidgeon*, whilst for the host nation, *Miho Shinzan* and the unbeaten provincially trained *Sakura Yukata* were widely touted as capable of keeping the £400,000 prize-money at home.

In the race the early pace was blistering with Japan's *Kushiro King* showing the way ahead of the British hope *Allez Milord*, who at 9-1 was preferred in the betting to *Jupiter Island*, sent off a 14-1 chance.

At one time the two leaders were six lengths clear, but approaching the far turn the field began to bunch with Greville Starkey kicking *Allez Milord* into a narrow lead. The New Zealander *Waverley Star* was poised in behind and Pat Eddery had begun to weave his way through from last place.

### A BRITISH SUCCESS

A furlong out it was Britain one and two with *Allez Milord* responding to Greville Starkey's urgings along the rails and *Jupiter Island* gaining inch by inch on his outside.

For a hundred yards or so the two were locked together, almost bumping for a stride or two, but as they approached the line *Jupiter Island* began to nose into the lead, and had won it by a head at the line.

Two days later a flight from Tokyo took *Jupiter Island* home to a career at stud. He had deserved it.

# CLASSIC JUMP RACES

*B*RITAIN *is certainly the leading country in steeplechase and hurdling. However, nations such as Ireland, which has produced so many top jockeys and horses, have long-standing races and traditions of their own. The fences jumped in the Maryland Hunt Cup are higher even than Aintree's and only one British horse has ever won Le Grand Steeplechase de Paris. . .*

THE GRAND NATIONAL

THE SCOTTISH GRAND NATIONAL

THE SCOTTISH CHAMPION HURDLE

THE CHELTENHAM GOLD CUP

THE CHAMPION HURDLE

THE QUEEN MOTHER
CHAMPION CHASE

THE KING GEORGE VI CHASE

THE IRISH GRAND NATIONAL

THE MARYLAND HUNT CUP

LE GRAND STEEPLECHASE DE PARIS

# AINTREE

Looking down anxiously from the start, jockeys see an awesome, challenging line of six fences stretching straight ahead of them; on their right, the canal embankment makes a natural grandstand for those spectators who prefer to be close to the action rather than up in the stands, and they give a tremendous, thrilling roar as the starter drops his flag and the horses surge off. The riders know that the last in that line of fences is Becher's Brook itself, 4ft 10in high but with that 7-foot drop to catch out the unwary. But fence number three is no pushover; standing 4ft 11in high, it has a gaping open ditch, guarded by a rail, in front of it. Even the first fence has a slight drop on landing, and many a horse has been caught out by it, especially when slightly unbalanced from the hectic cavalry charge that led up to it.

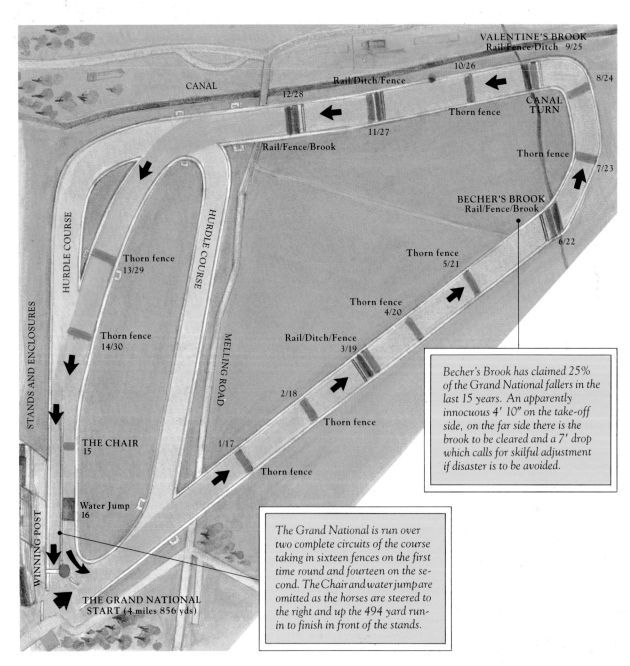

VALENTINE'S BROOK
Rail/Fence/Ditch 9/25

CANAL

10/26

Rail/Ditch/Fence

8/24

12/28

Thorn fence

CANAL TURN

11/27

7/23

Rail/Fence/Brook

Thorn fence

BECHER'S BROOK
Rail/Fence/Brook

6/22

HURDLE COURSE

HURDLE COURSE

Thorn fence
5/21

Thorn fence
13/29

Thorn fence
4/20

Thorn fence
14/30

Rail/Ditch/Fence
3/19

MELLING ROAD

2/18

STANDS AND ENCLOSURES

Thorn fence

THE CHAIR
15

1/17

Thorn fence

Becher's Brook has claimed 25% of the Grand National fallers in the last 15 years. An apparently innocuous 4' 10" on the take-off side, on the far side there is the brook to be cleared and a 7' drop which calls for skilful adjustment if disaster is to be avoided.

WINNING POST

Water Jump
16

The Grand National is run over two complete circuits of the course taking in sixteen fences on the first time round and fourteen on the second. The Chair and water jump are omitted as the horses are steered to the right and up the 494 yard run-in to finish in front of the stands.

THE GRAND NATIONAL
START (4 miles 856 yds)

**Above** *'The Chair' is the biggest fence on the Aintree course standing 5' 2" high and with a 6' wide open ditch on the take-off side. Though only jumped once, it invariably claims some fallers.* **Left** *Many of the Aintree fences have steep drops on the landing side. Captain Becher might have experienced such a view from the brook.*

## A COURSE OF AWESOME FENCES

The Aintree fences are not made of the birch that is used to build other steeplechase courses, but of thorn covered on top by a layer of spruce. Normal steeplechase fences are 4ft 6in high: the Chair at Aintree, jumped near the stands before the water, is the biggest of all, standing 5ft 2in high with an open ditch in front of it so wide that a Mini could fit into it and several of the fences stand five feet high. Nor are these the only hazards: the Canal Turn fence has a 45 degree left turn after it, calling for agility and horsemanship, and with more runners, and fallers, than in other races, loose horses are an additional hazard.

There are 30 fences in all, and because the water is only jumped once, there is an inordinately long run-in, with a jink known as the elbow half way up it; that final haul has proved too much for many a horse who has landed in front over the last fence.

# THE GRAND NATIONAL

IF EVER there was an appropriately named winner of a race it was *Lottery* in the first ever running of the Grand National, for that is how the world's most famous steeplechase is often seen to be.

Founded in 1839 by an enterprising hotel owner called William Lynn, the Grand National was a crowd puller from its very first beginnings. Though it lacked the mass media pre-publicity or modes of transport of today, to say nothing of sponsorship, the whole racing fraternity nevertheless was talking about and planning to attend the forthcoming race.

Until then, with steeplechasing on set courses only a decade or two old, St. Alban's had been the principal meeting. Already, equine and human heroes were emerging, among them *Lottery* and Jem Mason and Captain Becher and *Conrad*.

### THE FIRST 'NATIONAL'

The new race drew over 50 entries, including several horses from Ireland, and for days leading up to February 26, 1839, spectators flocked towards Liverpool by whatever means they could;

*In the first years of the Grand National, most of the fences were small banks topped by 2' palings.*

railway, steamer, coach, gig, wagon, horseback or on foot. The hotels did such a roaring trade that two, the Adelphi (still famed for its pre- and post-Grand National parties) and the Waterloo each let 100 beds, and it is said that in some cases, men were sleeping four to a bed.

By the bright, clear Tuesday morning of the race, hundreds of people were walking and running the three miles out to Aintree, every horse-drawn cab having long since been snapped up; it was the same at the races, where the grandstand (originally built for the flat racing there) was full to overflowing, and, failing to anticipate such a huge crowd, the caterers ran out.

Seventeen horses went to post, including four from Ireland; it was run over the same ground as today, four and a half miles long, but in many respects was different: there was a lot of plough-land to be crossed and, surprisingly perhaps, considering Aintree today is famed for the size of its jumps, most of the fences were very small, just

*Looking down the starting straight at that awesome line of fences. The field are just about to clear the 5th — but better not relax — it's Becher's next!*

little two-foot-high banks gorsed on top and with a small ditch in front; the last two fences were ordinary, upright sheep hurdles. But there were three exceptions: there was a big, five-foot-high solid wall in front of the stands, which took such a toll from the start that it only lasted a few years, and was replaced eventually by the water jump that is still there.

Then there were two wide brooks to be jumped, each faced by sizeable palings and thorn bushes. It was into one of these that Captain Becher was pitched headlong, vowed he never knew water tasted so foul without whiskey in it, and immortalized the fence known forever after as Becher's Brook.

It became a handicap four years after its inception and, until the emergence of the Cheltenham Gold Cup as a level weighted test of the best steeplechaser, was the most important chase in the National Hunt calendar. To millions of 'lay' people in all parts of the world it will always be the greatest horse race, conjuring up the biggest sense of excitement and anticipation, with its heroes and hard luck stories, its fairytales and fallers.

By the 1890s the course had been enclosed and the fences taken on the shape and form for which they are renowned today, and no longer could spectators gallop to vantage points around the course to watch from on horseback. The last piece of cultivated ground on the course was done away with in 1951; it was where the Topham family, who ran Aintree, used to grow their potatoes, and it was said to slow horses down on the headlong gallop from the start to the first fence. In 1951, the first year without it, no fewer than 12 horses fell or were brought down at the first fence!

Because there is an unusually long run from the start to the first, with a much bigger field of runners than in any other steeplechase (in 1929 a record sixty six horses took part), the jockeys are traditionally warned not to go flat out by the senior steward before the start of the race; and equally traditionally they ignore the advice. . .

## RED RUM

Just occasionally comes a horse — or human — who literally becomes a legend in his own life time. One such was *Red Rum*: winner of the Grand National a record three times and second twice; who set a new record time; who overcame harsh punishment with the whip by a succession of different jockeys; who endured a hard campaign on the flat as a sprinter; who was so lame it was feared he might never run again — and who in retirement is a better known and better paid 'show biz' personality than many human stars.

### HUMBLE BEGINNINGS

Few could have foretold *Red Rum's* greatness when he first dead-heated for a five furlong selling race, the lowliest of the low, as a two-year-old at Liverpool. What he did possess was that intangible quality — 'Heart' — the will to win, and the courage to overcome adversity.

By the miler *Quorum* out of a mare said to be virtually unrideable, he was not bred to be a stayer — yet galloped round Aintree's four-and-a-half miles five times with his ears pricked. In his ten year racing career he won three races on the flat, three over hurdles and 21 steeplechases and was placed 35 times. He was beaten a short head in the Hennessy Gold Cup, and won the Scottish Grand National, the only horse ever to do so in the same year as winning the National.

### THE 'McCAIN' FACTOR

He was ridden by 24 different jockeys, including Lester Piggott, and he never fell at a fence; once he slipped up on the flat, and once his jockey was knocked off. He had several trainers and owners, but it is with Donald 'Ginger' McCain and owner Noel le Mare that he is forever associated, and with whom he finally 'came good'.

Ginger's was a small stable in the suburbs of Southport in which the less formal atmosphere and individual attention coupled with the added new interest of doing his work on the beach and

*The 23-year-old Red Rum pictured eleven years after his last National with his trainer 'Ginger' McCain.*

*The perfectly balanced Red Rum, carrying 12 stone, clears Becher's Brook on his way to winning the 1974 Grand National from dual Gold Cup winner L'Escargot.*

over the sand dunes transformed him. Additionally, the sea water acted as a cure for the foot trouble which had been plaguing him for some time. He won five autumn chases off the reel so that by the arrival of Grand National day 1973 he started joint-favourite with the great Australian chaser *Crisp*.

## AN EPIC RACE

And what a race! Ridden by Brian Fletcher, *Red Rum* was set to carry 10st 5lbs and *Crisp*, with Richard Pitman up, was top weight with 12 stone. For many people, it was the year of *Crisp's* Grand National. Setting off like a train, he treated the awesome fences as if they were

upturned dandy brushes, and gave Richard Pitman the most exhilarating, thrilling ride of his life. With each fence, he jumped further into the lead; every time he saw one, he pulled harder and proceeded to devour the ground, fence and all, jumping so quickly and cleanly that, whether intended or not, he was in the lead as early as the second fence.

And there he stayed until a few yards short of the winning post over four miles later. The crowds were treated to the most breathtaking National in living memory that day. *Crisp* made it all look so easy. As they headed out into the country for the second time, he was an amazing 30 lengths clear. Away he went, flicking over that challenging line of fences that culminates in Becher's Brook, then angling over the Canal Turn, all the time saving ground on the inside. It was about this time that *Red Rum* began to break

119

free from the distant pack and to set off in pursuit of the long time leader.

It was at the second last fence that *Crisp* began to falter; the rhythmic, relentless gallop started to give way to fatigue. Now *Red Rum* was within earshot of him, still 20 lengths away but drawing closer, making up a length or two at a time. *Crisp* was still in front over the last but now he was drunk with exhaustion; he held on doggedly; literally two strides before the post, *Red Rum* came by to victory. The time was so fast that the first seven horses home all beat the previous course record!

*Red Rum, ridden by Tommy Stack, pictured before his third, record-breaking win in 1977. Aged 12, he carried 11 stone 8 lbs, the top weight, but ran on to win easily.*

## A SECOND TRIUMPH

If there were those who felt sorry for *Crisp* in 1973, the next four years belonged to *Red Rum*. In 1974, it was *Red Rum* who had to carry 12 stone — and he did so magnificently. Giving one pound to the former dual Cheltenham Gold Cup winner *L'Escargot*, he made the whole race look incredibly easy. The fast ground suited him, and he was going so well that in spite of the weight, he jumped into the lead at Becher's second time round. From there, he simply increased his lead, and won so easily that he was pulling up before the winning post, with jockey Brian Fletcher saluting the cheering crowds.

He came home in triumph to a hero's welcome more normally associated with returning soccer

teams. The streets were lined so deeply that some fans even shinned up drain pipes and climbed on to chimney stacks to get a better view.

## HEAVY GOING

In only one National did *Red Rum* find the going tough, and that was on the heavy ground he detested in 1975 when *L'Escargot*, receiving 11lbs, turned the tables on him. There was no disgrace in defeat, just the opposite rather, for at the half way stage, Brian Fletcher even thought of pulling him up, Red Rum was disliking conditions so. Yet he ploughed on to such effect that he was still just in front as the last fence was cleared.

In 1976, carrying top weight yet again, he ran a cracking race against *Rag Trade*. Just in the lead over the last, *Red Rum* was overtaken by the giant *Rag Trade*, receiving 12lbs, yet all the way up that long and gruelling run-in he was bravely regaining ground.

THE 1973 GRAND NATIONAL

**Prize Money:** £25,486
**Runners:** 38

1 RED RUM
(Quorum – Mared)
**Jockey:** B. Fletcher
**Starting Price:** 9-1
**Owner:** N. Le Mare
**Trainer:** D. McCain

2 CRISP
(Rose Argent – Wheatgerm)
**Jockey:** R. Pitman
**Starting Price:** 9-1
**Owner:** Sir C. Manifold
**Trainer:** F. Winter

3 L'ESCARGOT
(Escart III – What a Daisy)
**Jockey:** T. Carberry
**Starting Price:** 11-1
**Owner:** R. R. Guest
**Trainer:** D. Moore

**Finished:** 10
**Distances:** ¾ length, 25 lengths

## THE PEOPLE'S CHAMPION

In 1977, *Red Rum* was 12 years old, but feeling better than ever, and once again his whole season's programme was geared towards the Grand National.

A lot of uninformed opinion said 'Rummy' should be retired. But he was doing what he knew best and loving it. As Ginger McCain pointed out, 'he was fit and still relatively young, and Mr Le Mare, at eighty-eight years old, had given up golf. Red Rum was his only remaining pleasure and we were not abusing the horse.' He might have become a bit 'racewise' on park courses, but the challenge and heightened atmosphere of Aintree brought out all that was best in him.

So it proved again, and after the 1977 National there can have been few dry eyes among spectators, either at the meeting, or watching on world wide television coverage. It was one of those days when somehow connections, including the horse himself, just knew that he would win. His pre-race confidence was quite exceptional as he proudly walked round at the start, surveying the scene. He was the king and this was his kingdom.

There were 42 runners, but there might just as well have been only one. *Red Rum* met every fence perfectly, footsure and agile. Possessed of superior intelligence, he simply never met his fences wrong; he could shift his shoulders from four strides out to put himself right, and would change direction in mid-air if he spotted a faller on the other side. He was his own race reader and could sometimes make his jockey feel redundant. From Becher's second time round he drew further and further ahead, making the fences look like hurdles. He won as he liked by an incredible 25 lengths to tumultuous applause. It was a stupendous feat, the stuff of which fairy tales are truly made.

## HAPPY RETIREMENT

Had a minor ailment not caused his withdrawal at the eleventh hour the next year, *Red Rum*, again trained to perfection for the big occasion, looked all set to win again at the age of thirteen. Instead it was 'retirement' for 'Rummy', who has spent more than a decade since then playing to his audience with as much panache in his new role of superstar as he did when a racehorse. A professional opener of fêtes, functions and buildings, he appears on stage and television and parades in front of audiences as if to the manner born — truly a living legend.

## ALDANITI

Only four years after *Red Rum* bowed out of competitive action, the Grand National saw another fairy tale come true. This time it concerned a man who had recovered from near terminal cancer, and another horse who overcame lameness to share the Aintree limelight: jockey Bob Champion and *Aldaniti*.

Bob Champion had built a successful career as a jump jockey when in 1979 he received the news that was dramatically to alter his life: he had cancer; without treatment, he would die, and within a few months. Bob Champion did not feel ill and the news came as a complete shock, leaving him in stunned disbelief. He was in the prime of his life, doing a job for which no man had to be fitter. The treatment made him very ill indeed; but ultimately it cured him. They were long, dark days, and through his bleakest, weakest moments, one thought kept him going: riding this horse *Aldaniti*, for whom he had already predicted Grand National success. Bob would get better — and he would ride *Aldaniti* to victory in the National.

### BATTLE FOR RECOVERY

Trained by Josh Gifford, *Aldaniti* was also on the sidelines, recovering from tendon trouble. But whereas he was back in slow work, rebuilding his muscles and hardening his weakened legs, Bob found his muscles so wasted, his whole body so washed out and limp from his treatment that his ambition looked hopeless. The turning point came when he went to America, started riding out for a trainer friend — and made his comeback ride a winning one.

The fact that Bob Champion and *Aldaniti* even made it to the start of the 1981 Grand National was incredible enough; the result was pure fairytale. If the will of millions of viewers world wide could wish it hard enough, they would win. There are many more losers than winners in racing, many more hard luck stories than lucky ones. Occasionally dreams come true. This was one such occasion.

### FULFILLING A DREAM

Bob Champion himself felt only one thing: the certainty that he would win. Tommy Stack had felt it on *Red Rum* four years previously, and Bob felt it now.

**Above and right** *Bob Champion, having contracted cancer two years before and conquered it, fulfils a dream by riding Aldaniti to victory in the 1981 Grand National.*

Nevertheless, all their hopes and dreams nearly subsided at the first fence, when *Aldaniti* overjumped and 'paddled along with his feet on the ground'. Even at the second fence he dropped his hind legs, but he learnt his lesson, which was just as well, as the third fence is a big open ditch.

From then on he jumped like an old hand. In the early part of the race he tracked John Thorne on the favourite, hunter-chaser *Spartan Missile*, both of them running near the outside of the track. The ground was good, *Aldaniti* made light of 10st 13lbs, and by the 12th fence he had jumped his way to the front.

It was possibly a little early to be leading, but the horse was loving it. He gave the cheering crowds a treat by jumping the huge Chair in front of the stands superbly. He cleared the water, and set off on the second circuit full of running.

He met the last fence wrong and 'fiddled' it; then there was just that dreadful 856-yard run-in to come, and the pair set off boldly up it. Unbeknown to Bob, *Spartan Missile* was eating up the ground in hot pursuit, but *Aldaniti* was far enough clear, and they won by four memorable lengths, Bob's right arm raised in triumphant salute, his ever engaging smile spread across his glowing face for the world's cameras to capture.

## GLORY DAYS

As with *Red Rum*, there was to be considerable post-National glory for *Aldaniti*, but this time for his jockey, too. *Aldaniti* still takes part in many charity parades raising money for cancer, but the win changed Bob's life, too. He thereafter devoted much valuable time and energy to spreading the word: one does not necessarily die from cancer, but funds for medical research are always needed.

The win was considered such a fairytale that a successful film was made of the story, appropriately called 'Champions'.

# AYR

ALTHOUGH so far north, Ayr has one of the finest weather records, for it enjoys the benefits of being in the path of the Gulf Stream. So while courses further south and east can be blanketed in snow or frost, Ayr seldom is, and its excellent drainage means few meetings are lost to rain either.

Home of the Scottish Grand National, the Scottish Champion Hurdle, and of the Ayr Gold Cup founded in 1804 on the Flat, Ayr is Scotland's premier track, and has facilities to match its grade one status. It also has a reputation for being one of the best courses for looking after its owners and making them feel welcome.

Records show that racing began at Ayr in 1576 on ground that is now the Seafield Golf Course and Playing Fields, and it remained there until the present course at Craigie was opened in 1907.

Few records remain of the first two hundred years of Ayr racing, but in 1774, Ayr Town Council made a grant of five guineas for repairs to the course. Three years later a five day meeting was held in October and was recorded for the first time in the new Weatherby's Racing Calendar.

By 1800 there were three meetings held, in May, June, and a four day meeting in September. The Ayr Gold Cup was inaugurated four years later, run in two two-mile heats, won by Lord

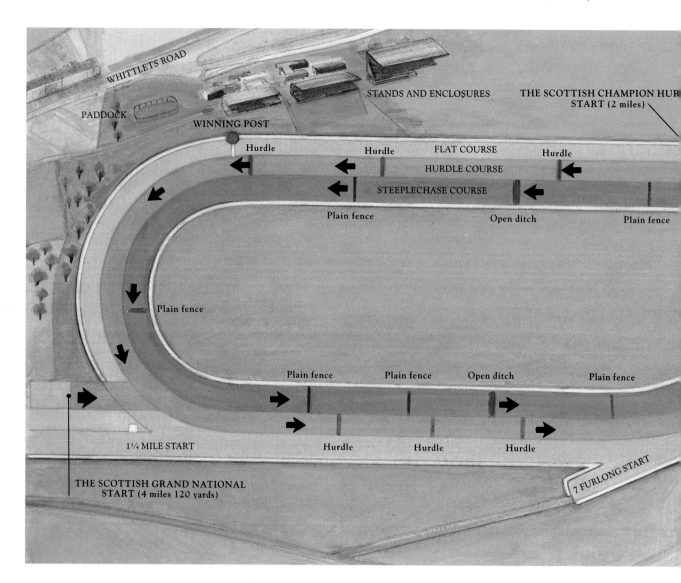

**Right** *The stands of Ayr racecourse pictured under a glowering western sky.*

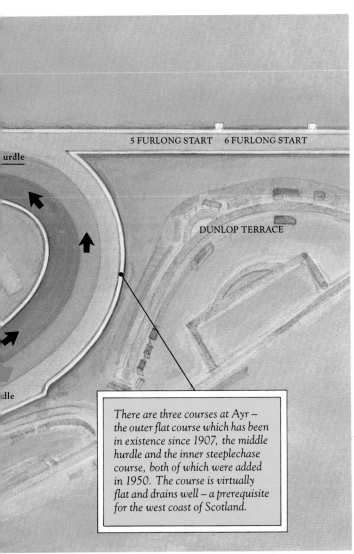

5 FURLONG START    6 FURLONG START

urdle

DUNLOP TERRACE

*There are three courses at Ayr – the outer flat course which has been in existence since 1907, the middle hurdle and the inner steeplechase course, both of which were added in 1950. The course is virtually flat and drains well – a prerequisite for the west coast of Scotland.*

Cassillis' *Chancellor*, who made it a double the next year. Racing thrived at Ayr during this period, and there were plenty of local cheers when Lord Eglinton won the Ayr Gold Cup of 1809 with his filly *Bit of Tartan*.

### THE WESTERN MEETING CLUB

The Western Meeting Club was formed in 1824 to further the interests of horse racing at Ayr, and over a century later, the club bought the racecourse outright. The Ayr Gold Cup became a handicap in 1855, and in 1908, its second year on the present course, its distance became six furlongs.

Although a hurdle race was staged on the old course in 1850, jumping did not come to the present course until exactly 100 years afterwards, when the new National Hunt course was opened in October 1950.

# THE SCOTTISH GRAND NATIONAL

THE SCOTTISH GRAND NATIONAL was staged at Bogside until 1965 but has found an ideal alternative at Ayr, where the almost flat track with gentle undulations is just enough testing over four miles 120 yards.

Its winners are littered with horses who have run well in the Grand National; sometimes, it is used by trainers to try and compensate owners for disappointment in the big one itself, coming, as it does, in mid April, just two or three weeks after Liverpool. Often that proves too short a period for a horse to recover fully, although 1987 brought just that sort of compensation for *Little Polveir*, who had run well in the Grand National. Ridden by Peter Scudamore, who headed off into the 1988-89 jumping season at frenetic, record-breaking speed in terms of winners, he was

*The 1982 Scottish Grand National field. Cockle Strand was the eventual winner of this testing 4 mile steeplechase.*

trained by John Edwards who frequently makes successful raids into Scotland from Ross-on-Wye.

*The Fossa*, *Arcturus* and *Playlord*, trained by Fred Rimell, Neville Crump and Gordon Richards, were all good winners of the Scottish National from 1967-69, and then fastest of all was *Young Ash Leaf*, who won in 1971, trained by Ken Oliver.

Since moving to Ayr, there have been two dual winners, *Barona* in 1975-76 and *Androma* in 1984-85. But the best remembered Scottish National winner of all is *Red Rum*, the only horse ever to have won the Grand National and Scottish National in the same season, 1974.

## PLAYLORD

The biggest weight carried to victory in the Scottish Grand National, the north's most valuable handicap steeplechase, was by *Playlord* in 1969. The eight-year-old's 12 stone was one pound more than that carried by *Red Rum* five years later when he became the only horse ever to win the race in the same year as winning the Grand National.

*Playlord*, a good class bay gelding sired by *Lord of Verona*, was trained for Mr P. Cussins by Sir Gordon Richards at his attractive gothic castellated yard in Greystoke between Penrith and the Lake District.

He had begun his season by winning at Doncaster in October and then, after finishing fourth in the Mackeson Gold Cup at Cheltenham in November, he added more victories at Catterick in December and the Great Yorkshire Chase in January when he beat *Domacorn*.

Having displayed this sort of form, he was among the shorter priced horses for the Cheltenham Gold Cup in which he finished a creditable third in bottomless and cloying ground. It was won by *What A Myth*, ridden by Paul Kelleway, whose unorthodox preparation by the astute trainer Ryan Price had been via the hunting field; *Domacorn* was second.

### TOP WEIGHT AT AYR

So it was no surprise to find *Playlord* burdened with top weight in the Scottish Grand National on April 19 when the ground rode good to firm.

There were 17 runners and *Playlord* started at 9-1 with a horse called *Fearless Fred*, ridden by Champion Jockey Terry Biddlecombe, the 3-1 favourite. Unfortunately, he was responsible for the biggest drama in the race.

All was well to begin with as the runners set off on their long trip, with *The Molar*, *Master Garter* and *Fearless Fred* all prominent and *Playlord* going easily within himself. *Two Springs* jumped into the lead at the thirteenth, running well with *Fearless Fred* close up.

### LUCKY FIFTEENTH

The fifteenth fence brought chaos; *Fearless Fred* fell and in the ensuing mêlée no fewer than four horses were brought down. *Master Garter* had no chance of avoiding him and within moments *African Patrol* who had won the race in 1966, *Harvest Gold* and *Game Purston* all found themselves with nowhere to land either.

It altered the whole complexion of the race but luckily *Playlord* had avoided the trouble. He

*Fearless Fred, ridden by Terry Biddlecombe, leads over the last at Fontwell. In the 1969 Scottish National his fall at the fifteenth fence proved fortunate for Playlord.*

gradually made ground on *Two Springs*, who only lost the lead momentarily until the second to last fence.

*The Molar*, carrying 10st 4lbs and ridden by the great Josh Gifford, was going as well as any until a bad mistake three from home put paid to his chances. Ron Barry — 'Big Ron' — was carefully and cleverly biding his time on *Playlord*, aware of the big weight he had to hump, and the horse was jumping beautifully.

He was bang in the picture by the nineteenth and at the second last, *The Molar* having blundered and *Two Springs* finally weakening, he jumped his way into the lead.

Running on well, he beat *Two Springs* (10st 10lbs) by two lengths, with *The Molar* a further eight lengths behind. *The Fossa*, who won in 1967, was fifth, out of only six finishers.

It was a fine victory for Gordon Richards in only his fifth season as a trainer. Having served an apprenticeship under Jack Waugh and Ivor Anthony, he had learnt things the right way, as he was to prove with later successes, which included Grand National wins with *Lucius* in 1978 and *Hallo Dandy* in 1984.

As it was with Gordon Richards, Ayr was a favourite racecourse for Ron Barry, who had ridden his first winner also only five years before; he was to break the record for the number of National Hunt winners ridden in a season four years later, 1972-73 with 125, which he held until Jonjo O'Neill, also northern-based, beat it with 149 in 1977-78.

In 1988-89, Peter Scudamore smashed all previous records out of sight by riding 100 winners before Christmas and beating Jonjo's record in February with another three months of the season still to run!

## BARONA

*Barona*, who won the Scottish Grand National in 1975 and 1976 was trained by Roddy Armytage, ridden by Paul Kelleway and was owned by one of the greatest patrons of the jumping game, Colonel Bill Whitbread.

He was responsible for introducing Britain's first major sponsored handicap steeplechase, the Whitbread Gold Cup run over 3 miles 5 furlongs at Sandown in April 1957 and in so doing, altered the whole face of the jumping game.

For until that time, the biggest prize for a trainer to aim at was also the riskiest, the Grand National. That, quite rightly, still is the most valuable race, but since the inauguration of the Whitbread Gold Cup, swiftly followed by the Hennessy Gold Cup and then over the years by many more, owners and trainers can now chase very worthwhile prizes without chancing their horses over the Aintree fences.

Colonel Whitbread was a true countryman and sportsman who rode several winners under National Hunt rules and twice completed the Grand National. In *Barona*, he had a genuine horse who also finished fourth in the 1976 Grand National and, only one week after winning his first Scottish Grand National in 1975, finished third in his own race, the Whitbread, behind *April Seventh* and *Captain Christy* with *Crisp* behind him in fourth.

### THE FIRST SCOTTISH NATIONAL

However, when he went to the starting post for his first Scottish Grand National on April 19,

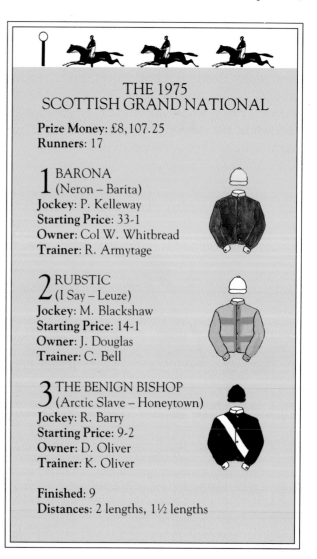

THE 1975
SCOTTISH GRAND NATIONAL

**Prize Money:** £8,107.25
**Runners:** 17

**1 BARONA**
(Neron – Barita)
**Jockey:** P. Kelleway
**Starting Price:** 33-1
**Owner:** Col W. Whitbread
**Trainer:** R. Armytage

**2 RUBSTIC**
(I Say – Leuze)
**Jockey:** M. Blackshaw
**Starting Price:** 14-1
**Owner:** J. Douglas
**Trainer:** C. Bell

**3 THE BENIGN BISHOP**
(Arctic Slave – Honeytown)
**Jockey:** R. Barry
**Starting Price:** 9-2
**Owner:** D. Oliver
**Trainer:** K. Oliver

**Finished:** 9
**Distances:** 2 lengths, 1½ lengths

1975, he was an unconsidered outsider on bottom weight having not won a race all season, Paul Kelleway having to put up 7lbs overweight to manage 10 stone.

Most eyes, naturally, were focused on *Red Rum,* who had just been beaten by *L'Escargot* in the Grand National, and was set to carry 12 stone. Ridden by Brian Fletcher, he started 3-1 favourite.

He looked a picture as usual, and a great credit to his trainer Ginger McCain, but although he made headway from halfway and was still in touch at the 20th fence, he was outpaced from there and finished seventh.

The race was remarkable for producing no fallers from the 17 runner field, as the six year old *Rubstic* carrying only 9st 8lb and *The Benign Bishop,* 11st 8lb, skipped along tirelessly amongst the leaders.

*Rubstic,* who was to win the Grand National four years later, was ridden by Martin Blackshaw, sadly killed in a car crash in France in January 1989, while Ron Barry rode *The Benign Bishop.*

*Rubstic* hit the front four fences from home but he made a bad mistake two out where *Barona* overtook both him and *The Benign Bishop* to run on gamely to victory.

*Paul Kelleway and Barona lead, safely on their way to their second Scottish Grand National victory in 1976. The victory was achieved shortly after Barona's 4th place finish in the Grand National.*

## DOUBLE SUCCESS

The following year *Barona* was better fancied in the field of 23, although again he had not won another race all season.

He was again ridden by Paul Kelleway, jumping's master at riding the waiting race. Often it would look as if he had left his run too late, only to come through at the last moment with perfect timing to snatch the spoils.

His second success on *Barona* in the Scottish Grand National was almost a carbon copy of his first. Behind early, he made headway from the 18th fence and again led between the last two to run on well.

*Bentley Boy,* whom he beat by six lengths, led four out but blundered badly at the penultimate fence which effectively ruined his chances. *Another Muddle* finished third ahead of long time leaders *Collingwood* and *Glanford Brigg.*

It was a very fine effort by *Barona* coming so soon after his fourth place finish in a gruelling race like the Grand National.

# THE SCOTTISH CHAMPION HURDLE

THE SCOTTISH CHAMPION HURDLE, founded in 1966 is run over 2 miles at level weights and has seen some true champions in its time. Among those on the roll of honour are *Captain Christy*, 1973, *Night Nurse*, 1976, and *Sea Pigeon* in 1977 and 1978.

In 1988, victory went to *Pat's Jester* whose jockey Brian Storey became the first rider ever to win both the Scottish Champion Hurdle and Scottish Grand National in the same year, the latter on *Mighty Mark.*

A former junior showjumping champion, Brian rode *Pat's Jester* with brilliant confidence, landing fourth over the last flight but galvanizing a run that wore down the 1984 winner *Rushmoor* to win by half a length.

Many 'ordinary' people enjoy racehorse ownership these days thanks to syndicates, partnerships and clubs, and *Pat's Jester* was owned by the Yorkshire Racing Club when he was successful on the Flat.

By the time he won the Scottish Champion Hurdle, he was owned by Mr Geoff Adam and trained by Dick Allan who, in 1969 was a stable lad in Gordon Richards's yard, 'doing his two', one of whom was Scottish National winner *Playlord!*

## NIGHT NURSE

For a flat-race bred colt to make only 1300 guineas as a yearling is almost unthinkable, that *Night Nurse* then went on to win the Champion Hurdle and Welsh Champion Hurdle twice, the Scottish Champion Hurdle, and the Irish Sweeps Hurdle, as well as some top class steeplechases and a second in the Cheltenham Gold Cup is part of racing's magic.

*Night Nurse*, a big brown horse, was unfashionably bred by *Falcon* out of *Florence Nightingale* and suffered a slight heart irregularity; as a result of this, it was 'almost impossible to give him away as a three-year-old', recalls his trainer's wife Mrs M. H. Easterby.

Indeed, there are a great many people now who can recall with some chagrin, 'I had the chance to buy *Night Nurse!*'

### FROM FLAT RACER TO HURDLER

In the end, Reg Spencer, an estate agent from York, was so impressed with him as a possible future hurdler as he walked round the parade ring for what turned out to be his only win on the Flat — at 20-1 — that he promptly bought him. He never regretted it!

*Night Nurse* in Jonjo O'Neill's words, 'jumped fences with the power of Concorde'. He won at his very first attempt over hurdles and after that victory never looked back, winning five of his seven runs in his first season, ridden by stable jockey Paddy Broderick whose partnership with the horse was one of jumping's great highlights, until unhappily a bad fall together ended Paddy's riding days.

### CHAMPION HURDLER

When *Night Nurse* made the long journey up to Ayr to contest the Scottish Champion Hurdle on the day that *Barona* won the Scottish National for the second time, his form was impeccable, having won all his previous eight races that season.

These included the Champion Hurdle, in which he had made all the running and a two horse race on the outcome of which there had been no betting; he had had more of a contest when beating *Comedy of Errors* and *Sea Pigeon* in the Fighting Fifth Hurdle at Newcastle; he had won the Welsh Champion Hurdle at odds of 5-1 on, and he had won the Sweeps Hurdle at Leopardstown.

So it was no surprise, although inevitably disappointing for spectators, that only one horse took him on in Scotland. This was *Nougat*, ridden by Ron Barry, but hard though he tried, he could never remotely get on terms with *Night Nurse*, out in front, jumping superbly, and giving what amounted to an exhibition round in the hands of 'Brod'.

After the sad enforced retirement of 'Brod', Jonjo O'Neill took over and, although he lacked the long legs of 'Brod' to 'wrap round' the big horse, he forged an equally successful partnership with him. *Night Nurse's* own powerful long legs would get lower to the ground like a greyhound as

he went into top gear in the closing stages of a race. He possessed an ideal mixture of speed, stamina, brilliant jumping and the will to win.

Jonjo recalls with fond admiration in his autobiography, 'He would take a flight of hurdles in his stride, not rising very high, just zipping over it at tremendous speed. Then in a flash it all happened. He landed, switched on an extra engine which accelerated him away from the hurdle the instant he touched down, and you

*Night Nurse, ridden by Jonjo O'Neill, pictured during his later steeplechasing days competing at Ayr.*

were powered back into the saddle. That was where he won his races, by leaving even the fastest hurdlers toiling as he roared away, his hurdles disappearing behind him in a mass of flying hooves and earth'.

It was this powerful and determined style that won £132,392 for his grateful owner, Reg Spencer.

131

## SEA PIGEON

Of all the equine stars that Jonjo O'Neill rode, his personal favourite was *Sea Pigeon*, with whom he enjoyed a real rapport.

Owned by white-haired Mr Pat Muldoon from Edinburgh, *Sea Pigeon*, unlike *Night Nurse*, was a good enough horse to have finished seventh in the 1973 Derby when trained by Jeremy Tree at Beckhampton, and in later years mixed jumping and flat racing with equal ease.

It was only Mr Muldoon's perseverance that got him *Sea Pigeon* — at the fourth time of asking! By that time the colt had been gelded and was taking a long time to recover.

### SON OF SEA BIRD II

*Sea Pigeon* was by the runaway Prix de l'Arc de Triomphe winner *Sea Bird II*, who also won the Derby, and was his best known son to go jumping.

He began his National Hunt career with Gordon Richards at Penrith and was later moved to Peter Easterby. *Sea Pigeon* was always an individual who liked to do things his own way — although when faced by a herd of cows on his first morning at Penrith, he did not know what to do!

He won both his Scottish Champion Hurdles before either of his Cheltenham ones, and in his first, he had only two rivals. Unlike *Night Nurse*, who was a bold front-runner, *Sea Pigeon* had to be 'held up' for his challenge, and on this occasion it was *Birds Nest*, ridden by Andy Turnell, who led until the last flight.

Jonjo produced *Sea Pigeon* there and accelerated away nicely, and although *Birds Nest* did not give up his effort, *Sea Pigeon* had a comfortable length and a half to spare at the line, with *Sabroso* third.

### A HARD-FOUGHT CONTEST

It was a much better contest in 1978 for with the rising Irish star *Golden Cygnet* in the field, unbeaten in six starts, as well as *Night Nurse*, *Beacon Light* and *Winter Melody* among the seven runners, a dramatic race was in prospect.

So it proved; *Sea Pigeon* and *Golden Cygnet* started at 7-4 joint favourites but with three

*Sea Pigeon (left of picture) on his way to his first Scottish Champion Hurdle success. He had started his career as a flat-racer and had finished seventh in the 1973 Derby.*

*Jonjo O'Neill poses aboard a healthy and sleek Sea Pigeon who looks every inch the son of 1965 Derby winner Sea Bird II.*

flights left it was a three horse race. *Night Nurse* was in the lead, but as he raced towards the penultimate flight first *Golden Cygnet* then *Sea Pigeon* loomed.

The expectant crowd, the 'home side' supporting the Scottish-owned *Sea Pigeon*, the Irish their young star, roared encouragement. *Golden Cygnet*, ridden by Irish amateur Niall Madden, quickened like a good one going to the last level with *Night Nurse* and about two lengths up on *Sea Pigeon*.

Then disaster! *Golden Cygnet* fell; his race was over and *Sea Pigeon* and Jonjo had to take quick evasive action to avoid being brought down. Even so, *Sea Pigeon* was able to recover, get into top gear, and still beat *Night Nurse* by half a length, with *Beacon Light* and *Winter Melody* running on to take a close third and fourth.

The biggest debate was what would the result have been had *Golden Cygnet* not fallen. Alas, it was never answered, for in the eagerly anticipated re-match *Golden Cygnet* suffered a second fall and sadly was killed.

*Sea Pigeon*, meanwhile, had at last won the Champion Hurdle twice after two seconds and the popular, versatile horse also won some top staying races on the Flat, including the Ebor Handicap, and the Chester Cup twice, sometimes ridden by his principal National Hunt jockey Jonjo O'Neill.

# CHELTENHAM

CHELTENHAM IS to National Hunt Racing what Newmarket is to the Flat. The natural amphitheatre beneath Cleeve Hill on the edge of the Cotswolds makes an ideal scenario. Simply to have a runner there is the ambition of many an owner, and to own a winner a dream come true.

In its earliest days, from about 1815, racing took place on top of the chilly and blustery hill

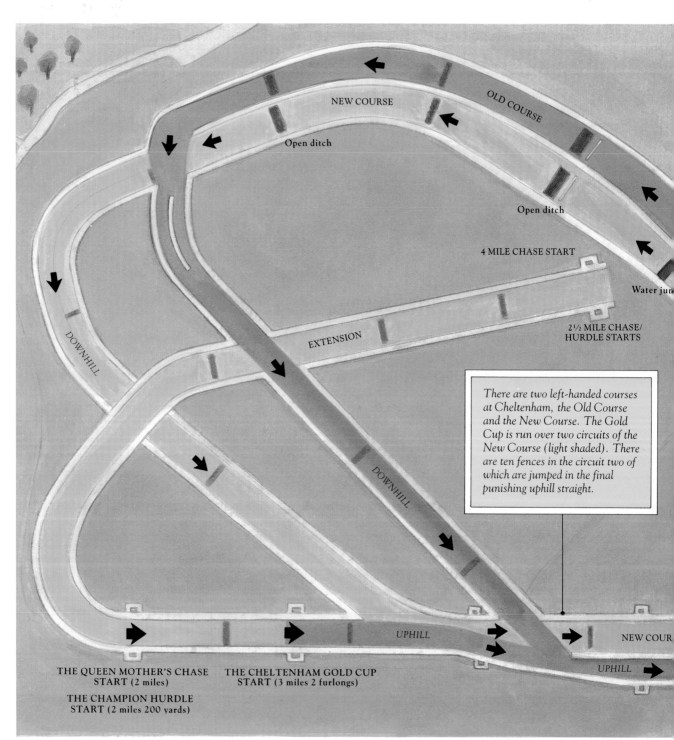

NEW COURSE

OLD COURSE

Open ditch

Open ditch

4 MILE CHASE START

Water jun

DOWNHILL

EXTENSION

2½ MILE CHASE/
HURDLE STARTS

DOWNHILL

There are two left-handed courses at Cheltenham, the Old Course and the New Course. The Gold Cup is run over two circuits of the New Course (light shaded). There are ten fences in the circuit two of which are jumped in the final punishing uphill straight.

UPHILL

NEW COUR

THE QUEEN MOTHER'S CHASE
START (2 miles)

THE CHELTENHAM GOLD CUP
START (3 miles 2 furlongs)

UPHILL

THE CHAMPION HURDLE
START (2 miles 200 yards)

above Prestbury but only flat racing took place at Cheltenham then, with a Cheltenham Gold Cup first run over three miles on the flat in 1819.

Twelve years later racing moved to the far better ambience below, complete with grandstand to accommodate 700 and declared the best in the land. For a time racing flourished, until that is, the coming of an evangelist, the Reverend (later Dean) Francis Close. A great orator, he preached far and wide about the sins of racing

> *The Champion Hurdle and the Queen Mother Champion Chase are both run over the Old Course. The hurdles course is set to the outside of the steeplechase course and is run over 1 circuit and 8 obstacles. The Queen Mother Chase is run over nine fences one of which is jumped in the final straight.*

*The stands and finishing straight at Cheltenham on a showery March afternoon.*

WINNING POST

STANDS AND ENCLOSURES

and the evils of gambling, with the result that, in 1829, his followers staged a demonstration on the course and the following year the grandstand was burnt down. Within a few years, the prevailing Victorian moral attitudes held sway, and racing ceased there altogether.

### HOME OF THE FESTIVAL

It had re-emerged by the turn of the century, and this time it was here to stay: the forerunner of the National Hunt Festival, the three day highlight of jumping's calendar each March, first took place in 1902. By 1914 new stands, promptly requisitioned by the Army during the Great War, were built and lasted until the 1970s.

Since then Cheltenham has undergone a major, multi-million pound facelift, with new stands complete with lifts, and bars, Tote and toilet facilities at every level. The paddock and weighing room complex was completely re-designed and re-sited, with viewing improved considerably. More facilities were opened for the 1989 Festival.

The course itself has two tracks, old and new, stretching away into the distance both uphill and down. Both courses are used, fresh ground coming into use for Gold Cup day, the last of the three day meeting at which the atmosphere has to be experienced first hand to be believed.

# THE CHELTENHAM GOLD CUP

THE FIRST RUNNING of the Cheltenham Gold Cup over jumps took place in 1924, won by *Red Splash*. The Cup quickly grew in stature, gradually taking over the mantle of the most important steeplechase from the Grand National. Nothing could detract from the National's unique standing, but, being a handicap, it was by no means always the best horse that won. With the Gold Cup run at level weights the winner, in theory at least, should be the best, and so it eventually became recognized as the Blue Riband race of steeplechasing. To win this race has become the ambition of every self-respecting owner.

## GOLDEN MILLER

*Golden Miller* was Irish bred, and a classical example of the type of staying chaser for which the period was famed. A bay with a white star, he was by *Goldcourt* out of *Miller's Pride*, and was brought to England as a three-year-old to be

*The impressive tiered grandstand at Cheltenham — part of a successful modernization programme that has helped the festival become a major sporting event.*

trained at his own stables by Basil Briscoe, one of whose owners was the Honourable Dorothy Paget, the most eccentric and influential woman in racing of her day, both on Flat and jumping courses.

Briscoe passed on *Golden Miller* and a horse called *Insurance* to her for £10,000; and as well as *Golden Miller*'s five Gold Cups, between 1932-1936, *Insurance* also won the Champion Hurdle twice! It is said that *Golden Miller* was the only male to whom Miss Paget ever outwardly showed any signs of affection. She was surrounded by an army of exclusively female servants, would order fish and chips in the middle of the night, was grossly overweight, wore shabby, battered clothes — and bet in telephone numbers.

## BEGINNING OF THE RUN

For this daughter of Lord Queenborough, Basil Briscoe did his best to train, and in 1932 the five-year-old *Golden Miller* went to Cheltenham with only four chases behind him, three of which he had won. The previous year's Grand National winner *Grakle* was favourite, and a horse called *Kingsford* second favourite. *Golden Miller* came next in the betting, and when *Grakle* lost his rider and *Kingsford* fell, Ted Leader rode *Golden Miller* home for a four-length victory.

With the demise of the two more fancied horses, the performance, good though it was, did not necessarily mark him out as a star. That was still to come, but it did not take long, for the next season he won his first five races, the fifth being his second Gold Cup.

*Golden Miller, the five times Gold Cup winner and the only horse ever to have won the Gold Cup and the Grand National in the same season.*

He blotted his copybook next time out when, still only six-years-old, he made his first attempt on the Grand National, one that ended with a fall, and Ted Leader predicting he would never be an Aintree 'natural'.

## A HISTORIC DOUBLE

Next year, in 1934, *Golden Miller* won the Gold Cup by a convincing six lengths and then set out for Aintree and an historic Grand National win in record time, the first and still the only horse to win both races in the same season. It stamped him a truly great horse. He carried 12st 2lbs to beat *Delaneige* (11st 6lbs) and *Thomond* (12st 4lbs).

At that time, the Grand National retained its status as the most important steeplechase in the calendar, as reflected by the prize money. In 1933, for instance, the Gold Cup was worth just £670, and the National £7,345. In 1988, it was £61,960 to the winner of the Gold Cup and

£68,740 for the National. So in the 1930s, the Gold Cup was still merely considered a stepping stone towards the ultimate goal.

### THE GREAT DUEL

The happenings of *Golden Miller* in 1935 were sensational. Believing nothing of note would oppose him in the Gold Cup, Basil Briscoe had been relatively light on *Golden Miller's* preparation, aiming to have him at his peak for the tilt at a second Grand National success.

The Gold Cup that year, however, turned into one of the greatest steeplechase duels of all time between *Golden Miller* and his old rival *Thomond II*. Neither were their three rivals small fry: *Southern Hero*, *Avenger* and *Kellsboro' Jack* were all useful horses, too.

Not surprisingly, a huge crowd turned out to watch the spectacle, many arriving by special train, disembarking right beside the course. Cleeve Hill made a noble backcloth to the drama that was to unfold, and the stands were filled with eager spectators. They were not to be disappointed.

From the start, the race was run at a great gallop on fast ground and with a mile to go all five still looked in with a chance. Cresting the top of the hill, and facing the downhill third last fence that has seen so many dreams crash over the years, *Golden Miller* and *Thomond* were neck and neck; they had the race to themselves, but which would be the first to weaken? Both brave, courageous horses, neither would give in lightly as they remained locked together around the long sweeping bend towards the last two fences. It was a battle royal, with both horses fencing fast and bravely, aided by their equally brave jockeys Gerry Wilson and Billy Speck.

They reached the rising ground and as they jumped the last fence they were still together; now only the final, stamina-sapping hill faced them, the roars of the cheering crowd rising to a crescendo as, with barely 100 yards to go, *Golden Miller* managed to get his head in front. On the line, he had three-quarters of a length to spare.

The time for the race was a record, eclipsing that of *Easter Hero*, considered by many as one of the best horses of all time and twice winner of the Gold Cup, by a full 27 seconds.

It is this sort of exhilarating spectacle that makes the Cheltenham Gold Cup so special. As the two jockeys are reported as saying afterwards, 'When we are old and grey, sitting back and enjoying a drink, we can tell them how we did ride at least one great horse race, one day in our lives'. Sadly, only one month later, Billy Speck was killed in a fall on the same course.

### AN UNBEATABLE RECORD?

*Golden Miller*, amid much controversy, never won the Grand National again, but he did win the next Gold Cup, his fifth, and might have done so again in 1937 had the race not been abandoned due to the weather. He turned out again in 1938, now aged 11, and was a creditable second, eventually having to concede to youth in the shape of *Morse Code*. He lived in contented retirement until the ripe old age of 30, the winner of 28 of his 52 races.

In 1989, a half life size statue of him was unveiled, to honour his memory, like that of *Arkle* and *Dawn Run*, already commemorated.

### ARKLE

*Cottage Rake* was to win the Gold Cup in three successive years from 1948-50 but it was the 1960s before another horse caught the public imagination as *Golden Miller* had in the Cheltenham Gold Cup. This was *Arkle*, surely the greatest chaser of all time.

*Arkle* was a star, and to watch him perform a lifelong privilege. He adored people, and people adored him. Wherever he went, there was an aura of regality about him, head held high, ears pricked, his whole bearing proud. In a race he was elegance personified, he jumped superbly, he galloped effortlessly.

### THE UNANSWERABLE QUESTION

*Arkle* won the Cheltenham Gold Cup three times before a broken pedal bone ended his career prematurely. A few will claim he was not the best of all time, for there are some who say *Golden Miller* was the greatest and, with the two horses foaled 30 years apart, many people were able to see both.

*Golden Miller* won five Gold Cups and a Grand National, in which *Arkle* was never risked by his devoted owner, Anne, Duchess of Westminster, but it is not so much the number of wins, but how they win that counts.

Only once was he beaten by making a jumping mistake, by *Mill House* in his first Hennessy, just twice he was beaten by crippling weight, and once he was beaten by injury. He never fell racing, and when he blundered wholesale as his attention was diverted by his cheering public, in his third Gold Cup, he learnt his lesson.

*Arkle* was bred at the lush grass growing County Dublin home of Mrs Mary Baker and as a gawky, gangly three-year-old was sent to Goff's Sales at Ballsbridge. Anne, Duchess of Westminster bought him, named him after a Scottish mountain and in due course sent him with another horse of hers, *Ben Stack*, to Tom Dreaper's yard at Kilsallaghan, as his mother and grandmother had been before him.

### AN EARLY SURPRISE

Not much notice was taken of the unexceptional youngster, for not much was expected of him. His grand-dam, *Greenogue Princess*, had won point-to-points ridden by Tom, and his dam *Bright Cherry*, could just about last home in a two-mile chase if the going was like concrete. Tom Dreaper, therefore, did not envisage him developing into a three-mile chaser at all, let alone a crack one.

When he was despatched to his first hurdle race at Navan, it was very much as the stable's second string — but he ploughed through the mud and, to the total bewilderment of all his connections, won as he liked.

The Navan victory had been unexpected but *Arkle* soon showed it was no fluke. He was also that paragon, a perfect horse to train, easy to care for in his box and to ride, a good 'grubber' and had a temperament to match. He ran in five more hurdles, won three of them, and later in his life won a maiden plate on the flat as a pre-season warm up.

*The much loved combination of Arkle and Pat Taaffe. Between 1964 and 1966 Arkle won the Gold Cup three times in succession and left behind him an indelible impression of character and intelligence.*

## STEEPLECHASE RIVALS

For his first ever steeplechase, he was taken to England, and won the Honeybourne Chase at Cheltenham in November, and then a chase at Leopardstown, before returning to Cheltenham for the National Hunt Festival. But although he won the Broadway Chase (now the Sun Alliance), he was not the talking horse of the meeting. That distinction went to a gentle giant of a horse trained by Fulke Walwyn called *Mill House* who at only six years old, the same age as *Arkle*, won the Cheltenham Gold Cup.

When *Mill House* and *Arkle* first met in the Hennessy Gold Cup at Newbury, amid great Press build up and speculation, it looked as if the English pundits were right. *Arkle*, who had won four more chases since the Broadway, slipped at the final open ditch and could finish only third to the mighty *Mill House*.

Naturally, when a renewed clash was lined up for the next Cheltenham Gold Cup, the English would not hear of defeat for their reigning champion even though *Arkle* had won his next three chases in Ireland.

## THE BIG CLASH

Ten minutes before the Gold Cup, as the horses paraded, it started snowing on the heavy ground and it was debated whether to let the horses race. But down at the start the snow stopped, and it was decided to let the race continue. *Mill House* and his competent rider Willie Robinson set off leading the four runners and jumping superbly. Winning looked a formality to his followers but not to those watching the Irish horse poised just behind, in the saddle his regular jockey, Pat Taaffe, a fine horseman, and an integral part of the long-standing success story at Kilsallaghan.

When Willie Robinson went for his whip between the last two fences, the writing was on the wall. Pat Taaffe had only to shake the reins for *Arkle* to take command and storm away up the hill for a five length win. *Pas Seul*, himself a previous Gold Cup winner, could only struggle in 25 lengths behind, such was the complete supremacy of the leading pair.

## A HORSE WITHOUT EQUALS

*Arkle* and *Mill House* met again in the Gold Cup of 1965. They set off together, but all poor *Mill House*'s efforts were futile; he struggled to keep in touch and, when Pat Taaffe pressed the button, *Arkle* simply drew away to win by 20 lengths.

By this time, many of his races in Ireland were becoming mere 'exercise canters', as *Arkle* was so far superior to everything else. An *Arkle* fan club had started; after his first Gold Cup win, the tiny road leading to the stables was blocked with cars full of admirers. All through the summer tourists from all over the world, including Japan, would come knocking at the door, and they were always shown '*Himself*' as *Arkle* became universally known. The fan mail arrived in droves, — one was addressed simply '*Arkle*, Ireland' — and all sorts of things would be sent through the post, like sugar lumps from a pensioner or a can of *Arkle*'s favourite Guinness, or a carrot.

## ALMOST AN UPSET

When *Arkle* went to post for his third Gold Cup, he started at 10-1 on. Realistically, only a fall could make him fail, and he had never fallen on the racecourse. How nearly he did that day!

Cruising into the last fence first time round, at

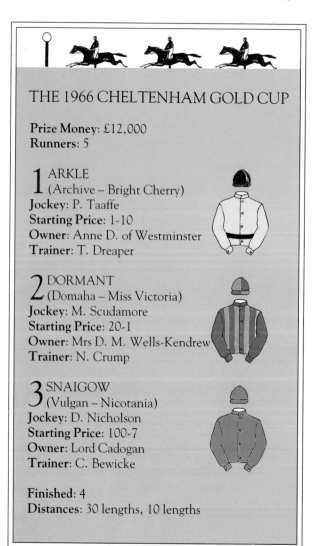

THE 1966 CHELTENHAM GOLD CUP

**Prize Money:** £12,000
**Runners:** 5

**1 ARKLE**
(Archive – Bright Cherry)
Jockey: P. Taaffe
Starting Price: 1-10
Owner: Anne D. of Westminster
Trainer: T. Dreaper

**2 DORMANT**
(Domaha – Miss Victoria)
Jockey: M. Scudamore
Starting Price: 20-1
Owner: Mrs D. M. Wells-Kendrew
Trainer: N. Crump

**3 SNAIGOW**
(Vulgan – Nicotania)
Jockey: D. Nicholson
Starting Price: 100-7
Owner: Lord Cadogan
Trainer: C. Bewicke

**Finished:** 4
**Distances:** 30 lengths, 10 lengths

*Arkle, seemingly out on his own whilst winning the 1965 Gold Cup. His eventual winning distance was 20 lengths.*

more or less the half way point in the race and closest to the crowds, a good few of whom were craning by the fence itself, *Arkle* simply looked at them and listened to the cheers, instead of taking off. His chest took the full force of the birch fence and breasted through it; he and Pat Taaffe between them subconsciously took every action possible to avoid a fall and miraculously they achieved what for a few breathtaking moments looked impossible.

It was a monumental mistake, but *Arkle* recovered himself and Pat Taaffe, adopting a good old hunting seat, shooting his legs forward and slipping the reins, remained in the saddle.

When he sauntered home by a record-breaking 30 lengths, it was still the mistake everyone was talking about. But there seemed no limit to what he could achieve, and surpassing *Golden Miller*'s record a distinct possibility.

### A SAD END

But it was not to be. Nine months later, running in the King George VI, at Kempton, he knocked his off fore foot so hard on a take-off board or guard rail that his pedal bone was broken. In the heat of the moment, with the adrenalin flowing, neither horse nor rider knew it. Nor did his ardent supporters from the stands who stared in disbelief as *Dormant* overtook him on the run-in and beat him by a length. Good, honest horse that *Dormant* was, he was not within stones of beating *Arkle*.

Moments later, as he pulled up, it was obvious to all that he was lame. *Arkle* stayed in his box at Kempton for six weeks with his leg in plaster, his door and walls smothered in Get Well cards.

It was hoped that he would be able to make a come-back, but arthritis set in and the dream was extinguished. Four years later, at 13 and in pain, he was put down and buried at the Duchess's farm in Maynooth, where he had spent his summer holidays and later his retirement.

It is in action that *Arkle* is forever remembered, for his superiority was truly stunning, as his record of 27 wins from 35 runs, no falls except once schooling over hurdles, and only once unplaced, in a hurdle race, shows.

141

# THE CHAMPION HURDLE

THREE YEARS AFTER the inauguration of the premier steeplechasing Classic, the Gold Cup, it was decided to stage a parallel race for hurdlers, the Champion Hurdle, in 1927. From the start it attracted high quality horses and lived up to its championship status.

Run over two miles, which is the minimum distance for any National Hunt race in England and the most usual one for hurdlers, Cheltenham's undulations put a test on the stamina and balance as well as speed, and on gameness as well as ability, as horses have to be brave to face the final hill after a fast run race.

It is run at level weights (with the general exception since 1984 that all mares receive a 5lb allowance), and is sponsored by Waterford Crystal, who put up beautiful pieces of its glassware each year for the winners.

*Dawn Run* is the only horse to have won both the Champion Hurdle and Gold Cup but generally it is the speedier, flat racer types who are

*Contenders for the 1988 Champion Hurdle circle the Cheltenham parade ring. The usual massive crowd is in attendance.*

more likely to win the Champion Hurdle than the chaser type.

Post war years have produced admirable multiple Champion Hurdlers: *Insurance* in 1931-32; *National Spirit* 1947-48; *Hatton's Grace* 1949-51; *Sir Ken* 1952-54; *Persian War* 1968-70; *Bula* 1971-2; *Comedy of Errors* 1973 and 75; *Night Nurse* 1976-7; *Monksfield* 1978-9; *Sea Pigeon* 1980-81; and *See You Then* 1985-87.

## SIR KEN

Possibly the greatest of all was *Sir Ken*, a horse bought cheaply in France who went on to win 16 hurdle races consecutively in England before tasting defeat. A good horse anywhere, *Sir Ken* was brilliant at Cheltenham where the supreme test brought the best out of him.

It was trainer Willie Stephenson who spotted him in France, and he sold him on to Maurice Kingsley while retaining his training.

When *Sir Ken* first lined up for the Champion Hurdle in 1952 he already possessed a considerable reputation, and although opposed by *National Spirit* and *Hatton's Grace*, who between them had won the previous five runnings of the race, he started favourite. *National Spirit*, in fact, ran in six consecutive Champion Hurdles, while *Hatton's Grace* had been transformed by the Irish maestro Vincent O'Brien to win his Champions at an advanced age.

*Sir Ken*'s regular rider Tim Moloney rode a peach of a race, producing him with exquisite timing at the last flight to beat *Noholme* by two lengths, with *National Spirit* and *Hatton's Grace* both falling along the way.

In 1953, still unbeaten and, at 5-2 on, the shortest priced favourite in the history of the race, *Sir Ken* produced a carbon copy of a race, this time beating *Galation* by two lengths with *Teapot II* third. The first three jockeys were amongst the finest over fences, Tim Moloney, Brian Marshall and Pat Taaffe, but could 'produce the goods' over hurdles too.

*Sir Ken* was a tough, courageous type who stood a lot of work, but before the 1954 Champion he met his first three defeats, the first at 7-1 on. He suffered another defeat at the hands of *Noholme* who was in receipt of 11 lbs. A mixture of firm ground and big weight burdens were largely responsible but it was a different story back at his favourite Cheltenham, where, of course, the Champion was run at level weights.

*Tim Moloney aboard Sir Ken wins the 1954 Champion Hurdle.*

143

### TRIPLE ATTEMPT

In spite of his defeats, *Sir Ken* not only started favourite but was again odds-on, this time at 9-4 on. His fans were not to be disappointed; behind him came *Impney*, who had been responsible for his first defeat, and *Galation*, second to him the previous year. He was given a hero's welcome.

*Sir Ken* ran again the following year but this time could finish only fourth, and he then embarked on a successful chasing career, winning four of his first six including the Cotswold (now Arkle) at his favourite Cheltenham Festival. In 1957 he became one of several horses to attempt the Champion Hurdle/Gold Cup double, but the fire had lost much of its fuel, and *Sir Ken* deservedly was retired to the hunting field.

### MONKSFIELD

One of the most courageous battlers ever to grace the jumping world was *Monksfield*, winner of the Champion Hurdle in 1978 and 1979, and of some other very brave races, too. His was one of racing's fairy tales: bought as an unbroken two-year-old for 740 guineas, his new owner Des

*Sir Ken, winner of three successive Champion Hurdles (1952-1954). He later went on to pursue a successful steeplechase career.*

McDonagh took him back to the wild country of northern County Meath, where he had a few stables and some very wet land alongside his bungalow. He sold him on to first time owner Dr Michael Mangan a radiologist from Newfoundland, who had only to lift the phone to hear his new purchase as he contentedly munched hay in the box nearest to McDonagh's home.

*Monksfield* was always a good eater, so much so that he often carried surplus flesh in early season, but he was anyway a spring horse. Often referred to as little, there was a good frame behind his neat head, and he was in beautiful proportion. Luckily for the National Hunt breeding world, he remained a full horse, and his temperament was so good that anyone could walk into his box.

To the surprise of all, he won his only race as a two-year-old at Punchestown, paying 647-1 on the Tote. He won his first two hurdles in Ireland then finished second in the four-year-olds' Classic, the Daily Express Triumph Hurdle at the

144

Cheltenham Festival. Next year, he tried the Champion for the first time, only to finish second again, this time to *Night Nurse* who was winning it for the second time. Three weeks later came one of the most stirring hurdle races of all time when, over a longer distance, the pair dead-heated at Liverpool.

### A MEETING OF CHAMPIONS

These two were both in the Champion again the next year, 1978, along with another all time National Hunt hero, *Sea Pigeon*. The great and gutsy *Monksfield* went hammer and tongs at *Night Nurse* from way out, and had that horse beaten before the penultimate hurdle. But had he taken too much out of himself? *Sea Pigeon* was looming,

*Sea Pigeon (left) challenges Monksfield during the 1978 Champion Hurdle. Monksfield went on to win and then repeated the same feat against the same horse in 1979.*

and the pair of them jumped the last flight stride for stride, *Monksfield* straining away to keep level. A few moments later, it was all over. 'Monkey', as he was affectionately known, attacked that final hill to the winning line as if it was his breakfast, and victory was his.

Again, the same two protagonists fought out the finish of the 1979 Champion; it was truly an era of great hurdlers, and again this pair raced stride for stride, as they headed for the last flight and that stamina-sapping hill. But this time it was *Sea Pigeon* who was cruising, and *Monksfield* who had to be slapped sharply. He responded with as great a bravery as has ever been witnessed. He would not give in. He jumped that last flight like dynamite then dourly faced the hill under the greatest pressure; he was not one to shirk the issue, instead he tried his heart out. The victory that looked impossible became deservedly his, his resolution rewarded.

*Monksfield, ridden by D. T. Hughes, hurdling with plenty to spare during his 1979 Champion Hurdle victory.*

It was a memorable Champion Hurdle — and *Monksfield*, the last entire horse to win it, went on to stand at stud; one of his first successful progeny being *Broadsword*.

## DAWN RUN

Of all the unlikely prospects to be the first — and so far only — horse to bring off the Champion Hurdle/Gold Cup double, it was the mare, *Dawn Run*, in 1984 and 1986.

Big, ungainly, bred to be a chaser, she nevertheless produced the turn of foot to become Champion Hurdler of three countries. Bravery, determination and the will to win were the attributes that enabled her to succeed and to set her and her owner, the diminutive Charmian Hill, apart from the fold.

### THE SPIRIT TO SUCCEED

*Dawn Run* first visited Cheltenham from her native Ireland where she was trained in County Kilkenny by Paddy Mullins to contest the top novice hurdle, the Sun Alliance, in which she finished a determined second. Even by then, she had shown the spirit that is needed to succeed in life — or even to live at all. For as a foal, she had

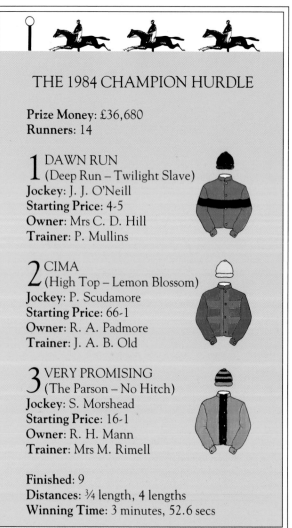

### THE 1984 CHAMPION HURDLE

**Prize Money:** £36,680
**Runners:** 14

**1 DAWN RUN**
(Deep Run – Twilight Slave)
**Jockey:** J. J. O'Neill
**Starting Price:** 4-5
**Owner:** Mrs C. D. Hill
**Trainer:** P. Mullins

**2 CIMA**
(High Top – Lemon Blossom)
**Jockey:** P. Scudamore
**Starting Price:** 66-1
**Owner:** R. A. Padmore
**Trainer:** J. A. B. Old

**3 VERY PROMISING**
(The Parson – No Hitch)
**Jockey:** S. Morshead
**Starting Price:** 16-1
**Owner:** R. H. Mann
**Trainer:** Mrs M. Rimell

**Finished:** 9
**Distances:** ¾ length, 4 lengths
**Winning Time:** 3 minutes, 52.6 secs

such a high fever that she was not expected to live through the night. Her breeder's wife sat up with her nursing her at their home in Co. Cork.

When she first went into training, nothing too high was thought of her: she would be a nice ride for her owner, Mrs Charmian Hill, that's all. Mrs Hill was already past 60 and a grandmother several times over, but had come back from near death in a racing fall and rode *Dawn Run* herself to the mare's first victory, a two-mile amateur's flat race at Tralee. Thereafter, Mrs Hill was forced to concede to anno domini when the Irish stewards refused to renew her licence, but that did not stop her riding *Dawn Run* in her gallops.

The mare progressed to hurdle races and soon showed she could win in England as well as Ireland. Although hurdling was only ever considered a means towards an end, a stepping stone and schooling ground towards chasing, *Dawn Run* gave clear notice at the end of her first season that she possessed a turn of foot, too, when running that year's Champion Hurdler *Gaye Brief* to a length at Liverpool in April.

In 1984, however, *Gaye Brief* was clear ante-post favourite for the Champion Hurdle. But a brilliant win by *Dawn Run* at Kempton on Boxing Day, followed by victory in the Irish Champion Hurdle in February, meant a number of tipsters and punters were beginning to sit up and take notice of the Irish mare.

### CHAMPION HURDLER
In the end, *Gaye Brief* could not start for the Champion Hurdle, and it was left to *Dawn Run* to take advantage of the new 5 lbs mares' allowance in throwing off challenge after challenge; nearly all the runners tried at one stage or another to take over, but none succeeded: she beat the gallant *Cima* three-quarters of a length, with *Very Promising* third and her old Irish sparring partner *Buck House* fourth. She and her jockey, Irishman and leading National Hunt jockey in England, the popular Jonjo O'Neill returned to a welcome fit for a heroine and hero.

When it was decided to take *Dawn Run* to France that June it was to tackle the strange 'hurdles', more like mini chase fences but which could be jumped from both ways, that have been the downfall of many an English challenge.

One of the respects in which *Dawn Run* proved

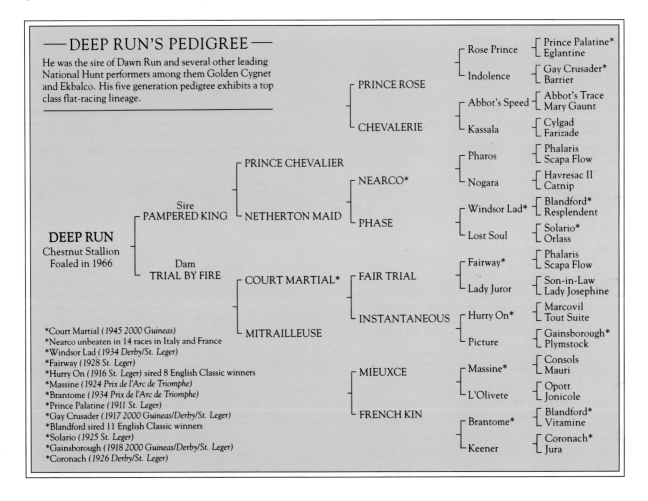

**— DEEP RUN'S PEDIGREE —**

He was the sire of Dawn Run and several other leading National Hunt performers among them Golden Cygnet and Ekbalco. His five generation pedigree exhibits a top class flat-racing lineage.

**DEEP RUN**
Chestnut Stallion
Foaled in 1966

Sire
PAMPERED KING

Dam
TRIAL BY FIRE

PRINCE CHEVALIER

NETHERTON MAID

COURT MARTIAL*

MITRAILLEUSE

NEARCO*

PHASE

FAIR TRIAL

INSTANTANEOUS

MIEUXCE

FRENCH KIN

PRINCE ROSE

CHEVALERIE

Rose Prince — Prince Palatine* / Eglantine

Indolence — Gay Crusader* / Barrier

Abbot's Speed — Abbot's Trace / Mary Gaunt

Kassala — Cylgad / Farizade

Pharos — Phalaris / Scapa Flow

Nogara — Havresac II / Catnip

Windsor Lad* — Blandford* / Resplendent

Lost Soul — Solario* / Orlass

Fairway* — Phalaris / Scapa Flow

Lady Juror — Son-in-Law / Lady Josephine

Hurry On* — Marcovil / Tout Suite

Picture — Gainsborough* / Plymstock

Massine* — Consols / Mauri

L'Olivete — Opott / Jonicole

Brantome* — Blandford* / Vitamine

Keener — Coronach* / Jura

*Court Martial (1945 2000 Guineas)
*Nearco unbeaten in 14 races in Italy and France
*Windsor Lad (1934 Derby/St. Leger)
*Fairway (1928 St. Leger)
*Hurry On (1916 St. Leger) sired 8 English Classic winners
*Massine (1924 Prix de l'Arc de Triomphe)
*Brantome (1934 Prix de l'Arc de Triomphe)
*Prince Palatine (1911 St. Leger)
*Gay Crusader (1917 2000 Guineas/Derby/St. Leger)
*Blandford sired 11 English Classic winners
*Solario (1925 St. Leger)
*Gainsborough (1918 2000 Guineas/Derby/St. Leger)
*Coronach (1926 Derby/St. Leger)

so remarkable was her adaptability, and when she treated the French race like any other, it was greeted wholeheartedly by the French spectators and the vociferous Irish band. It might not have provoked the excited scenes that Cheltenham did, but there was very little staid decorum about it either.

### FROM HURDLER TO CHASER

It was in November 1984, after her summer holiday back home in Co. Waterford, that *Dawn Run* made her chasing début at Navan, and it was unforgettable: she ran in only seven steeplechases in her life and gained a poor jumping reputation, yet on that first day it was as if to the manner born. She put *Dark Ivy* and *Buck House* emphatically in their places; ironically, all three horses were to be dead within three months of each other three years later.

Immediately a 'new Arkle' was hailed, the 'Dawn' of a new era; already odds were quoted for the 1985 Gold Cup. A minor setback kept her off the course for 13 months. She immediately won her first two chases in Ireland on her comeback and when she was quoted favourite for the Gold Cup there were those who derided that

as absurd for such a novice. Fuel was added to the fire when, meeting stiffer fences in a 'prep' race at Cheltenham in January, she unseated Tony Mullins.

Her next race, with only four chases behind her, was the Gold Cup itself — and Jonjo O'Neil was booked to ride.

### GOLD CUP CHALLENGE

What crowds there were on Thursday March 13, 1986: a record 41,732 had come to see 'The Mare' and her supporting cast. It proved to be a race that will be remembered for all time in the annals of horseracing. With *Run and Skip* in the race, *Dawn Run* could not have things all her own way, as that gallant little horse set off living up to his name in the lead.

The mare was soon in front where she likes to be, or disputing affairs and, had it been any other horses or any other race, one would have thought they must 'cut each other's throats'. *Dawn Run* made a slight mistake at the eighteenth, allowing *Run and Skip* back into the lead, but then fought

**Below and right** *Dawn Run pictured before and after the race in which she became the only horse to have won both the Champion Hurdle and Cheltenham Gold Cup.*

back, and her supporters' hopes remained high as she led over the penultimate.

But the pack was closing on her tail.

### A DESPERATE FINISH

Suddenly, she was no longer all over the winner. For once, she had no answer, as first *Wayward Lad* and then previous winner, *Forgive 'n Forget*, overtook her going into the last. She would, at best, be an honourable, but well beaten third, failing like *Night Nurse*, *Sea Pigeon* and *Bula* before her to bring off the double; perhaps too much euphoria had been allowed to surround her in the run-up to the race.

*Dawn Run* appeared out of it and most eyes were on the two new leaders as they landed over the last fence, with only that morale-sapping uphill slog to the winning post remaining. But suddenly 'The Mare' was running on again; *Dawn Run* was *storming* up the hill, galvanized by Jonjo O'Neill as only he knew how. And he had the partner to answer his call. This, the greatest racehorse battler *refused* to be beaten. What had been unthinkable a few moments before happened: *Dawn Run* had WON!

### CROWNING GLORY

All the pent-up emotion was released now into scenes of crazy cheering and frantic running as hordes of fans scrambled to reach the winner's enclosure to greet her: the first horse ever to win the dual hurdling/chasing crown, a mare, no less,

who had also clipped nearly two seconds off the record time.

It was indeed the crowning glory for *Dawn Run*, and who is to say she would not again have won the title in years to come? She was not another *Arkle*, that had long since been conceded, but she had her own special brand of enthusiasm and fire, one that endeared her to her scores of followers.

She won a specially arranged match against *Buck House* in Ireland over only two miles. The shorter distance might have suited the winner of the Queen Mother Champion Chase but *Dawn Run* showed herself as versatile as ever. Reunited with Tony Mullins, Jonjo O'Neill having now retired, the pair left *Buck House* standing even though crack Irish jockey Tommy Carmody more than once tried to steal through on the inside.

### TRAGEDY STRIKES

So it was back to France in June in an attempt to repeat her French Champion Hurdle win of two years previously. The going was perfect and *Dawn Run* looked a picture. She went into every flight sharing the lead, and came out of each one two lengths clear — until, that is, the flight on the far side, the fifth from home. Then she never reappeared at all. She had 'missed one out' and paid the ultimate price, for her neck was broken.

It is not for her death that *Dawn Run* should be remembered. Hers was a truly remarkable career, not least because it was so unlikely . . .

# THE QUEEN MOTHER CHAMPION CHASE

WHILE THE CHELTENHAM GOLD CUP is the acknowledged Blue Riband of steeple-chasing, and the Champion Hurdle is the hurdlers' crown, the Queen Mother Champion Chase is the top accolade for two-mile steeplechasers.

The very fact that they are speed merchants rather than stayers makes for some truly exhilarating races around Cheltenham and there have been some splendid spectacles.

Run from its inauguration in 1959 to 1980 as the National Hunt Two Mile Champion Chase, it changed its name in order to commemorate the 80th birthday of National Hunt racing's favourite lady.

### RACING'S FIRST LADY

There is no better loved or respected person in jump racing than the 'Queen Mum'; she enjoys racing so much, come rain or shine, that the only real problem lies in security, especially as she loves to stop and have an informal chat amongst the crowd if she so wishes.

Her love and knowledge of the sport over the years has been rewarded by some splendid victories from her own horses, since that day in the 1949-50 season when *Monaveen*, owned jointly with the Queen, gave her her first victory.

Her second was *Manicou*, who, although a full horse, won the King George VI Steeplechase at Kempton Park and went on to be a successful sire, as did a later National Hunt horse owned by her, *Sunnyboy*.

Other favourites were *Double Star, The Rip, Gay Record, Laffy, Makaldar, Chaou II, Black Magic, Game Spirit, Inch Arran, Isle of Man* and *Special Cargo*. The best remembered by the public is 'the horse who didn't win the Grand National', *Devon Loch*, who, ridden by Dick Francis, sprawled to the ground inexplicably within yards of winning the 1956 race.

Once or twice she has come close to winning 'her' race, without quite succeeding to date; in 1976 *Game Spirit* came second and the following year *Isle of Man* finished third, the winner both times being the Irish-trained *Skymas*.

### A SPECIALIST'S RACE

It is something of a race for specialists and one in which the Irish have a good record. *Drinny's Double* won twice, and others to do so include the late Edward Courage's *Royal Relief* who also finished second no less than three times and third once, *Hilly Way* and, in 1987 and '88, *Pearlyman*, while *Badsworth Boy* between 1983-85 achieved a hat-trick.

### CRISP

One of the most memorable victories came in 1971 from *Crisp*; he was the magnificent Australian chaser who was to lose to *Red Rum* in perhaps the most tear-jerking Grand National of all two years later.

In the spring of 1971, he was still very much National Hunt's 'new boy', but already he had given notice that he was something rather out of the ordinary.

Owned by Sir Chester Manifold, *Crisp* was considered a freak in Australia, where jumping very much plays second fiddle to the Flat. A strapping big horse by *Rose Argent*, he was tall and angular with great shoulders, and as strong as they come. On the gallops he would work with his head low to the ground, pulling his rider's arms out.

There was nothing in the least malicious about him: he was gentle by nature, with kind eyes and loppy ears, and one of life's characters.

### AUSTRALIAN EXPORT

He won all there was to win in Australia and his sporting owner decided to see just how good he was by sending him to England not for the Grand National, as many would imagine, but for the Cheltenham Gold Cup, the 'class' race in which, ultimately, he never ran.

His journey over was by way of America, where he jumped ship to run third in the Colonial Cup, South Carolina, and he finally arrived at Fred Winter's yard in November 1970 as a seven-year-old. It took him a long time to acclimatize, and his coat grew so long that it waved in the breeze like a field of corn, but he was almost impossible to clip.

At the time, Fred Winter was in the fortunate position of housing the very best of British jumpers in his yard, such as *Pendil, Bula* and *Killiney*, and so his staff were a little sceptical of the new arrival — until they saw what he was made of.

*Crisp leads the field in the 1972 Champion Chase. Held back by his jockey for fear of his not lasting the distance, he lost interest and came in a disappointing fifth.*

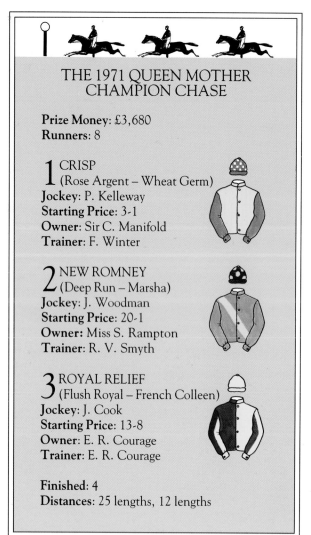

## THE 1971 QUEEN MOTHER CHAMPION CHASE

**Prize Money:** £3,680
**Runners:** 8

**1 CRISP**
(Rose Argent – Wheat Germ)
**Jockey:** P. Kelleway
**Starting Price:** 3-1
**Owner:** Sir C. Manifold
**Trainer:** F. Winter

**2 NEW ROMNEY**
(Deep Run – Marsha)
**Jockey:** J. Woodman
**Starting Price:** 20-1
**Owner:** Miss S. Rampton
**Trainer:** R. V. Smyth

**3 ROYAL RELIEF**
(Flush Royal – French Colleen)
**Jockey:** J. Cook
**Starting Price:** 13-8
**Owner:** E. R. Courage
**Trainer:** E. R. Courage

**Finished:** 4
**Distances:** 25 lengths, 12 lengths

### AN EYE-OPENING RACE

*Crisp*'s first run was in a handicap chase at Wincanton on March 11 where he automatically had to carry top weight of 12st 7lbs because he had not had the requisite number of three runs to give the handicapper enough assessable form.

No-one in the stable quite knew what to expect from *Crisp*; what happened was a real eye-opener. Ridden by Paul Kelleway, he took up the running after a mile and, making light of the handicapper's burden, then drew further and further ahead to win by 15 lengths.

From the start, he made himself famous for his galloping and his style of running, and it was nothing unusual for track records to be toppled by him; he simply pulverized his opposition, galloping them into the ground and outjumping them.

Here was the arch chaser of the type that money cannot buy; his jumping was electrical and he gave his regular jockeys Paul Kelleway and Richard Pitman many magical moments.

### A FRUSTRATING CAREER

In the March of his first spring in England just after Wincanton he was lined up for the Two Mile Champion Chase. Seven opponents lined up against him and, ridden by Paul Kelleway, he led from the tenth fence to gallop to a 25 lengths victory. *Straight Fort* fell at the ninth, while *Muir*, winner two years before, finished tailed off.

*New Romney* and *Royal Relief*, the favourite, followed *Crisp* home.

One outcome of his sparkling performances over two miles was that it was felt his style might not enable him to stay an extended three miles. He was entered for the 1972 Gold Cup, but it was

decided to stick to the Champion Chase, and to try 'holding him up'. It was not a success. Like many a front-runner before him, he resented being restrained, felt thoroughly frustrated, and eventually gave up the fight, coming in fifth.

This had the effect of further compounding the theory that he did not stay, something his former Australian rider, the ex-British Tommy McGinley, was firmly convinced was wrong, contending that if allowed to bowl along, he would get the distance. What subsequently happened in the Grand National in his epic run in which he almost succeeded in making all, and was at one time 40 lengths clear only to succumb to *Red Rum*

yards from the line, would certainly lend support to that view.

But that was in the future and in the meantime, at the National Hunt Festival of 1973, it was again decided to run him in the Champion Chase instead of in the Gold Cup. The story was much as before, and this time he finished third behind *Inkslinger* and his old rival, *Royal Relief*.

He will go down as the greatest chaser by far that Australia ever produced, and in the view of his trainer Fred Winter was the best horse he ever saw in the Grand National — that from a man who not only rode two, but also trained two winners of the race himself.

*Crisp, ridden by his Grand National partner, Richard Pitman, leads the Top Rank steeplechase at Ascot. His connections felt for a long time that he was a two-mile specialist until proved wrong by his Grand National performance.*

# KEMPTON PARK

IDEALLY SITUATED for London, Kempton Park offers both flat and National Hunt racing of the highest calibre. The right-handed track is flat with tight bends and its fast draining sandy soil nearly always ensures good, fast ground, more likely to suit the handy speed merchant than the long striding stayer.

### THE HYDE LEGACY
It was in 1872 that a Mr S. H. Hyde, a would-be politician and then secretary to the Bristol Race-

course Company, was in London for Derby week; while there, he travelled by river steamer to Hampton Court, then hired a carriage and drove out into the surrounding countryside. On the road towards Sunbury he saw a sign advertising 400 acres for sale or lease at Kempton Park: six years later, as a result of that chance discovery, the first race meeting was held on the site.

Three generations of Hydes were secretaries, and the course was nine years old when it staged the first running of the Jubilee Stakes, founded to

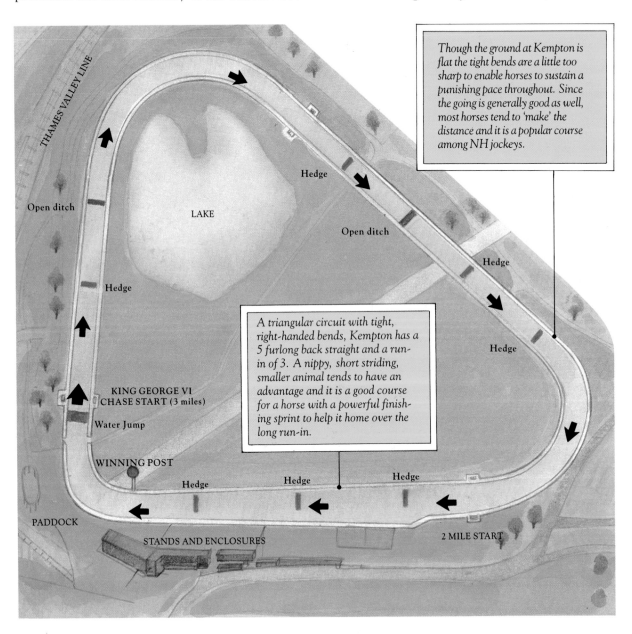

Though the ground at Kempton is flat the tight bends are a little too sharp to enable horses to sustain a punishing pace throughout. Since the going is generally good as well, most horses tend to 'make' the distance and it is a popular course among NH jockeys.

A triangular circuit with tight, right-handed bends, Kempton has a 5 furlong back straight and a run-in of 3. A nippy, short striding, smaller animal tends to have an advantage and it is a good course for a horse with a powerful finishing sprint to help it home over the long run-in.

THAMES VALLEY LINE

Open ditch

LAKE

Hedge

Hedge

Open ditch

Hedge

Hedge

KING GEORGE VI
CHASE START (3 miles)

Water Jump

WINNING POST

PADDOCK

Hedge

Hedge

Hedge

STANDS AND ENCLOSURES

2 MILE START

**Right** *The parade ring at Kempton Park. The nearest course to Central London and considered, by some, one of the least attractive, it was thought so highly of by one German p.o.w. housed there in the last war that he continued to live happily in the grandstand a fortnight after the general repatriation.*

commemorate the 50th year of Queen Victoria's reign and won by *Bendigo*. Two years later, in 1889, the course was visited by the Prince of Wales and the Shah of Persia. With only 21 days notice, Mr Hyde had a Royal Box built and furnished in time.

The grandstand and restaurants were destroyed by fire in 1932 and the new ones opened eight months later. The course was requisitioned by the War Office during both the First and Second World Wars; during the latter it housed prisoners of war, and one prisoner was discovered still living happily in the grandstand two weeks after the rest had been repatriated.

**Below** *Suburbia's tentacles have not yet begun to enclose the racecourse in this early twentieth century painting of horses going out at Kempton by Sir Alfred Munnings.*

# THE KING GEORGE VI CHASE

THE KING GEORGE VI STEEPLECHASE has had an interrupted career since it was founded in 1938, first because of the War and sometimes the weather, yet it is one of the country's premier steeplechases, and had hailed horses of the highest class on its roll of honour.

Held on Boxing Day, it is for countless racing fans their Christmas treat, if the weather does not intervene. It is run over three miles and, like the Cheltenham Gold Cup, is at level weights, but with penalties. However, although there have been winners of both, such as *Cottage Rake*, *Mill House*, *Arkle*, *Captain Christy* and *Burrough Hill Lad*, the two courses are inclined to suit different types of horses; Cheltenham, with its extra quarter mile, several undulations and stiff uphill finish, to say nothing of its frequent heavy going, puts much more emphasis on stamina.

*Pendil*, who won the King George in 1972 and '73, *Silver Buck*, successful in 1979 and '80, and *Wayward Lad*, three times winner in the 1980s, tried their hardest to win the Gold Cup too but

failed, sometimes by the narrowest of margins.

The 1950 King George winner *Manicou* was unusual because the horse was an entire; although some colts run over hurdles, it is most unusual in steeplechases, as they are not unnaturally inclined to be wary about hurting their undercarriage. *Manicou*, owned by Queen Elizabeth the Queen Mother was, at five, the youngest winner. He went on to become a successful National Hunt sire.

### DESERT ORCHID

On Boxing Day 1988 the stunning grey, *Desert Orchid*, joined the select band of dual King George VI winners.

He was promptly installed favourite for the

*Gerry Newman and Captain Christy clearing the open ditch during the 1975 King George VI Chase. After a distinguished hurdling career "the Captain" went on to win the 1974 Gold Cup and the "King George" twice.*

156

1989 Cheltenham Gold Cup although, at that time, it was not clear that he would run. For this former top class two-mile chaser, and one time Champion Hurdle contender, had a far inferior record on the left-handed Cheltenham track compared with his supremacy elsewhere.

### A 'SPIRITED' INHERITANCE

Father and son James and Richard Burridge and friend Simon Bullimore own the fabulous grey whose grand-dam, *Grey Orchid*, James originally went to see in a field in Nottinghamshire as a potential hunter.

She was by *No Orchid* whose dam was by a sprinter, but her famous grandson now can cope with any distance, as his incredible victory in the 3 miles 5 furlongs Whitbread Gold Cup in April 1988 under a heavy burden testified. *Grey Orchid* had won a point-to-point but was considered largely unrideable, and Mr Burridge, relishing a challenge, parted with £175 to buy her.

It was a brave move, for although a competent polo player, he had not ridden a thoroughbred before, and when he first mounted *No Orchid* he remained in the saddle for about ten seconds flat — she went over backwards and deposited him

*Desert Orchid ridden by his regular partner Simon Sherwood. Descended from a line of self-willed and impetuous hunters he has become the most popular steeplechaser since Arkle.*

ignominiously in a manure heap.

Eventually he made her tractable enough to hunt, and even won a point-to-point on her himself and then decided to breed from her. The first foal died, and for the second mating, he simply sent the mare to the nearest, cheapest stallion. From this hit or miss arrangement came *Flower Child* who, though not as bad as her mother, proved a pretty impetuous hunter. She was nine years old when Mr Burridge somewhat belatedly put her in training, won two races with her, and then put her in foal.

This time he was far more fastidious about the breeding, and pored over the blood lines before selecting *Grey Mirage*, standing for a fee of £350: the resultant progeny was *Desert Orchid*.

### A SINGULAR HORSE

He was a gangling, backward youngster but when Mr Burridge's son Richard saw him take off in the field like greased lightning after being stung, he felt a hunch about him and bought a 50 per cent

157

share, Mr Burridge senior and Mr Bullimore having a quarter each.

When *Desert Orchid* was sent to trainer David Elsworth, who at that time was virtually unknown, he was portly, backward, and had some peculiar quirks — and from the start was prone to resemble a scalded cat, just about his one pace being that of flat out.

David Elsworth had only taken out a training licence in 1978, having been a professional jump jockey, but has built up his Fordingbridge, Hampshire stable into a highly successful one both on the Flat and National Hunt.

*Desert Orchid* first ran at Kempton at 50-1 in 1983 in a 4-year-old hurdle. It looked likely to be his last for, having set off like a lunatic, he galloped himself off his own legs, fell at the second last and lay as if for dead for ten minutes.

Much of his subsequent transformation was due to the patient care of head lad Rodney Boult who rides him in his work at home — yet still at Kempton on Boxing Day 1988 he did his best to run away on the way to the start!

The 1985-86 season was probably his worst, finishing tailed off in the Champion Hurdle, pulled up in the Welsh Champion Hurdle and 13th in the Irish Sweeps Hurdle. He was switched to novice chasing and by the time of the 1986 King George VI Chase, had established himself

as a class chaser — one who, with his eye-catching colour and flamboyant style of running, was becoming increasingly popular with the crowds. They were thrilled to see him make virtually all the running on Boxing Day, and at 16-1, thrilled to see him quicken from in front to beat *Door Latch* by 15 lengths. *Bolands Cross* was third ahead of 1985 Cheltenham Gold Cup winner *Forgive 'n Forget*, with the favourite, *Wayward Lad* only fifth.

There was a real upset in the 1987 race, however, for 'Dessie' was caught near the finish by the French challenger *Nupsala*. This was a fine feat of training and riding by his connections as the English fences are very different from those *Nupsala* had encountered at home.

## 1988 — THE PEOPLE'S CHAMPION

The pair were due to clash again in the 1988 event but due to a clerical error, *Nupsala*'s entry was sent to the wrong place and not received in time. If it lessened the prospect of a fine duel, it did nothing to diminish the glorious performance of *Desert Orchid*.

He was unbeaten in all his previous races that season and started odds-on. Thousands of people

*Desert Orchid pictured at Sandown on his way to winning the 1988 Whitbread Gold Cup.*

poured into Kempton not to bet on him but simply to watch him.

What followed was spectacular, and a real, spine-tingling, tear-jerking Christmas treat. *Desert Orchid*, sweating in his eagerness, could hardly wait to get to the start, but Simon Sherwood just managed to restrain him sufficiently to get there safely and without using up too much valuable energy.

At the start, *'Dessie'* galloped straight into the lead as usual, as the recalcitrant *Vodkatini*, his trainer Josh Gifford at his head, also got off successfully.

*Cavvies Clown* made a mistake at the first as *'Dessie'* swept on imperiously with his ears pricked and *Vodkatini* was pulling hard. *Kildimo* ran in third ahead of Cheltenham Gold Cup holder *Charter Party* having his seasonal début, then there was a gap to *Cavvies Clown*.

Coming to the water, *Vodkatini* moved up alongside the beautiful grey, but *'Dessie'*, on the inside, outjumped him.

Running to the sixth from home, *Desert Orchid* saw a long stride and put in a stupendous leap spectacular even by his standards. With three fences left to jump, neither *Vodkatini* or *Kildimo* were done with yet as they mounted their challenges, but *'Dessie'* put in another special leap at the second last and from there he swept all challenge aside. He stormed home to a tremendous ovation, without doubt the most popular horse currently gracing the jumping scene.

## 1989 – THE GOLD CUP CHALLENGE

Three months later, his unbeaten record still intact, he capped even that glorious Kempton performance when he won the Cheltenham Gold Cup in the style that sorts the truly great from the very good, with all the odds heavily stacked against him. For it was well known that Desert Orchid disliked left-handed courses – he had never won at left-handed Cheltenham in five attempts – and detested heavy ground, yet it not only rained hard before the race but there had been a considerable fall of snow that morning.

Therefore on the day, his participation at all was in doubt, with the official going altered to heavy and the fire brigade having pumped away surplus water from around the second last fence.

His owner, Richard Burridge, was keen that Desert Orchid should be given his chance to join the Gold Cup greats but he was also concerned about the threat posed to life and limb by such

### THE 1988 KING GEORGE VI CHASE

**Prize Money:** £37,280
**Runners:** 5

**1 DESERT ORCHID**
(Grey Mirage – Flower Child)
**Jockey:** S. Sherwood
**Starting Price:** 1-2
**Owner:** R. Burridge
**Trainer:** D. Elsworth

**2 KILDIMO**
(Le Bavard – Leuze)
**Jockey:** J. Frost
**Starting Price:** 8-1
**Owner:** Lady Harris
**Trainer:** G. B. Balding

**3 VODKATINI**
(Dubasoff – Olympic Visualise)
**Jockey:** P. Hobbs
**Starting Price:** 7-1
**Owner:** Dick Richardson
 Horse Racing Ltd
**Trainer:** J. T. Gifford

**Finished:** 5
**Distances:** 4 lengths, 5 lengths
**Winning Time:** 5 minutes, 50 secs

awful conditions.

He did run, however, and the rest is now happy history, marred only by the fall of Ten Plus when in the lead three from home. In fact, there was an unusually high number of fallers in the world's premier steeplechase. No mere novices, Golden Frieze fell at the sixth and the Irish hope Carvill's Hill went at the one after that. Then The Thinker fell at the tenth, Slalom fell at the 17th, and Ten Plus at the notorious downhill fence three from home where he brought down the unfortunate Bally-hane.

Most of this time Desert Orchid was leading, his ears pricked in spite of the mud splattering up, and he was giving an exhibition of jumping, but when first Ten Plus and then Yahoo took up the running, defeat looked imminent. Soon the crowds roared as, in a finish reminiscent of Dawn Run's three years earlier, he refused to be beaten, tackled that final hill, wore down Yahoo – and became the best-loved English winner for years.

# FAIRYHOUSE

F AIRYHOUSE: the very name conjures up pictures of Irish leprechauns, and the place has an atmosphere to live up to that image. Set in the countryside of County Meath, not far from Dublin, Fairyhouse is renowned for its friendly, informal atmosphere, more like that of a point-

to-point than the venue for a race as important as the Irish Grand National. All the family, kids, dogs and all, come along to Fairyhouse.

The course appears to be in the middle of nowhere, and is approached off the Dublin to Navan road by narrow, minor roads. It has been

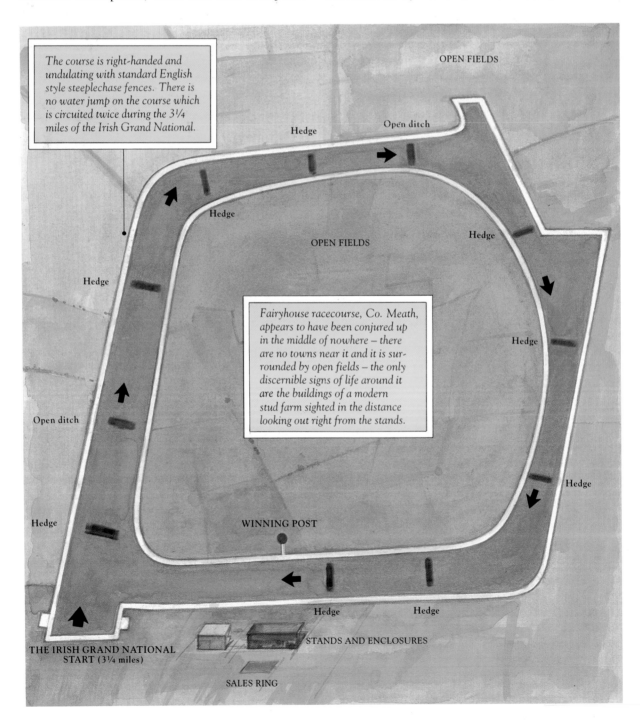

*The course is right-handed and undulating with standard English style steeplechase fences. There is no water jump on the course which is circuited twice during the 3¼ miles of the Irish Grand National.*

OPEN FIELDS

Hedge

Open ditch

Hedge

OPEN FIELDS

Hedge

Hedge

Hedge

*Fairyhouse racecourse, Co. Meath, appears to have been conjured up in the middle of nowhere – there are no towns near it and it is surrounded by open fields – the only discernible signs of life around it are the buildings of a modern stud farm sighted in the distance looking out right from the stands.*

Hedge

Open ditch

Hedge

Hedge

Hedge

WINNING POST

Hedge

Hedge

STANDS AND ENCLOSURES

THE IRISH GRAND NATIONAL
START (3¼ miles)

SALES RING

*The spectacular new stand at Fairyhouse pictured under smiling skies the day following the 1989 Irish Grand National.*

there since the 1860s and was on a site opposite for about ten years before that. Old Fairyhouse then became the training venue of Dan Moore, and since 1988 has been transformed by the opening of a brand new Sales complex by Tattersalls.

The course itself is right-handed and undulating, the flat and hurdle course being one mile seven furlongs round, and the chase course two miles round. The chase jumps consist of standard English style fences. There are nine fences in total with no water jump but two open ditches to be contended with. The Irish Grand National which is the premier event held at the course starts to the left of the stands and is run over two circuits of the course.

Flat racing only began there in the 1970s and until recently, no racing took place during the summer months. This was because the grandstand and straight was in different ownership, and a condition of the racecourse company leasing it was that racing was only allowed in winter.

The racecourse trust has now bought out the lease, stipulating that the land may be used for equestrian sport only, and in 1988 built a new grandstand for opening in 1989 and it is planned to hold about ten meetings per year.

# THE IRISH GRAND NATIONAL

TRADITIONALLY, the Irish Grand National is held on Easter Monday although 1988 was an exception, when it was held later in an attempt to avoid being too close to the Grand National and so lure more English runners over for the £100,000 prize money.

It was not felt to be a success, and in 1989 reverted to the traditional date. For 100 years, it was the only meeting held at Fairyhouse, then in the early 60s it was made a two day meeting.

Run over three and a half miles, history was made in 1984, when Anne Ferris, daughter of Willie Rooney, won the race riding *Benton Boy*.

During the 60s and 70s, the race was domin-ated by the Dreaper family, first Tom, in honour of whom the T.W. Dreaper Memorial Chase is also run on the course, and latterly by his son, Jim who took over the stables.

Tom won it for the first time in 1942 with *Prince Regent*, in the 1950s with Lord Bicester's *Royal Approach* and Mr J. Rank's *Shagreen*, then successively from 1960 to 1966 with *Olympia*, *Fortria*, *Kerforo*, *Last Link*, *Arkle*, *Splash* and *Flyingbolt*. Tom's son Jim then went on to win the race in 1974, '75, '76, and '78.

*Rhyme n' Reason, winner of the 1985 Irish Grand National and the 1988 Aintree Grand National.*

*Prince Regent, winner of the 1943 Irish Grand National and the first success in this race for the prolific Irish trainer, Tom Dreaper.*

## FLYINGBOLT

In *Arkle*'s heyday, there was only one horse who could be mentioned in the same breath as him, and that was his own stable companion in Dreaper's yard, *Flying-bolt*.

The English often import horses from Ireland, but with *Flyingbolt* it was the other way round. Bred near Newmarket, he was by the 1946 Derby winner *Airborne*. He was the last foal of his 19-year-old dam *Eastlock* (who had herself been a 50 guinea purchase) and so there could never be valuable younger half brothers or sisters to *Flyingbolt* for sale. He was also the last racehorse bred by Mr Robert Way who then sold the stud.

*Flyingbolt* was a wishy washy chestnut with a lot of white about him, and was a gawky, gangly yearling when he went to the Newmarket Sales. From there he was brought by Mrs T. G. Wilkinson whose husband, a retired Lieutenant Colonel in the Durham Light Infantry and the King's

African Rifles, had ridden as an amateur in Britain, India and East Africa and was Master of Fox Hounds of the North Kilkenny Hunt.

They sent *Flyingbolt* to be trained by Tom Dreaper, where the two years older *Arkle* was establishing himself as a rising star. New horses are allocated to stable lads at random, and it was pure co-incidence that the lad who 'did' *Arkle* also took over the raw-boned newcomer.

If *Flyingbolt* looked as if he needed time to fill out and mature, his racecourse performances belied that: he went through his first two seasons unbeaten.

### EARLY SUCCESSES

In his first season he showed he had the speed to be a successful hurdler. At Leopardstown, he won the Scalp hurdle in a canter beating old, high-class, experienced hurdlers on worse terms than in a handicap.

He travelled to Cheltenham in March and won his division of the Gloucester Hurdle with such ease that it was clear he was the top novice in both England and Ireland. Bred to be a chaser, he might nevertheless be a Champion Hurdler.

163

In fact, he nearly was, although his chance to prove it did not come just yet because the following year he was put straight to fences. If anything, his progress in this field was even more stunning. He won the top novices chase, the Broadway (now the Sun Alliance) at Cheltenham in runaway fashion in 1965, the Black and White Gold Cup at Ascot and the Massey Ferguson Gold Cup.

This was a real eyeopener, for not only was the ground dreadfully wet, but *Flyingbolt* was set to carry 12st 6lb — yet he won by 15 lengths. People were now beginning to seriously compare him with *Arkle*.

In January, he slaughtered the opposition for the Thystes Chase at Gowran Park in ground so heavy that one fence had to be omitted. He carried 12 stone and beat *Height O'Fashion*, a good, consistent mare who was receiving two stone, by a distance, with *Flying Wild*, on 9st 3lbs another 25 lengths back.

### A GREAT ALL-ROUNDER

In the spring, as *Arkle* was winning his third Cheltenham Gold Cup, *Flyingbolt* also won for the third successive year at the Festival at the age of only seven, this time taking the Two Mile Champion Chase by a stunning 15 lengths.

It was at this meeting that he almost became Champion Hurdler, too, for he turned out again the day after his Two Mile success to take on the crack hurdlers and, despite his age and the fact that he was now regularly jumping fences, which require a more deliberate technique, he was nevertheless installed favourite.

He looked like achieving it, too, as he came to the last flight in the lead but perhaps the edge had been taken off him through running the day before, and he was overtaken by *Salmon Spray* and *Sempervivum* on the hill to the line, to finish a most honourable third in what was an exceedingly unusual venture.

### DREAPER'S RUN

His season had not finished yet, and his next outing was to be for the race his trainer Tom Dreaper had virtually made his own, the Irish Grand National.

*Arkle* had won it two years before, also as a seven-year-old, as part of an incredible run of six successive victories by Dreaper-trained horses in the race.

Could *Flyingbolt* make it seven in a row? Yet again the ground was heavy, and yet again *Flyingbolt* was set to carry 12st 7lbs and to concede lumps of weight to his rivals, who were no mean performers themselves.

The mare *Height O'Fashion* was again in the line up, and this time she was carrying 9st 9lbs. The crowds flocked into Fairyhouse amid a holiday atmosphere. They sensed they were in for a real treat, and how right they were.

Tom Dreaper was a very popular trainer in Ireland. Small, with twinkling eyes and a delightful smile, and usually smoking a pipe, he looked very much a leprachaun himself. Those hordes of fans who followed his fortunes on that particular day were paid handsome dividends, for his horses won five of the races.

One of them was won by a young horse called *Vulture*, a nephew of *Arkle* himself, and it was his racecourse début; but it was the big race people had mainly turned out for, and all eyes were on one horse, *Flyingbolt*.

He did not disappoint them; splashing through the mud, he brought up Dreaper's seventh successive win and added another laurel in a glorious career beating the mare, *Height O'Fashion* by two lengths whilst the previous year's winner, *Splash*, wallowed ten lengths behind in third.

*Flyingbolt, being ridden in 1966 by Pat Taaffe. He was the only horse of his generation to be seriously compared with Arkle and came from the same stables. His victory in the 1966 Irish Grand National gave his trainer, Tom Dreaper, his seventh successive win.*

# WORTHINGTON VALLEY

MUCH OF THE countryside in the state of Maryland is rolling pasture fenced by the white painted panel railings of the numerous horse farms. It is home, too, of America's oldest and most famous jumping race, the Maryland Hunt Cup. Like steeplechasing in Britain, it owes its origin to hunting, for the colonists who imported horses and hounds also liked to wager between themselves to determine whose was the best horse.

The Elkridge Hunt, founders of the Maryland Hunt Cup, dictated that the course for the race should be 'about four miles, flagged at intervals, with no artificial jumps'. After various venues had been tried the race eventually settled in 1922 at its present home of Worthington Valley where it is traditionally held each year on the third Saturday in April.

### A UNIQUE COURSE

With luck, the sun can then be expected to shine, and the crowds pour in for what has become a popular social occasion. From the banks above the valley, they have excellent

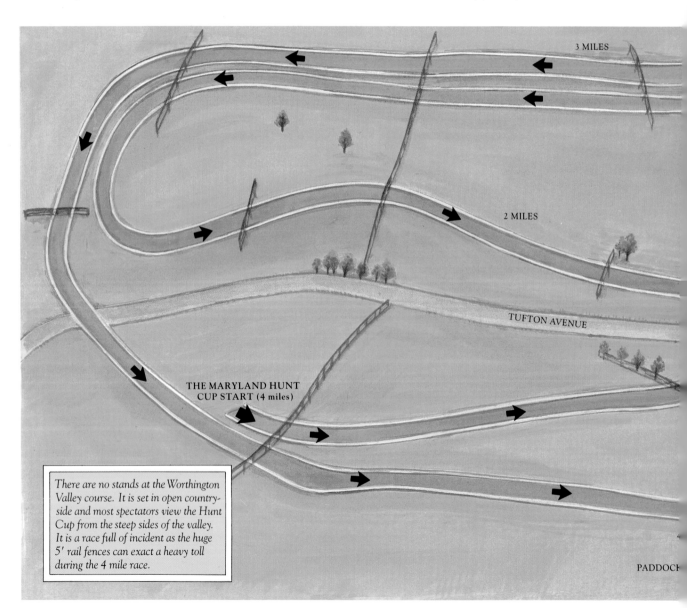

3 MILES

2 MILES

TUFTON AVENUE

THE MARYLAND HUNT
CUP START (4 miles)

There are no stands at the Worthington Valley course. It is set in open country-side and most spectators view the Hunt Cup from the steep sides of the valley. It is a race full of incident as the huge 5' rail fences can exact a heavy toll during the 4 mile race.

PADDOCK

A crowded Worthington Valley course pictured during the 1965 Hunt Cup. This was the year Jay Trump travelled to England to win the National.

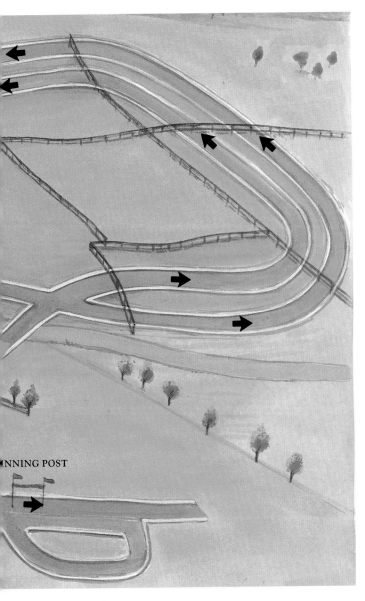

NNING POST

viewing of the course, which is most unlike that of anywhere else in the world. The broad meadow land over which the race is run is not the pampered turf of Aintree or Newmarket. However, it is excellent grass for galloping over even on wet days, the going being surprisingly firm.

All the fences are made of solid timber and a horse who hits one hard has little chance of remaining upright, unlike in steeplechasing, when a horse brushing through the birch has at least a sporting chance of survival. The fences are either four or five rails in height. The top rail is usually a round chestnut log six inches in depth. The fence posts are sunk deep in the ground and it is hard to imagine any of the construction breaking though from time to time under attack from a half-ton horse travelling at 30 mph they do!

To stand beside the highest fence standing bolt upright at five feet, is an awesome experience; to gallop towards it at racing pace in the middle of the pack, is strictly only for the brave!

167

# THE MARYLAND HUNT CUP

ALTHOUGH THE Maryland Hunt Cup is a race of long standing and great prestige, National Hunt racing in the USA is on nothing like the scale of jumping in England, nor, even, of point-to-pointing other than in prize money to be won.

1988 saw record jumping prize money of $3.2 million distributed in 241 races, of which $2.6 million went to 39 hunt meetings and $½ million to the seven racetracks offering National Steeplechase and Hunt Association races. These were Beulah Park, Rockingham Park, Belmont Park, all down the Eastern side of the States.

Fairhill in Maryland, whence Michael Dickinson went to train, is designated a hunt meeting, and in 1986 the Breeders' Cup Steeplechase was staged there, corresponding with the Breeders' Cup Series on the Flat.

In 1988, this steeplechase was worth $¼ million, with the first prize of half that amount going to the ex-English horse *Jimmy Lorenzo*, ridden by Graham McCourt. Foreign runners in

*A Worthington Valley tradition — Huntsman, Les Grimes, blows the competitors to post for the 1966 race won by Jay Trump.*

the race came from Italy, France, and Sweden.

America's leading trainer for 16 consecutive years up to and including 1988 was Englishman Jonathan Shepherd. In that year, he earned record prize money of $830,000 from 39 wins, Jonathan Smart was leading jockey with 25 wins.

## JAY TRUMP

The best known winner of America's leading jumping race was *Jay Trump* whose story is another of racing's fairytales. Found running round little downbeat tracks and getting nowhere fast in half mile races, he turned into America's jumping legend winning a hat-trick of Maryland Hunt Cups as well as the Aintree Grand National.

Crompton 'Tommy' Smith, who bought him

cheaply for Mrs Mary Stephenson as a timber prospect, schooled him so well and patiently that when he arrived at Fred Winter's yard in England prior to his assault on the Grand National, he was a dream horse for the staff there. Used to quickly-broken yearlings, they found *Jay Trump* beautifully schooled, balanced and mannered.

This was the horse who had been drumming round sordid dirt tracks; who had been almost killed when caught up in a piece of tin on a racecourse; who was modestly bred and whose future looked bleak until the day that he came into Tommy Smith's life. Tommy lived for the good looking bay horse with the big white star.

Tommy himself had been hunting since he was six months old and loved anything to do with the chase — and that included steeplechasing.

## THE EARLY DAYS

*Jay Trump*'s first public appearance over fences was in a hunter trial when, as a four-year-old he proceeded to win the Green Hunter and Middle-weight Hunter classes, earning in the process the Master's Trophy and the title Grand Champion of the Trial.

After that he was hunted no fewer than 25 times with the Green Spring Hounds, putting his innate good manners and adaptability to good use and gaining invaluable experience in extricating himself from tricky situations.

It seemed an ideal schooling ground for timber racing yet that spring, running in a ladies' race on his début, he appeared all at sea, at a loss as to what was expected of him. Thereafter Tommy Smith took the ride — and they won their

*Crompton 'Tommy' Smith, Jay Trump's trainer and the jockey who rode him to his Grand National and three Hunt Cup victories.*

*Mountain Dew jumps the 13th fence in the 1965 Cup. He too was a three times winner but always came off second best to Jay Trump.*

remaining four races that season. So here was a good horse after all — but how good?

America's supreme jumping test, one to be highly respected in any quarter of the world, is the Maryland Hunt Cup. At six years old, *Jay Trump* was young to tackle such a gruelling test as that, but Tommy felt he was ready for it, and so he took his place in the line up along with a very good horse called *Mountain Dew*.

### GREAT RIVALS

As so often happens in the annals of classic horse racing, this pair were destined to be great rivals. Indeed, their heyday was so dominant that lesser horses were frightened off. *Mountain Dew* had finished third in 1961 as a six year old and won the following year, so in 1963, when they met for the first time, *Mountain Dew* at eight was in his prime, while *Jay Trump* was the young upstart.

Little could anyone then know how the pair would dominate the race. *Jay Trump* won on his only three appearances, in 1963, '64 and '66.

*Mountain Dew* won without him in 1962, 1965 (when *Jay Trump* was in England) and again in 1967 after *Jay Trump* had retired. Both horses were fast, tough competitors, great fencers, and both possessed abundant courage.

### A LEGEND IS BORN

On that clear day in April 1963, when the ground was hard and riding fast, no-one could have guessed a legend was in the making. Only five horses went to post, and two of them fell at the tenth. *Jay Trump* was young, keen and eager. The fences might be solid, upright and high but he held no fear of them. Tommy tried to restrain him, to no avail. They went at a sizzling pace. *Bushwheeler* crashed at the tenth and *Red Lion Mike*, in trying to avoid him, crossed his legs and fell too.

*Mountain Dew* showed the way along the side of the woods on the second circuit with *Hurdy Gurdy* and *Jay Trump*, now under better control, able to make his move when signalled to do so by his rider. The signal came at the 19th, when *Jay Trump* jumped into the lead on the inside, but it was not all over for the other pair continued to press him. At the last, *Jay Trump* and *Mountain*

170

*Dew* were upsides with *Hurdy Gurdy* close behind; for a moment it looked as if *Mountain Dew* would produce his renowned finishing spurt, but the younger horse outran him, putting four lengths between them at the post. The race had been a cracker, and set a new record time.

In later years, as told in 'Maryland Hunt Cup Past and Present', Tommy Smith, the consummate horseman, admitted frankly, '*Jay Trump* scared me that day, he was just plain getting too confident — too bold. He took off with me and I was strictly a passenger. And jump big! Sometimes he stood back two or three strides. At the 12th he stood so far back that he landed on the top rail. It staggered him, and scratched him up to his stifle. The rail didn't break. He's awfully strong or he would have been down for sure. After that he jumped more sanely, but he was running too fast for his own safety'.

In 1964, fitted with a pelham bit, *Jay Trump* toyed with the opposition, and the following year he made his triumphant visit to England when he beat the gallant Scottish hunter chaser *Freddie* in a memorable race for the Grand National.

### A TRUE CHAMPION

He was back in America for 1966 when he and *Mountain Dew* once more renewed rivalry, producing some fiercely contested preparatory races with first one and then the other winning before coming to the Maryland Hunt Cup.

The ground this time was a different kettle of fish to the rattle on which *Jay Trump* first won the classic, and it is the mark of a true champion when a horse can win on any ground. In 1966 it was bottomless. It rained for a week and only stopped just before the race, but at that moment, fog rolled in. Few of the expectant hillside crowds could see much of the re-match between the two great rivals.

Again, only three horses took on the pair and one of them, *El Moro*, crashed heavily at the high third fence, almost spelling disaster for *Jay Trump* who cleverly avoided the faller. He slipped going into the sixth, hit it, and lost his confidence for a while, and *Mountain Dew* was going the better as they raced along by the woods for the first time. But Tommy Smith was patient, *Jay Trump* got back into his stride, and by the sixteenth he was ready to challenge.

The pair went full tilt down by the woods for the second time, so fast that both of them rapped the eighteenth, but this time it was *Mountain Dew* who fared worse, and *Jay Trump* began to draw away. By the post, he had put a convincing 12 lengths between them, and on that resplendent note the retirement of this great jumper was immediately announced.

*Jay Trump and Tommy Smith take the 13th fence in the 1964 race — the second of their three wins.*

171

# AUTEUIL

AUTEUIL IS France's premier jumping track, situated in the Bois de Boulogne in the smart suburbs of Paris. It is served by the Métro from the city centre and is close to the south-bound motorways. Most of the horses are trained in the area, only about one fifth in the provinces, and although there are about 170 tracks around the country altogether, many of these are in use only once a year in conjunction with a local fair or festival. Some of their jumping races are open to half breeds and even Anglo Arabs.

Thanks to the 'tote' monopoly in France, more money is ploughed back into facilities and prize money than in countries like Britain where much of the cash spent on betting fills book-makers' satchels. Consequently, Auteuil boasts magnificent stands with every convenience,

overlooking its broad strip of green grass capable of accommodating 30 runners with ease, criss-crossed by its jumps.

### FRENCH STEEPLECHASING

The 'hurdles' are more like mini chase fences, but upright, standing three foot eight inches high and almost four foot wide, and with a two-foot open ditch and white guard rail on both sides, so that they can be, and sometimes are, jumped from both directions during the course of one race.

The steeplechase fences are bigger but softer than British ones, and besides birch, there is also a stone wall, a bank and a huge 'bullfinch' where the top several feet of thin birch are brushed through. No wonder so few outsiders succeed

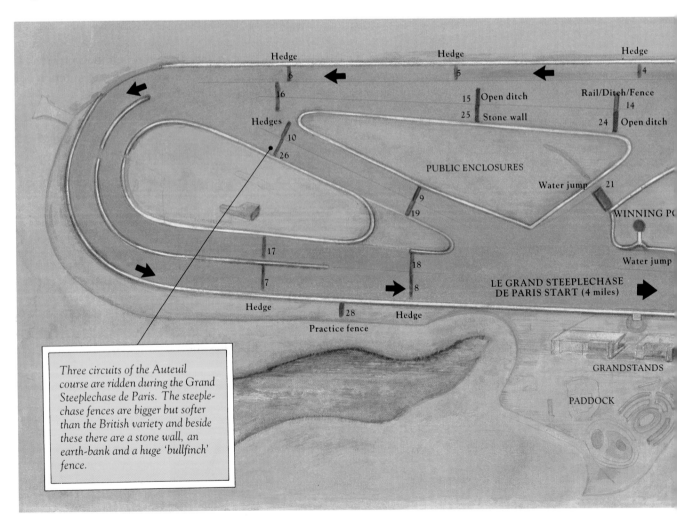

Three circuits of the Auteuil course are ridden during the Grand Steeplechase de Paris. The steeplechase fences are bigger but softer than the British variety and beside these there are a stone wall, an earth-bank and a huge 'bullfinch' fence.

172

*Horses line up in front of the crowded grandstand at Auteuil, the leading steeplechase course in France.*

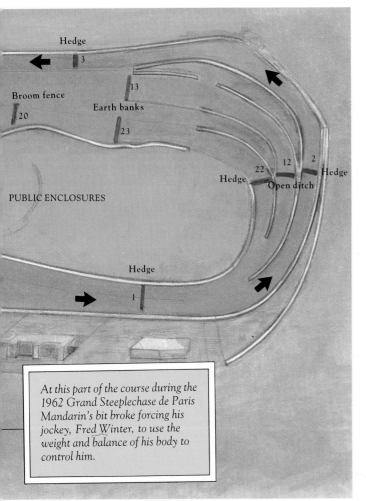

At this part of the course during the 1962 Grand Steeplechase de Paris Mandarin's bit broke forcing his jockey, Fred Winter, to use the weight and balance of his body to control him.

there — even though horses customarily jump a practice fence on their way to the start!

The most important of the races held at Auteuil is Le Grand Steeplechase de Paris. It was run for the first time in 1874 over 6000 metres and under the title of the 'Grand National' but in 1876 changed its name to what it is today.

The difficulties posed by this individualistic course perhaps explain why so few horses have succeeded here more than once. Since the foundation of the race only six horses have achieved this feat, the last being *Huron* in 1969 and 1970.

The race is normally staged on the third Sunday in June and is run over twenty three fences and a distance of 5800 metres.

# LE GRAND STEEPLECHASE DE PARIS

VERY FEW British or Irish horses succeed on this beautifully maintained course for the simple reason that it is so totally different to anything they have encountered elsewhere. To *Mandarin* in the 'French Grand National' and *Dawn Run* in the 'French Champion Hurdle' alone belong this distinction, although many others have tried, including *Tied Cottage* and *Spartan Missile* in the former, and *Gaye Chance*, *Gaye Brief* and *For Auction* in the hurdle.

## MANDARIN

Of all the feats in the history of horse racing, one of the greatest came at Auteuil on a flaming June day in 1962 when *Mandarin* won the Grand Steeplechase de Paris — the French Grand National — with a broken bit dangling from his mouth, a tendon strained, and a jockey ill from wasting.

It was a blazing hot day, and Fred Winter was due to ride at a low weight in the following race; he had wasted so hard that it finally made him ill and he was up all the night before.

There is no steeplechase course in the world quite like Auteuil, making it extremely difficult for foreign challengers. *Mandarin*, bred in France by his owner Mme Peggy Hennessy, had been to Auteuil once three years before but had otherwise seen nothing but conventional English hurdles and fences in his career, and that was already a long one.

He was 11 years old, well set in his ways, his early jumping problems having long since been ironed out and, a small horse with abundant courage, he was a favourite with National Hunt followers. Most British steeplechasers are out at grass enjoying their summer holidays at that time of year but *Mandarin* looked lean and hard as he paraded round the Paris ring.

### WEIGHT PROBLEMS

Fred Winter, one of nature's gentlemen who has done so much good for National Hunt racing both as jockey and trainer, had felt as limp as a rag doll as he walked the course in a dense, humid heat on the morning of the race.

Having wasted all week, he had decided to have one good meal the night before, and that was his undoing, for his stomach was unused to it and reacted violently. He came out in a cold sweat and 'thought I was going to die'.

What's more, the partly eaten meal had put 2lbs of weight on him, so it was back to the Turkish baths, and then most of the night was spent being violently ill. He always believes that the half a bottle of champagne he drank the next morning on the flight to France is what 'really saved my life'.

He walked every inch of the four mile course,

checking the various routes and inspecting the strange variety of fences. *Mandarin* was a hard pulling front runner, and he quite expected to be blazing the trail.

The first thing he noticed when he went into the paddock was how drawn *Mandarin* was looking compared with when he won the Gold Cup three months before. Soon they were on the way to the start and circling nervously before the tapes flew up and they were off, with *Mandarin* running on the inside.

### STEERING PROBLEMS
The first was one of the French 'hurdles', and *Mandarin*, as expected, bowled along in front. He was still at the head of affairs as they headed for the fourth, a large privet hedge with a white post and rail in front of it.

Fred Winter recalls in 'My Greatest Race', 'All of a sudden, going to this fence, my reins became slack and I realised that somehow the bit had broken in half'.

It left Fred with no means of either steering or stopping, and left him as little more than a passenger on the twisty track. *Mandarin* jumped the big fence well, and then a most extraordinary thing happened. Instead of continuing to pull hard and lead, he allowed himself to settle in behind a few other runners. It saved the day.

They negotiated the bank with a small brush fence on top of it, and then came the Grande Rivière in front of the stands, followed by a sharp left bend. Here, to his great credit, one of the French jockeys flanked him on his outside, to help guide *Mandarin* round the corner.

Next, the course split three ways, and it was necessary to take the centre track that opened out in front of them. Using the swing of his body,

*Fred Winter steers a bitless Mandarin home to win the 1962 Grand Steeplechase de Paris. The bit had broken just before the fourth fence leaving 20 fences and a complicated course to negotiate.*

much as a motor cyclist does, Fred Winter managed to give some steering assistance, and *Mandarin* himself obliged by keeping within the pack, and jumping perfectly, bar an awkward jump at the big water second time round.

The worst moment of worry came where the courses again diverged, and for an awful moment it looked as if *Mandarin* would gallop innocently down the wrong one. By this time, the spectators in the stands were aware of Fred's dilemma, and held their collective breath. With an almighty twist in the saddle, forcing his weight the way he wanted his horse to go, Fred managed to get him on the right track.

### INJURY PROBLEMS

But this manoeuvre also cost *Mandarin* his soundness, for almost certainly it was then that he 'broke down', that is, strained his tendon in a front leg. There were four fences left and *Mandarin* bravely galloped on, about six lengths

*Mandarin, who holds the unique distinction of being the only ever winner of both the Cheltenham Gold Cup and the Grand Steeplechase de Paris.*

behind the leaders. The penultimate was the huge 'bullfinch', a fence of very high, thin birch, through the top few feet of which the horses have to brush.

They negotiated it and then, to the roars of the madly excited crowd, including an astounded and naturally partisan British contingent, set off in earnest after the leaders. Only a 'hurdle' remained, and about 100 yards before it, *Mandarin* took the lead.

Fred Winter rode for dear life, but on the run-in, as Mandarin's damaged leg finally began to take its toll, several horses were challenging. One drew right up to him, and they passed the post locked together, neither jockey knowing whose horse had won.

And then the verdict came: *Mandarin* by a head! It was a stupendous piece of horsemanship by Fred and of bravery by *Mandarin*.

As Fred Winter said, 'I think he had more courage than any horse I ever rode — he just didn't know what it was to be beaten'.

Happily, *Mandarin* lived in retirement to a ripe old age, his strength boosted by a daily supply of stout. He was a true hero.

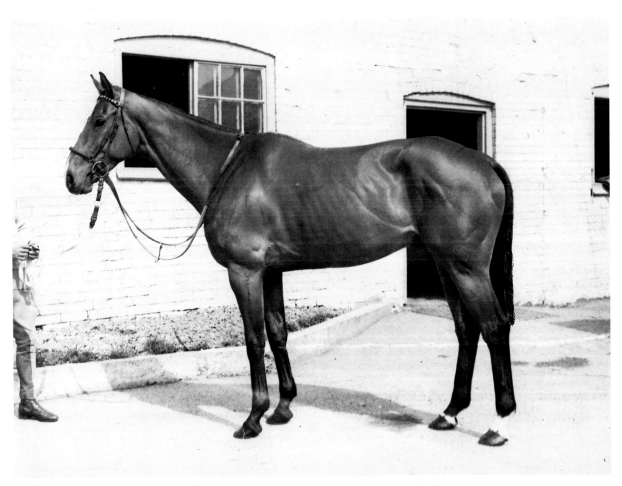

# CLASSIC RACE RECORDS

## CLASSIC FLAT RACES

### THE DERBY

|  |  | OWNER | TRAINER | JOCKEY |
|---|---|---|---|---|
| 1946 | Airborne | J. E. Ferguson | R. Perryman | T. Lowrey |
| 1947 | Pearl Diver | Baron G. de Waldner | P. Carter | G. Bridgeland |
| 1948 | My Love | H.H. Aga Khan | R. Carver | W. R. Johnstone |
| 1949 | Nimbus | Mrs M. Glenister | G. Colling | E. C. Elliott |
| 1950 | Galcador | M. Boussac | C. H. Semblat | W. R. Johnstone |
| 1951 | Arctic Prince | J. McGrath | W. Stephenson | C. Spares |
| 1952 | Tulyar | H.H. Aga Khan | M. Marsh | C. Smirke |
| 1953 | Pinza | Sir V. Sassoon | N. Bertie | Sir G. Richards |
| 1954 | Never Say Die | R. S. Clark | J. Lawson | L. Piggott |
| 1955 | Phil Drake | Mme. L. Volterra | F. Mathet | F. Palmer |
| 1956 | Lavandin | P. Wertheimer | A. Head | W. R. Johnstone |
| 1957 | Crepello | Sir V. Sassoon | C. F. N. Murless | L. Piggott |
| 1958 | Hard Ridden | Sir V. Sassoon | J. M. Rogers | C. Smirke |
| 1959 | Parthia | Sir H. de Trafford | C. Boyd-Rochfort | W. H. Carr |
| 1960 | St. Paddy | Sir V. Sassoon | C. F. N. Murless | L. Piggott |
| 1961 | Psidium | Mme. A. Plesch | H. Wragg | R. Poincelet |
| 1962 | Larkspur | R. R. Guest | M. V. O'Brien | N. Sellwood |
| 1963 | Relko | F. Dupré | F. Mathet | Y. Saint-Martin |
| 1964 | Santa Claus | J. Ismay | J. M. Rogers | A. Breasley |
| 1965 | Sea-Bird | J. Ternynck | E. Pollet | T. P. Glennon |
| 1966 | Charlottown | Lady Z. Wernher | G. Smyth | A. Breasley |
| 1967 | Royal Palace | H. J. Joel | C. F. N. Murless | G. Moore |
| 1968 | Sir Ivor | R. R. Guest | M. V. O'Brien | L. Piggott |
| 1969 | Nijinsky | A. M. Budgett | A. M. Budgett | E. Johnson |
| 1970 | Blakeney | C. W. Engelhard | M. V. O'Brien | L. Piggott |
| 1971 | Mill Reef | P. Mellon | I. Balding | G. Lewis |
| 1972 | Roberto | J. W. Galbreath | M. V. O'Brien | L. Piggott |
| 1973 | Morston | A. M. Budgett | A. M. Budgett | E. Hide |
| 1974 | Snow Knight | Mrs. N. F. Phillips | P. Nelson | B. Taylor |
| 1975 | Grundy | C. Vittadini | P. Walwyn | P. Eddery |
| 1976 | Empery | N. B. Hunt | M. Zilber | L. Piggott |
| 1977 | The Minstrel | R. E. Sangster | M. V. O'Brien | L. Piggott |
| 1978 | Shirley Heights | Lord Halifax | J. Dunlop | G. Starkey |
| 1979 | Troy | Sir M. Sobell | W. R. Hern | W. Carson |
| 1980 | Henbit | Mme. A. Plesch | W. R. Hern | W. Carson |
| 1981 | Shergar | H.H. Aga Khan | M. Stoute | W. R. Swinburn |
| 1982 | Golden Fleece | R. E. Sangster | M. V. O'Brien | P. Eddery |
| 1983 | Teenoso | E. B. Moller | G. Wragg | L. Piggott |
| 1984 | Secreto | L. Miglietti | D. V. O'Brien | C. Roche |
| 1985 | Slip Anchor | Lord Howard de Walden | H. Cecil | S. Cauthen |
| 1986 | Shahrastani | H.H. Aga Khan | M. Stoute | W. R. Swinburn |
| 1987 | Reference Point | L. Freedman | H. Cecil | S. Cauthen |
| 1988 | Kahyasi | H.H. Aga Khan | L. Cumani | R. Cochrane |
| 1989 | Nashwan | Hamdan Al-Maktoum | W. Hern | W. Carson |
| 1990 | Quest For Fame | Khalid Abdullah | R. Charlton | P. Eddery |

### THE OAKS

| 1946 | Steady Aim | Sir A. Butt | Frank Butters | H. Wragg |
|---|---|---|---|---|
| 1947 | Imprudence | Mme. P. Corbière | J. Lieux | W. R. Johnstone |
| 1948 | Masaka | H.H. Aga Khan | Frank Butters | W. Nevett |
| 1949 | Musidora | N. P. Donaldson | C. F. Elsey | E Britt |
| 1950 | Asmena | M. Boussac | C. H. Semblat | W. R. Johnstone |

| | | OWNER | TRAINER | JOCKEY |
|---|---|---|---|---|
| 1951 | Neasham Bell | L. B. Holliday | G. Brooke | S. Clayton |
| 1952 | Frieze | A. M. Keith | C. F. Elsey | E. Britt |
| 1953 | Ambiguity | Lord Astor | R. J. Colling | J. Mercer |
| 1954 | Sun Cap | Mme. R. Forget | Reg Carver | W. R. Johnstone |
| 1955 | Meld | Lady Z. Wernher | C. Boyd-Rochfort | W. H. Carr |
| 1956 | Sicarelle | Mme. L. Volterra | F. Mathet | F. Palmer |
| 1957 | Carrozza | H.M. The Queen | C. F. N. Murless | L. Piggott |
| 1958 | Bella Paola | F. Dupré | F. Mathet | M. Garcia |
| 1959 | Petite Etoile | Prince Aly Khan | C. F. N. Murless | L. Piggott |
| 1960 | Never Too Late | Mrs. H. E. Jackson | E. Pollet | R. Poincelet |
| 1961 | Sweet Solera | Mrs. S. M. Castello | R. Day | W. Rickaby |
| 1962 | Monade | G. P. Goulandris | J. Lieux | Y. Saint-Martin |
| 1963 | Noblesse | Mrs. J. M. Olin | P. J. Prendergast | G. Bougoure |
| 1964 | Homeward Bound | Sir F. Robinson | J. Oxley | G. Starkey |
| 1965 | Long Look | J. Cox Brady | M. V. O'Brien | J. Purtell |
| 1966 | Valoris | C. Clore | M. V. O'Brien | L. Piggott |
| 1967 | Pia | Gräfin M. Batthyany | C. W. C. Elsey | E. Hide |
| 1968 | La Lagune | H. Berlin | F. Boutin | G. Thiboeuf |
| 1969 | Sleeping Partner | Lord Rosebery | D. Smith | J. Gorton |
| 1970 | Lupe | Mrs. S. Joel | C. F. N. Murless | A. Barclay |
| 1971 | Altesse Royale | F. R. Hue-Williams | C. F. N. Murless | G. Lewis |
| 1972 | Ginevra | C. A. B. St. George | H. R. Price | A. Murray |
| 1973 | Mysterious | G. A. Pope, jr. | C. F. N. Murless | G. Lewis |
| 1974 | Polygamy | L. Freedman | P. Walwyn | P. Eddery |
| 1975 | Juliette Marny | J. I. Morrison | A. J. Tree | L. Piggott |
| 1976 | Pawneese | D. Wildenstein | A. Penna | Y. Saint-Martin |
| 1977 | Dunfermline | H.M. The Queen | W. R. Hern | W. Carson |
| 1978 | Fair Salinia | S. Hanson | M. Stoute | G. Starkey |
| 1979 | Scintillate | J. I. Morrison | A. J. Tree | P. Eddery |
| 1980 | Bireme | R. D. Hollingsworth | W. R. Hern | W. Carson |
| 1981 | Blue Wind | Mrs. B. R. Firestone | D. K. Weld | L. Piggott |
| 1982 | Time Charter | R. Barnett | H. Candy | W. Newnes |
| 1983 | Sun Princess | Sir M. Sobell | W. R. Hern | W. Carson |
| 1984 | Circus Plume | Sir R. McAlpine | J. Dunlop | L. Piggott |
| 1985 | Oh So Sharp | Sheikh Mohammed | H. Cecil | S. Cauthen |
| 1986 | Midway Lady | H.H. Ranier | B. Hanbury | R. Cochrane |
| 1987 | Unite | Sheikh Mohammed | M. Stoute | W. R. Swinburn |
| 1988 | Diminuendo | Sheikh Mohammed | H. Cecil | S. Cauthen |
| 1989 | Aliysa | H.H. Aga Khan | M. Stoute | W. R. Swinburn |
| 1990 | Salsabil | Hamdan Al-Maktoum | J. Dunlop | W. Carson |

# THE 2000 GUINEAS

| | | | | |
|---|---|---|---|---|
| 1946 | Happy Knight | Sir W. Cooke | H. Jellis | T. Weston |
| 1947 | Tudor Minstrel | J. A. Dewar | F. Darling | G. Richards |
| 1948 | My Babu | H.H. Maharaja of Baroda | F. Armstrong | C. Smirke |
| 1949 | Nimbus | Mrs. M. Glenister | G. Colling | E. C. Elliott |
| 1950 | Palestine | H.H. Aga Khan | M. Marsh | C. Smirke |
| 1951 | Ki Ming | Ley On | M. Beary | A. Breasley |
| 1952 | Thunderhead | E. Constant | E. Pollet | R. Poincelet |
| 1953 | Nearula | W. Humble | C. F. Elsey | E. Britt |
| 1954 | Darius | Sir P. Loraine | H. Wragg | E. Mercer |
| 1955 | Our Babu | D. Robinson | G. Brooke | D. Smith |
| 1956 | Gilles de Retz | A. G. Samuel | Mrs. G. T. Johnson Houghton | F. Barlow |
| 1957 | Crepello | Sir V. Sassoon | C. F. N. Murless | L. Piggott |
| 1958 | Pall Mall | H.M. The Queen | C. Boyd-Rochfort | D. Smith |
| 1959 | Taboun | Prince Aly Khan | A. Head | G. Moore |
| 1960 | Martial | R. N. Webster | P. J. Prendergast | R. Hutchinson |
| 1961 | Rockavon | T. C. Yuill | G. Boyd | N. Stirk |
| 1962 | Privy Councillor | G. Glover | T. Waugh | W. Rickaby |
| 1963 | Only for Life | Miss M. Sheriffe | A. J. Tree | J. Lindley |
| 1964 | Baldric | Mrs. H. E. Jackson | E. Fellows | W. Pyers |
| 1965 | Niksar | W. Harvey | W. Nightingall | D. Keith |
| 1966 | Kashmir | P. Butler | C. W. Bartholomew | J. Lindley |
| 1967 | Royal Palace | H. J. Joel | C. F. N. Murless | G. Moore |
| 1968 | Sir Ivor | R. R. Guest | M. V. O'Brien | L. Piggott |
| 1969 | Right Tack | J. R. Brown | J. R. Sutcliffe | G. Lewis |
| 1970 | Nijinsky | C. W. Engelhard | M. V. O'Brien | L. Piggott |

| | | OWNER | TRAINER | JOCKEY |
|---|---|---|---|---|
| 1971 | Brigadier Gerard | Mrs. J. L. Hislop | W. R. Hern | J. Mercer |
| 1972 | High Top | Sir J. Thorn | B. van Cutsem | W. Carson |
| 1973 | Mon Fils | Mrs. B. M. L. Davis | R. Hannon | F. Durr |
| 1974 | Nonoalco | Mme. M. F. Berger | F. Boutin | Y. Saint-Martin |
| 1975 | Bolkonski | C. d'Alessio | H. Cecil | G. Dettori |
| 1976 | Wollow | C. d'Alessio | H. Cecil | G. Dettori |
| 1977 | Nebbiolo | N. Schibbye | K. Prendergast | G. Curran |
| 1978 | Roland Gardens | J. Hayter | D. Sasse | F. Durr |
| 1979 | Tap on Wood | A. D. Shead | B. W. Hills | S. Cauthen |
| 1980 | Known Fact | K. Abdullah | A. J. Tree | W. Carson |
| 1981 | To-Agori-Mou | Mrs. A. Muinos | G. Harwood | G. Starkey |
| 1982 | Zino | G. A. Oldham | F. Boutin | F. Head |
| 1983 | Lomond | R. E. Sangster | M. V. O'Brien | P. Eddery |
| 1984 | El Gran Senor | R. E. Sangster | M. V. O'Brien | P. Eddery |
| 1985 | Shadeed | Maktoum Al Maktoum | M. Stoute | L. Piggott |
| 1986 | Dancing Brave | K. Abdullah | G. Harwood | G. Starkey |
| 1987 | Don't Forget Me | J. Horgan | R. Hannon | W. Carson |
| 1988 | Doyoun | H.H. Aga Khan | M. Stoute | W. R. Swinburn |
| 1989 | Nashwan | Hamdan Al-Maktoum | W. Hern | W. Carson |
| 1990 | Tirol | J. Horgan | R. Hannon | M. Kinane |

# THE 1000 GUINEAS

| | | | | |
|---|---|---|---|---|
| 1946 | Hypericum | H.M. The King | C. Boyd-Rochfort | D. Smith |
| 1947 | Imprudence | Mme. P. Corbière | J. Lieux | W. R. Johnstone |
| 1948 | Queenpot | Sir P. Loraine | C. F. N. Murless | G. Richards |
| 1949 | Musidora | N. P. Donaldson | C. F. Elsey | E. Britt |
| 1950 | Camarée | J. Ternynck | A. Lieux | W. R. Johnstone |
| 1951 | Belle of All | H. S. Tufton | N. Bertie | G. Richards |
| 1952 | Zabara | Sir M. McAlpine | V. Smyth | K. Gethin |
| 1953 | Happy Laughter | H. D. H. Wills | J. Jarvis | E. Mercer |
| 1954 | Festoon | J. A. Dewar | N. Cannon | A. Breasley |
| 1955 | Meld | Lady Z. Wernher | C. Boyd-Rochfort | W. H. Carr |
| 1956 | Honeylight | Sir V. Sassoon | C. F. Elsey | E. Britt |
| 1957 | Rose Royale | H.H. Aga Khan | A. Head | C. Smirke |
| 1958 | Bella Paola | F. Dupré | F. Mathet | S. Boullenger |
| 1959 | Petite Etoile | Prince Aly Khan | C. F. N. Murless | D. Smith |
| 1960 | Never Too Late | Mrs. H. E. Jackson | E. Pollet | R. Poincelet |
| 1961 | Sweet Solera | Mrs. S. M. Castello | R. Day | W. Rickaby |
| 1962 | Abermaid | R. More O'Ferrall | H. Wragg | W. Williamson |
| 1963 | Hula Dancer | Mrs. P. A. B. Widener | E. Pollet | R. Poincelet |
| 1964 | Pourparler | Beatrice, Lady Granard | P. J. Prendergast | G. Bougoure |
| 1965 | Night Off | L. B. Holliday | W. Wharton | W. Williamson |
| 1966 | Glad Rags | Mrs. J. P. Mills | M. V. O'Brien | P. Cook |
| 1967 | Fleet | R. C. Boucher | C. F. N. Murless | G. Moore |
| 1968 | Caergwrle | Mrs. C. F. N. Murless | C. F. N. Murless | A. Barclay |
| 1969 | Full Dress | R. B. Moller | H. Wragg | R. Hutchinson |
| 1970 | Humble Duty | Jean, Lady Ashcombe | P. Walwyn | L. Piggott |
| 1971 | Altesse Royale | F. R. Hue-Williams | C. F. N. Murless | Y. Saint-Martin |
| 1972 | Waterloo | Mrs. R. Stanley | J. W. Watts | E. Hide |
| 1973 | Mysterious | G. A. Pope, jr. | C. F. N. Murless | G. Lewis |
| 1974 | Highclere | H.M. The Queen | W. R. Hern | J. Mercer |
| 1975 | Nocturnal Spree | Mrs. D. D. O'Kelly | H. V. S. Murless | J. Roe |
| 1976 | Flying Water | D. Wildenstein | A. Penna | Y. Saint-Martin |
| 1977 | Mrs McArdy | Mrs. E. Kettlewell | M. W. Easterby | E. Hide |
| 1978 | Enstone Spark | R. A. N. Bonnycastle | B. W. Hills | E. Johnson |
| 1979 | One in a Million | Helena Springfield Ltd | H. Cecil | J. Mercer |
| 1980 | Quick as Lightning | O. M. Phipps | J. Dunlop | B. Rouse |
| 1981 | Fairy Footsteps | H. J. Joel | H. Cecil | L. Piggott |
| 1982 | On the House | Sir P. Oppenheimer | H. Wragg | J. Reid |
| 1983 | Ma Biche | Maktoum Al Maktoum | Mme C. Head | F. Head |
| 1984 | Pebbles | M. D. Lemos | C. Brittain | P. Robinson |
| 1985 | Oh So Sharp | Sheikh Mohammed | H. Cecil | S. Cauthen |
| 1986 | Midway Lady | H.H. Ranier | B. Hanbury | R. Cochrane |
| 1987 | Miesque | S. S. Niarchos | F. Boutin | F. Head |
| 1988 | Ravinella | Ecurie Aland | Mme. C. Head | G. Moore |
| 1989 | Musical Bliss | Sheikh Mohammed | M. Stoute | W. R. Swinburn |
| 1990 | Salsabil | Hamdan Al-Maktoum | J. Dunlop | W. Carson |

| | OWNER | TRAINER | JOCKEY |
|---|---|---|---|

# THE ST LEGER

| | | OWNER | TRAINER | JOCKEY |
|---|---|---|---|---|
| 1946 | Airborne | J. E. Ferguson | R. Perryman | T. Lowrey |
| 1947 | Sayajirao | H.H. Maharaja of Baroda | F. Armstrong | E. Britt |
| 1948 | Black Tarquin | W. Woodward | C. Boyd-Rochfort | E. Britt |
| 1949 | Ridge Wood | G. R. H. Smith | C. F. N. Murless | M. Beary |
| 1950 | Scratch | M. Boussac | C. H. Semblat | W. R. Johnstone |
| 1951 | Talma | M. Boussac | C. H. Semblat | W. R. Johnstone |
| 1952 | Tulyar | H.H. Aga Khan | M. Marsh | C. Smirke |
| 1953 | Premonition | W. P. Wyatt | C. Boyd Rochfort | E. Smith |
| 1954 | Never Say Die | R. S. Clark | J. Lawson | C. Smirke |
| 1955 | Meld | Lady Z. Wernher | C. Boyd-Rochfort | W. H. Carr |
| 1956 | Cambremer | R. B. Strassburger | G. Bridgland | F. Palmer |
| 1957 | Ballymoss | J. McShain | M. V. O'Brien | T. P. Burns |
| 1958 | Alcide | Sir H. de Trafford | C. Boyd Rochfort | W. H. Carr |
| 1959 | Cantelo | W. Hill | C. F. Elsey | E. Hide |
| 1960 | St. Paddy | Sir V. Sassoon | C. F. N. Murless | L. Piggott |
| 1961 | Aurelius | Mrs. V. Lilley | C. F. N. Murless | L. Piggott |
| 1962 | Hethersett | L. B. Holliday | W. R. Hern | W. H. Carr |
| 1963 | Ragusa | J. R. Mullion | P. J. Prendergast | G. Bougoure |
| 1964 | Indiana | C. W. Engelhard | J. F. Watts | J. Lindley |
| 1965 | Provoke | J. J. Astor | W. R. Hern | J. Mercer |
| 1966 | Sodium | R. J. Sigtia | G. Todd | F. Durr |
| 1967 | Ribocco | C. W. Engelhard | R. F. Johnson Houghton | L. Piggott |
| 1968 | Ribero | C. W. Engelhard | R. F. Johnson Houghton | L. Piggott |
| 1969 | Intermezzo | G. A. Oldham | H. Wragg | R. Hutchinson |
| 1970 | Nijinsky | C. W. Engelhard | M. V. O'Brien | L. Piggott |
| 1971 | Athens Wood | Mrs. J. Rogerson | H. Thomson Jones | L. Piggott |
| 1972 | Boucher | O. Phipps | M. V. O'Brien | L. Piggott |
| 1973 | Peleid | W. E. Behrens | C. W. C. Elsey | F. Durr |
| 1974 | Bustino | Lady Beaverbrook | W. R. Hern | J. Mercer |
| 1975 | Bruni | C. A. B. St. George | H. R. Price | A. Murray |
| 1976 | Crow | D. Wildenstein | A. Penna | Y. Saint-Martin |
| 1977 | Dunfermline | H.M. The Queen | W. R. Hern | W. Carson |
| 1978 | Julio Mariner | M. D. Lemos | C. Brittain | E. Hide |
| 1979 | Son of Love | A. Rolland | R. Collet | A. Lequeux |
| 1980 | Light Cavalry | H. J. Joel | H. Cecil | J. Mercer |
| 1981 | Cut Above | Sir J. J. Astor | W. R. Hern | J. Mercer |
| 1982 | Touching Wood | Maktoum Al Maktoum | H Thomson Jones | P. Cook |
| 1983 | Sun Princess | Sir M. Sobel | W. R. Hern | W. Carson |
| 1984 | Commanche Run | I. W. Allen | L. Cumani | L. Piggott |
| 1985 | Oh So Sharp | Sheikh Mohammed | H. Cecil | S. Cauthen |
| 1986 | Moon Madness | Lavinia, Duchess of Norfolk | J. Dunlop | P. Eddery |
| 1987 | Reference Point | L. Freedman | H. Cecil | S. Cauthen |
| 1988 | Minster Son | Lady Beaverbrook | W. R. Hern | W. Carson |
| 1989 | Michelozzo | C.A.B. St. George | H. Cecil | S. Cauthen |
| 1990 | Snurge | M. Arbib | P. F. I. Cole | T. Quinn |

# THE KING GEORGE VI AND
# QUEEN ELIZABETH DIAMOND STAKES

| | | OWNER | TRAINER | JOCKEY |
|---|---|---|---|---|
| 1951 | Supreme Court | Mrs. T. Lilley | E. Williams | C. Elliott |
| 1952 | Tulyar | H.H. Aga Khan | M. Marsh | C. Smirke |
| 1953 | Pinza | Sir V. Sassoon | N. Bertie | G. Richards |
| 1954 | Aureole | H.M. The Queen | C. B-Rochfort | E. Smith |
| 1955 | Vimy | P. Wertheimer | A. Head | R. Poincelet |
| 1956 | Ribot | Marchese della Rocchetta | U. Penco | E. Camici |
| 1957 | Montaval | R. Strassburger | G. Bridgland | F. Palmer |
| 1958 | Ballymoss | J. McShain | M. V. O'Brien | A. Breasley |
| 1959 | Alcide | Sir H. de Trafford | C. B-Rochfort | W. Carr |
| 1960 | Aggressor | Sir H. Wernher | J. Gosden | J. Lindley |
| 1961 | Right Royal V | Mme. J. Couturie | E. Pollett | R. Poincelet |
| 1962 | Match III | F. Dupré | F. Mathet | Y. Saint-Martin |
| 1963 | Ragusa | J. Mullion | P. J. Prendergast | G. Bougoure |
| 1964 | Nasram II | Mrs. H. Jackson | E. Fellows | W. Pyers |
| 1965 | Meadow Court | G. Bell | P. J. Prendergast | L. Piggott |
| 1966 | Aunt Edith | Lt.-Col. J. Hornung | N. Murless | L. Piggott |
| 1967 | Busted | S. Joel | N. Murless | G. Moore |
| 1968 | Royal Palace | H. Joel | N. Murless | A. Barclay |

|  |  | OWNER | TRAINER | JOCKEY |
|---|---|---|---|---|
| 1969 | Park Top | Duke of Devonshire | B. van Cutsem | L. Piggott |
| 1970 | Nijinsky | C. W. Engelhard | M. V. O'Brien | L. Piggott |
| 1971 | Mill Reef | P. Mellon | I. Balding | G. Lewis |
| 1972 | Brigadier Gerard | Mrs. J. Hislop | W. Hern | J. Mercer |
| 1973 | Dahlia | N. B. Hunt | M. Zilber | W. Pyers |
| 1974 | Dahlia | N. B. Hunt | M. Zilber | L. Piggott |
| 1975 | Grundy | Dr. C. Vittadini | P. Walwyn | P. Eddery |
| 1976 | Pawneese | D. Wildenstein | A. Penna | Y. Saint-Martin |
| 1977 | The Minstrel | R. Sangster | M. V. O'Brien | L. Piggott |
| 1978 | Ile de Bourbon | D. McCall | R. Johnson-Houghton | J. Reid |
| 1979 | Troy | Sir M. Sobell | W. Hern | W. Carson |
| 1980 | Ela-Mana-Mou | S. Weinstock | W. Hern | W. Carson |
| 1981 | Shergar | H.H. Aga Khan | M. Stoute | W. R. Swinburn |
| 1982 | Kalaglow | A. Ward | G. Harwood | G. Starkey |
| 1983 | Time Charter | R. Barnett | H. Candy | J. Mercer |
| 1984 | Teenoso | E. Moller | G. Wragg | L. Piggott |
| 1985 | Petoski | Marcia, Lady Beaverbrook | W. Hern | W. Carson |
| 1986 | Dancing Brave | K. Abdullah | G. Harwood | P. Eddery |
| 1987 | Reference Point | L. Freedman | H. Cecil | S. Cauthen |
| 1988 | Mtoto | Sheikh Ahmed Al Maktoum | A. C. Stewart | M. Roberts |
| 1989 | Nashwan | Hamdan Al-Maktoum | W. Hern | W. Carson |
| 1990 | Belmez | Sheikh Mohammed | H. Cecil | M. Kinane |

# THE ASCOT GOLD CUP

|  |  |  |  |  |
|---|---|---|---|---|
| 1946 | Caracalla II | M. Boussac | C. Semblat | C. Elliott |
| 1947 | Souverain | F. R. Schmitt | H. Delavaud | M. Lollieron |
| 1948 | Arbar | M. Boussac | C. Semblat | C. Elliott |
| 1949 | Alycidon | Lord Derby | W. Earl | D. Smith |
| 1950 | Supertello | W. Harvey | J. C. Waugh | D. Smith |
| 1951 | Pan II | M. E. Constant | E. Pollet | R. Poincelet |
| 1952 | Aquino II | H.H. Maharanee of Baroda | F. Armstrong | G. Richards |
| 1953 | Souepi | G. Digby | G. Digby | C. Elliott |
| 1954 | Elpenor | M. Boussac | C. Elliott | J. Doyasbere |
| 1955 | Botticelli | Marchese della Rocchetta | U. Penco | E. Camici |
| 1956 | Macip | M. Boussac | C. Elliott | S. Boullenger |
| 1957 | Zarathustra | T. J. Gray | C. B-Rochfort | L. Piggott |
| 1958 | Gladness | J. McShain | M. V. O'Brien | L. Piggott |
| 1959 | Wallaby II | Baron G. de Waldner | P. Carter | F. Palmer |
| 1960 | Sheshoon | H.H. Aga Khan | A. Head | G. Moore |
| 1961 | Pandofell | H. Warwick-Daw | F. Maxwell | L. Piggott |
| 1962 | Balto | M. Bonaventure | M. Bonaventure | F. Palmer |
| 1963 | Twilight Alley | Lady Sassoon | N. Murless | L. Piggott |
| 1964 | No race |  |  |  |
| 1965 | Fighting Charlie | Lady Mairi Bury | F. Maxwell | L. Piggott |
| 1966 | Fighting Charlie | Lady Mairi Bury | F. Maxwell | G. Starkey |
| 1967 | Parbury | Major H. P. Holt | D. Candy | J. Mercer |
| 1968 | Pardallo II | Mme. L. Volterra | C. Bartholomew | W. Pyers |
| 1969 | Levmoss | S. McGrath | S. McGrath | W. Williamson |
| 1970 | Precipice Wood | J. J. McAlpine | Mrs. R. Lomax | J. Lindley |
| 1971 | Random Shot | Mrs. G. Benskin | A. Budgett | G. Lewis |
| 1972 | Erimo Hawk | Y. Yammamoto | G. Barling | P. Eddery |
| 1973 | Lassalle | Z. Yoshida | R. Carver | J. Lindley |
| 1974 | Ragstone | Duke of Norfolk | J. Dunlop | R. Hutchinson |
| 1975 | Sagaro | G. A. Oldham | F. Boutin | L. Piggott |
| 1976 | Sagaro | G. A. Oldham | F. Boutin | L. Piggott |
| 1977 | Sagaro | G. A. Oldham | F. Boutin | L. Piggott |
| 1978 | Shangamuzo | Mrs. E. Charles | M. Stoute | G. Starkey |
| 1979 | Le Moss | C. d'Alessio | H. Cecil | L. Piggott |
| 1980 | Le Moss | C. d'Alessio | H. Cecil | J. Mercer |
| 1981 | Ardross | C. St. George | H. Cecil | L. Piggott |
| 1982 | Ardross | C. St. George | H. Cecil | L. Piggott |
| 1983 | Little Wolf | Lord Porchester | W. Hern | W. Carson |
| 1984 | Gildoran | R. Sangster | B. Hills | S. Cauthen |
| 1985 | Gildoran | R. Sangster | B. Hills | B. Thomson |
| 1986 | Longboat | R. Hollingsworth | W. Hern | W. Carson |
| 1987 | Paean | Lord H. de Walden | H. Cecil | S. Cauthen |
| 1988 | Sadeem | Sheikh Mohammed | G. Harwood | G. Starkey |
| 1989 | Sadeem | Sheikh Mohammed | G. Harwood | W. Carson |
| 1990 | Ashal | Hamdan Al-Maktoum | H. Thomson Jones | R. Hills |

| | OWNER | TRAINER | JOCKEY |
|---|---|---|---|

# THE ECLIPSE STAKES

| | | OWNER | TRAINER | JOCKEY |
|---|---|---|---|---|
| 1946 | Gulf Stream | Lord Derby | W. Earl | H. Wragg |
| 1947 | Migoli | H.H. Aga Khan | F. Butters | C. Smirke |
| 1948 | Petition | Sir A. Butt | F. Butters | K. Gethin |
| 1949 | Djeddah | M. Boussac | C. Semblat | C. Elliott |
| 1950 | Flocon | Baron G. de Waldner | P. Carter | F. Palmer |
| 1951 | Mystery IX | Mrs. E. Esmond | P. Carter | L. Piggott |
| 1952 | Tulyar | H.H. Aga Khan | M. Marsh | C. Smirke |
| 1953 | Argur | M. Boussac | J. Glynn | C. Elliott |
| 1954 | King Of The Tudors | F. Dennis | W. Stephenson | K. Gethin |
| 1955 | Darius | Sir P. Loraine | H. Wragg | L. Piggott |
| 1956 | Tropique | Baron G. de Rothschild | G. Watson | P. Blanc |
| 1957 | Arctic Explorer | Lt.-Col. G. Loder | N. Murless | L. Piggott |
| 1958 | Ballymoss | J. McShain | M. V. O'Brien | A. Breasley |
| 1959 | Saint Crespin III | Prince Aly Khan | A. Head | G. Moore |
| 1960 | Javelot | Baron G. de Waldner | P. Carter | F. Palmer |
| 1961 | St. Paddy | Sir V. Sassoon | N. Murless | L. Piggott |
| 1962 | Henry The Seventh | H. Joel | W. Elsey | E. Hide |
| 1963 | Khalkis | Lord Elvedon | P. J. Prendergast | G. Bougoure |
| 1964 | Ragusa | J. Mullion | P. J. Prendergast | G. Bougoure |
| 1965 | Canisby | H.M. The Queen | C. B-Rochfort | S. Clayton |
| 1966 | Pieces of Eight | Comtesse de la Valdene | M. V. O'Brien | L. Piggott |
| 1967 | Busted | S. Joel | N. Murless | W. Rickaby |
| 1968 | Royal Palace | H. Joel | N. Murless | A. Barclay |
| 1969 | Wolver Hollow | Mrs. C. Iselin | H. Cecil | L. Piggott |
| 1970 | Connaught | H. Joel | N. Murless | A. Barclay |
| 1971 | Mill Reef | P. Mellon | I. Balding | G. Lewis |
| 1972 | Brigadier Gerard | Mrs. J. Hislop | W. R. Hern | J. Mercer |
| 1973 | Scottish Rifle | A. Struthers | J. Dunlop | R. Hutchinson |
| 1974 | Coup de Feu | F. Sasse | D. Sasse | P. Eddery |
| 1975 | Star Appeal | W. Zeitelhack | T. Greiper | G. Starkey |
| 1976 | Wollow | C. d'Alessio | H. Cecil | G. Dettori |
| 1977 | Artaius | Mrs. G. Getty II | M. V. O'Brien | L. Piggott |
| 1978 | Gunner B | Mrs. P. Barratt | H. Cecil | J. Mercer |
| 1979 | Dickens Hill | Mme. J. Binet | M. O'Toole | A. Murray |
| 1980 | Ela-Mana-Mou | S. Weinstock | W. R. Hern | W. Carson |
| 1981 | Master Willie | R. Barnett | H. Candy | P. Waldron |
| 1982 | Kalaglow | A. Ward | G. Harwood | G. Starkey |
| 1983 | Solford | R. Sangster | M. V. O'Brien | P. Eddery |
| 1984 | Sadlers Wells | R. Sangster | M. V. O'Brien | P. Eddery |
| 1985 | Pebbles | Sheikh Mohammed Al Maktoum | C. Brittain | S. Cauthen |
| 1986 | Dancing Brave | K. Abdullah | G. Harwood | G. Starkey |
| 1987 | Mtoto | Sheikh Ahmed Al Maktoum | A. Stewart | M. Roberts |
| 1988 | Mtoto | Sheikh Ahmed Al Maktoum | A. Stewart | M. Roberts |
| 1989 | Nashwan | Hamdan Al-Maktoum | W. R. Hern | W. Carson |
| 1990 | Elmaamul | Hamdan Al-Maktoum | W. R. Hern | G. Mosse |

# THE IRISH DERBY

| | | TRAINER | JOCKEY |
|---|---|---|---|
| 1946 | Bright News | D. Rogers | M. Wing |
| 1947 | Sayajirao | F. Armstrong | E. Britt |
| 1948 | Nathoo | Frank Butters | W. R. Johnstone |
| 1949 | Hindostan | Frank Butters | W. R. Johnstone |
| 1950 | Dark Warrior | P. J. Prendergast | J. W. Thompson |
| 1951 | Fraise du Bois | H. Wragg | C. Smirke |
| 1952 | Thirteen of Diamonds | P. J. Prendergast | J. Mullane |
| 1953 | Chamier | M. V. O'Brien | W. Rickaby |
| 1954 | Zarathustra | M. Hurley | P. Powell, jr. |
| 1955 | Panaslipper | S. McGrath | J. Eddery |
| 1956 | Talgo | H. Wragg | E. Mercer |
| 1957 | Ballymoss | M. V. O'Brien | T. P. Burns |
| 1958 | Sindon | M. Dawson | L. Ward |
| 1959 | Fidalgo | H. Wragg | J. Mercer |
| 1960 | Chamour | A. S. O'Brien | G. Bougoure |
| 1961 | Your Highness | H. L. Cottrill | H. Holmes |
| 1962 | Tambourine | E. Pollet | R. Poincelet |

| | | TRAINER | JOCKEY |
|---|---|---|---|
| 1963 | Ragusa | P. J. Prendergast | G. Bougoure |
| 1964 | Santa Claus | J. M. Rogers | W. Burke |
| 1965 | Meadow Court | P. J. Prendergast | L. Piggott |
| 1966 | Sodium | G. Todd | F. Durr |
| 1967 | Ribocco | R. F. Johnson Houghton | L. Piggott |
| 1968 | Ribero | R. F. Johnson Houghton | L. Piggott |
| 1969 | Prince Regent | E. Pollet | G. Lewis |
| 1970 | Nijinsky | M. V. O'Brien | L. Ward |
| 1971 | Irish Ball | P. Lallié | A. Gibert |
| 1972 | Steel Pulse | A. Breasley | W. Williamson |
| 1973 | Weavers' Hall | S. McGrath | G. McGrath |
| 1974 | English Prince | P. Walwyn | Y. Saint-Martin |
| 1975 | Grundy | P. Walwyn | P. Eddery |
| 1976 | Malacate | F. Boutin | P. Paquet |
| 1977 | The Minstrel | M. V. O'Brien | L. Piggott |
| 1978 | Shirley Heights | J. Dunlop | G. Starkey |
| 1979 | Troy | W. R. Hern | W. Carson |
| 1980 | Tyrnavos | B. Hobbs | A. Murray |
| 1981 | Shergar | M. Stoute | L. Piggott |
| 1982 | Assert | D. V. O'Brien | C. Roche |
| 1983 | Shareef Dancer | M. Stoute | W. R. Swinburn |
| 1984 | El Gran Senor | M. V. O'Brien | P. Eddery |
| 1985 | Law Society | M. V. O'Brien | P. Eddery |
| 1986 | Shahrastani | M. Stoute | W. R. Swinburn |
| 1987 | Sir Harry Lewis | B. W. Hills | J. Reid |
| 1988 | Kahyasi | L. Cumani | R. Cochrane |
| 1989 | Old Vic | H. Cecil | S. Cauthen |
| 1990 | Salsabil | J. Dunlop | W. Carson |

# PRIX DE L'ARC DE TRIOMPHE

| 1946 | Caracalla | C. H. Semblat | E. C. Elliott |
|---|---|---|---|
| 1947 | Le Paillon | W. Head | F. Rochetti |
| 1948 | Migoli | Frank Butters | C. Smirke |
| 1949 | Coronation | C. H. Semblat | R. Poincelet |
| 1950 | Tantième | F. Mathet | J. Doyasbère |
| 1951 | Tantième | F. Mathet | J. Doyesbère |
| 1952 | Nuccio | A. Head | R. Poincelet |
| 1953 | La Sorellina | E. Pollet | M. Larraun |
| 1954 | Sica Boy | P. Pelat | W. R. Johnstone |
| 1955 | Ribot | V. U. Penco | E. Camici |
| 1956 | Ribot | V. U. Penco | E. Camici |
| 1957 | Oroso | D. Lescalle | S. Boullenger |
| 1958 | Ballymoss | M. V. O'Brien | A. Breasley |
| 1959 | Saint Crespin | A. Head | G. Moore |
| 1960 | Puissant Chef | C. W. Bartholomew | M. Garcia |
| 1961 | Molvedo | A. Maggi | E. Camici |
| 1962 | Soltikoff | R. Pelat | M. Depalmas |
| 1963 | Exbury | G. Watson | J. Deforge |
| 1964 | Prince Royal | G. Bridgland | R. Poincelet |
| 1965 | Sea-Bird | E. Pollet | T. P. Glennon |
| 1966 | Bon Mot | W. Head | F. Head |
| 1967 | Topyo | C. W. Bartholomew | W. Pyers |
| 1968 | Vaguely Noble | E. Pollet | W. Williamson |
| 1969 | Levmoss | S. McGrath | W. Williamson |
| 1970 | Sassafras | F. Mathet | Y. Saint-Martin |
| 1971 | Mill Reef | I. Balding | G. Lewis |
| 1972 | San San | A. Penna | F. Head |
| 1973 | Rheingold | B. Hills | L. Piggott |
| 1974 | Allez France | A. Penna | Y. Saint-Martin |
| 1975 | Star Appeal | T. Grieper | G. Starkey |
| 1976 | Ivanjica | A. Head | F. Head |
| 1977 | Alleged | M. V. O'Brien | L. Piggott |
| 1978 | Alleged | M. V. O'Brien | L. Piggott |
| 1979 | Three Troikas | Mme. C. Head | F. Head |
| 1980 | Detroit | O. Douieb | P. Eddery |
| 1981 | Gold River | A. Head | G. W. Moore |
| 1982 | Akiyda | F. Mathet | Y. Saint-Martin |

|  |  | TRAINER | JOCKEY |
|---|---|---|---|
| 1983 | All Along | P. Biancone | W. R. Swinburn |
| 1984 | Sagace | P. Biancone | Y. Saint-Martin |
| 1985 | Rainbow Quest | A. J. Tree | P. Eddery |
| 1986 | Dancing Brave | G. Harwood | P. Eddery |
| 1987 | Trempolino | A. Fabre | P. Eddery |
| 1988 | Tony Bin | L. Camici | J. Reid |
| 1989 | Carroll House | M. Jarvis | M. Kinane |

# THE KENTUCKY DERBY

| 1946 | Assault | M. Hirsch | W. Mehrtens |
|---|---|---|---|
| 1947 | Jet Pilot | T. Smith | E. Guerin |
| 1948 | Citation | B. A. Jones | E. Arcaro |
| 1949 | Ponder | B. A. Jones | S. Brooks |
| 1950 | Middleground | M. Hirsch | W. Boland |
| 1951 | Count Turf | S. Rutchick | C. McCreary |
| 1952 | Hill Gail | B. A. Jones | E. Arcaro |
| 1953 | Dark Star | E. Hayward | H. Moreno |
| 1954 | Determine | W. Molter | R. York |
| 1955 | Swaps | M. A. Tenney | W. Shoemaker |
| 1956 | Needles | H. L. Fontaine | D. Erb |
| 1957 | Iron Liege | H. A. Jones | W. Hartack |
| 1958 | Tim Tam | H. A. Jones | I. Valenzuela |
| 1959 | Tomy Lee | F. Childs | W. Shoemaker |
| 1960 | Venetian Way | V. J. Sovinski | W. Hartack |
| 1961 | Carry Back | J. A. Price | J. Sellers |
| 1962 | Decidedly | H. A. Luro | W. Hartack |
| 1963 | Chateaugay | J. P. Conway | B. Baeza |
| 1964 | Northern Dancer | H. A. Luro | W. Hartack |
| 1965 | Lucky Debonair | F. Catrone | W. Shoemaker |
| 1966 | Kauai King | H. Forrest | D. Brumfield |
| 1967 | Proud Clarion | L. Gentry | R. Ussery |
| 1968 | Forward Pass | H. Forrest | I. Valenzuela |
| 1969 | Majestic Prince | J. Longden | W. Hartack |
| 1970 | Dust Commander | D. Combs | M. Manganello |
| 1971 | Canonero | J. Arias | G. Avila |
| 1972 | Riva Ridge | L. Laurin | R. Turcotte |
| 1973 | Secretariat | L. Laurin | R. Turcotte |
| 1974 | Cannonade | W. C. Stephens | A. Cordero |
| 1975 | Foolish Pleasure | L. Jolley | J. Vasquez |
| 1976 | Bold Forbes | L. S. Barrera | A. Cordero |
| 1977 | Seattle Slew | W. H. Turner | J. Cruguet |
| 1978 | Affirmed | L. S. Barrera | S. Cauthen |
| 1979 | Spectacular Bid | G. G. Delp | R. J. Franklin |
| 1980 | Genuine Risk | L. Jolley | J. Vasquez |
| 1981 | Pleasant Colony | J. P. Campo | J. Velasquez |
| 1982 | Gato Del Sol | E. Gregson | E. Delahoussaye |
| 1983 | Sunny's Halo | D. C. Cross | E. Delahoussaye |
| 1984 | Swale | W. C. Stephens | L. Pincay |
| 1985 | Spend a Buck | C. Gambolati | A. Cordero |
| 1986 | Ferdinand | C. Whittingham | W. Shoemaker |
| 1987 | Alysheba | J. C. Van Berg | C. McCarron |
| 1988 | Winning Colors | D. W. Lukas | G. Stevens |
| 1989 | Sunday Silence | C. Whittingham | P. Valenzuela |
| 1990 | Unbridled | C. Nafzoer | C. Perret |

# THE PREAKNESS STAKES

| 1946 | Assault | M. Hirsch | W. Mehrtens |
|---|---|---|---|
| 1947 | Faultless | H. A. Jones | D. Dodson |
| 1948 | Citation | H. A. Jones | E. Arcaro |
| 1949 | Capot | J. M. Gaver | T. Atkinson |
| 1950 | Hill Prince | J. H. Hayes | E. Arcaro |
| 1951 | Bold | P. M. Burch | E. Arcaro |
| 1952 | Blue Man | W. C. Stephens | C. McCreary |
| 1953 | Native Dancer | W. C. Winfrey | E. Guerin |
| 1954 | Hasty Road | H. Trotsek | J. Adams |
| 1955 | Nashua | J. Fitzsimmons | E. Arcaro |
| 1956 | Fabius | H. A. Jones | W. Hartack |

|  |  | TRAINER | JOCKEY |
|---|---|---|---|
| 1957 | Bold Ruler | J. Fitzsimmons | E. Arcaro |
| 1958 | Tim Tam | H. A. Jones | I. Valenzuela |
| 1959 | Royal Orbit | R. Cornell | W. Harmatz |
| 1960 | Bally Ache | H. J. Pitt | R. Ussery |
| 1961 | Carry Back | J. A. Price | J. Sellers |
| 1962 | Greek Money | V. W. Raines | J. Rotz |
| 1963 | Candy Spots | M. A. Tenney | W. Shoemaker |
| 1964 | Northern Dancer | H. A. Luro | W. Hartack |
| 1965 | Tom Rolfe | F. Y. Whiteley | R. Turcotte |
| 1966 | Kauai King | H. Forrest | D. Brumfield |
| 1967 | Damascus | F. Y. Whiteley | W. Shoemaker |
| 1968 | Forward Pass | H. Forrest | I. Valenzuela |
| 1969 | Majestic Prince | J. Longden | W. Hartack |
| 1970 | Personality | J. W. Jacobs | E. Belmonte |
| 1971 | Canonero | J. Arias | G. Avila |
| 1972 | Bee Bee Bee | D. W. Carroll | E. Nelson |
| 1973 | Secretariat | L. Laurin | R. Turcotte |
| 1974 | Little Current | L. Rondinello | M. Rivera |
| 1975 | Master Derby | W. E. Adams | D. McHargue |
| 1976 | Elocutionist | P. T. Adwell | J. Lively |
| 1977 | Seattle Slew | W. H. Turner | J. Cruguet |
| 1978 | Affirmed | L. S. Barrera | S. Cauthen |
| 1979 | Spectacular Bid | G. G. Delp | R. J. Franklin |
| 1980 | Codex | D. W. Lukas | A. Cordero |
| 1981 | Pleasant Colony | J. P. Campo | J. Velasquez |
| 1982 | Aloma's Ruler | J. J. Lenzini | J. Kaenel |
| 1983 | Deputed Testamony | W. J. Boniface | D. Miller |
| 1984 | Gate Dancer | J. C. Van Berg | A. Cordero |
| 1985 | Tank's Prospect | D. W. Lukas | P. Day |
| 1986 | Snow Chief | M. Stute | A. Solis |
| 1987 | Alysheba | J. C. Van Berg | C. McCarron |
| 1988 | Risen Star | L. J. Roussell III | E. Delahoussaye |
| 1989 | Sunday Silence | C. Whittingham | P. Valenzuela |
| 1990 | Summer Squall | N. Howard | P. Day |

# THE BELMONT STAKES

| 1946 | Assault | M. Hirsch | W. Mehrtens |
|---|---|---|---|
| 1947 | Phalanx | S. E. Veitch | R. Donoso |
| 1948 | Citation | H. A. Jones | E. Arcaro |
| 1949 | Capot | J. M. Gaver | T. Atkinson |
| 1950 | Middleground | M. Hirsch | W. Boland |
| 1951 | Counterpoint | S. E. Veitch | D. Gorman |
| 1952 | One Count | O. White | E. Arcaro |
| 1953 | Native Dancer | W. C. Winfrey | E. Guerin |
| 1954 | High Gun | M. Hirsch | E. Guerin |
| 1955 | Nashua | J. Fitzsimmons | E. Arcaro |
| 1956 | Needles | H. L. Fontaine | D. Erb |
| 1957 | Gallant Man | J. A. Nerud | W. Shoemaker |
| 1958 | Cavan | T. J. Barry | P. Anderson |
| 1959 | Sword Dancer | J. E. Burch | W. Shoemaker |
| 1960 | Celtic Ash | T. J. Barry | W. Hartack |
| 1961 | Sherluck | H. Young | B. Baeza |
| 1962 | Jaipur | W. F. Mulholland | W. Shoemaker |
| 1963 | Chateaugay | J. P. Conway | B. Baeza |
| 1964 | Quadrangle | J. E. Burch | M. Ycaza |
| 1965 | Hail to All | E. Yowell | J. Sellers |
| 1966 | Amberoid | L. Laurin | W. Boland |
| 1967 | Damascus | F. Y. Whiteley | W. Shoemaker |
| 1968 | Stage Door Johnny | J. M. Gaver | H. Gustines |
| 1969 | Arts and Letters | J. E. Burch | B. Baeza |
| 1970 | High Echelon | J. W. Jacobs | J. L. Rotz |
| 1971 | Pass Catcher | E. Yowell | W. Blum |
| 1972 | Riva Ridge | L. Laurin | R. Turcotte |
| 1973 | Secretariat | L. Laurin | R. Turcotte |
| 1974 | Little Current | L. Rondinello | M. Rivera |
| 1975 | Avatar | A. T. Doyle | W. Shoemaker |
| 1976 | Bold Forbes | L. S. Barrera | A. Cordero |

| | | TRAINER | JOCKEY |
|---|---|---|---|
| 1977 | Seattle Slew | W. H. Turner | J. Cruguet |
| 1978 | Affirmed | L. S. Barrera | S. Cauthen |
| 1979 | Coastal | D. A. Whiteley | R. Hernandez |
| 1980 | Temperence Hill | J. B. Cantey | E. Maple |
| 1981 | Summing | L. Barrera | G. Martens |
| 1982 | Conquistador Cielo | W. C. Stephens | L. Pincay |
| 1983 | Caveat | W. C. Stephens | L. Pincay |
| 1984 | Swale | W. C. Stephens | L. Pincay |
| 1985 | Creme Fraiche | W. C. Stephens | E. Maple |
| 1986 | Danzig Connection | W. C. Stephens | C. McCarron |
| 1987 | Bet Twice | W. A. Croll | C. Perret |
| 1988 | Risen Star | L. J. Roussell III | E. Delahoussaye |
| 1989 | Easy Goer | C. McGaughey | P. Day |
| 1990 | Go and Go | D. Weld | M. Kinane |

# THE MELBOURNE CUP

| 1946 | Russia | E. Hush | D. Munro |
|---|---|---|---|
| 1947 | Hiraji | J. W. McCurley | J. Purtell |
| 1948 | Rimfire | S. Boyden | R. Neville |
| 1949 | Foxzami | D. Lewis | W. Fellows |
| 1950 | Comic Court | J. M. Cummings | T. P. Glennon |
| 1951 | Delta | M. McCarten | N. Sellwood |
| 1952 | Dalray | C. C. McCarthy | W. Williamson |
| 1953 | Wodalla | R. Sinclair | J. Purtell |
| 1954 | Rising Fast | I. J. Tucker | J. Purtell |
| 1955 | Toparoa | T. J. Smith | N. Sellwood |
| 1956 | Evening Peal | E. D. Lawson | G. Podmore |
| 1957 | Straight Draw | J. M. Mitchell | N. McGrowdie |
| 1958 | Baystone | J. Green | M. Schumacher |
| 1959 | MacDougal | R. W. Roden | T. P. Glennon |
| 1960 | Hi Jinx | T. H. Knowles | W. A. Smith |
| 1961 | Lord Fury | F. B. Lewis | R. Selkrig |
| 1962 | Even Stevens | A. McGregor | L. Coles |
| 1963 | Gatum Gatum | H. G. Heagney | J. Johnson |
| 1964 | Polo Prince | J. P. Carter | R. W. Taylor |
| 1965 | Light Fingers | J. B. Cummings | R. Higgins |
| 1966 | Galilee | J. B. Cummings | J. Miller |
| 1967 | Red Handed | J. B. Cummings | R. Higgins |
| 1968 | Rain Lover | M. L. Robins | J. Johnson |
| 1969 | Rain Lover | M. L. Robins | J. Johnson |
| 1970 | Baghdad Note | R. Heasley | E. J. Didham |
| 1971 | Silver Knight | E. Templeton | R. B. Marsh |
| 1972 | Piping Lane | G. M. Hanlon | J. Letts |
| 1973 | Gala Supreme | R. J. Hutchins | F. Reys |
| 1974 | Think Big | J. B. Cummings | H. White |
| 1975 | Think Big | J. B. Cummings | H. White |
| 1976 | Van Der Hum | L. H. Robinson | R. J. Skelton |
| 1977 | Gold and Black | J. B. Cummings | J. Duggan |
| 1978 | Arwon | G. M. Hanlon | H. White |
| 1979 | Hyperno | J. B. Cummings | H. White |
| 1980 | Beldale Ball | C. S. Hayes | J. Letts |
| 1981 | Just a Dash | T. J. Smith | P. Cook |
| 1982 | Gurner's Lane | G. T. Murphy | L. Dittman |
| 1983 | Kiwi | E. S. Lupton | J. Cassidy |
| 1984 | Black Knight | G. M. Hanlon | P. Cook |
| 1985 | What a Nuisance | J. F. Meagher | P. Hyland |
| 1986 | At Talaq | C. S. Hayes | M. Clarke |
| 1987 | Kensei | L. J. Bridge | L. Olsen |
| 1988 | Empire Rose | L. K. Laxon | T. Allen |
| 1989 | Tawrrific | D. Freedman | R. Dye |

# CLASSIC JUMP RACES

## THE GRAND NATIONAL

| | | OWNER | TRAINER | JOCKEY |
|---|---|---|---|---|
| 1946 | Lovely Cottage | J. Morant | T. Rayson | Captain R. Petre |
| 1947 | Caughoo | J. McDowell | H. McDowell | E. Dempsey |
| 1948 | Sheila's Cottage | J. Proctor | N. Crump | A. Thompson |
| 1949 | Russian Hero | W. Williamson | G. Owen | L. McMorrow |
| 1950 | Freebooter | Mrs. L. Brotherton | R. Renton | J. Power |
| 1951 | Nickel Coin | J. Royle | J. O'Donoghue | J. Bullock |
| 1952 | Teal | H. Lane | N. Crump | A. Thompson |
| 1953 | Early Mist | J. Griffin | M. V. O'Brien | B. Marshall |
| 1954 | Royal Tan | J. Griffin | M. V. O'Brien | B. Marshall |
| 1955 | Quare Times | Mrs. W. Welman | M. V. O'Brien | P. Taaffe |
| 1956 | E.S.B. | Mrs. L. Carver | F. Rimell | D. Dick |
| 1957 | Sundew | Mrs. G. Kohn | F. Hudson | F. Winter |
| 1958 | Mr What | D. Coughlan | T. Taaffe | A. Freeman |
| 1959 | Oxo | J. Bigg | W. Stephenson | M. Scudamore |
| 1960 | Merryman II | Miss W. Wallace | N. Crump | G. Scott |
| 1961 | Nicolaus Silver | C. Vaughan | F. Rimell | H. Beasley |
| 1962 | Kilmore | N. Cohen | Ryan Price | F. Winter |
| 1963 | Ayala | P. Raymond | K. Piggott | P. Buckley |
| 1964 | Team Spirit | J. Goodman | F. Walwyn | W. Robinson |
| 1965 | Jay Trump | Mrs. M. Stephenson | F. Winter | C. Smith |
| 1966 | Angio | S. Levy | F. Winter | T. Norman |
| 1967 | Foinavon | C. Watkins | J. Kempton | J. Buckingham |
| 1968 | Red Alligator | J. Manners | Denys Smith | B. Fletcher |
| 1969 | Highland Wedding | T. McKoy | G. Balding | E. Harty |
| 1970 | Gay Trip | R. Chambers | F. Rimell | P. Taaffe |
| 1971 | Specify | F. Pontin | J. Sutcliffe | J. Cook |
| 1972 | Well To Do | T. Forster | T. Forster | G. Thorner |
| 1973 | Red Rum | N. le Mare | D. McCain | B. Fletcher |
| 1974 | Red Rum | N. le Mare | D. McCain | B. Fletcher |
| 1975 | L'Escargot | R. Guest | D. Moore | T. Carberry |
| 1976 | Rag Trade | P. Raymond | F. Rimell | J. Burke |
| 1977 | Red Rum | N. le Mare | D. McCain | T. Stack |
| 1978 | Lucius | Mrs. D. Whitaker | G. W. Richards | B. R. Davies |
| 1979 | Rubstic | J. Douglas | S. J. Leadbetter | M. Barnes |
| 1980 | Ben Nevis | R. Stewart jr. | T. Forster | C. Fenwick |
| 1981 | Aldaniti | S. N. Embiricos | J. Gifford | R. Champion |
| 1982 | Grittar | F. Gilman | F. Gilman | Mr. C. R. Saunders |
| 1983 | Corbiere | B. Burrough | Mrs. J. Pitman | B. de Haan |
| 1984 | Hallo Dandy | R. Shaw | G. W. Richards | N. Doughty |
| 1985 | Last Suspect | Anne, D. of Westminster | T. Forster | H. Davies |
| 1986 | West Tip | P. Luff | M. Oliver | R. Dunwoody |
| 1987 | Maori Venture | H. J. Joel | A. Turnell | S. C. Knight |
| 1988 | Rhyme 'N Reason | Miss J. Reed | D. Elsworth | B. Powell |
| 1989 | Little Polveir | E. Harvey | T. Balding | J. Frost |
| 1990 | Mr. Frisk | Mrs. L. Duffey | K. Bailey | Mr. M. Armytage |

## THE SCOTTISH GRAND NATIONAL

| 1947 | Rowland Boy | A. Boley | F. Walwyn | R. Black |
|---|---|---|---|---|
| 1948 | Magnetic Fun | N. Willis | W. Hall | L. Vick |
| 1949 | Wot No Sun | Captain T. Wilson | N. Crump | A. Thompson |
| 1950 | Sanvina | J. Oliver | J. Wight | J. Oliver |
| 1951 | Court Painter | Major E. H.-St. John | C. Bewicke | F. Carroll |
| 1952 | Flagrant Mac | Lord Grimthorpe | R. Renton | J. Power |
| 1953 | Queen's Taste | W. Bailey | H. Clarkson | T. Robson |
| 1954 | Queen's Taste | W. Bailey | H. Clarkson | G. Slack |
| 1955 | Bar Point | Sir S. Bell | R. Renton | D. Ancil |
| 1956 | Queen's Taste | W. Bailey | H. Clarkson | R. Curran |
| 1957 | Bremontier | B. Nichols | P. Taylor | A. Rossio |
| 1958 | Game Field | Lady Barber | J. Fawcus | J. Boddy |
| 1959 | Merryman II | Miss W. Wallace | N. Crump | G. Scott |

| | | OWNER | TRAINER | JOCKEY |
|---|---|---|---|---|
| 1960 | Finchman | Mrs. M. Green | J. Wight | M. Batchelor |
| 1961 | Kinmont Willie | A. Stephenson | A. Stephenson | C. Stobbs |
| 1962 | Sham Fight | R. Jeffrey | T. Robson | T. Robson |
| 1963 | Pappageno's Cottage | W. King | J. Oliver | T. Brookshaw |
| 1964 | Popham Down | W. Turriff | F. Walwyn | J. Haine |
| 1965 | Brasher | E. Gosschalk | T. Robson | J. Fitzgerald |
| 1966 | African Patrol | Miss A. Robertson | R. Fairbairn | J. Leech |
| 1967 | The Fossa | R. Greatbeach | F. Rimell | A. Turnell |
| 1968 | Arcturus | Lady Hay | N. Crump | P. Buckley |
| 1969 | Playlord | P. Cussins | G. W. Richards | R. Barry |
| 1970 | The Spaniard | W. Rimmer | K. Oliver | B. Brogan |
| 1971 | Young Ash Leaf | R. McDonald | K. Oliver | P. Ennis |
| 1972 | Quick Reply | W. Thyne | C. Bell | M. Barnes |
| 1973 | Esban | Miss D. Squires | R. Clay | J. Bourke |
| 1974 | Red Rum | N. le Mare | D. McCain | B. Fletcher |
| 1975 | Barona | W. Whitbread | R. Armytage | P. Kelleway |
| 1976 | Barona | W. Whitbread | R. Armytage | P. Kelleway |
| 1977 | Sebastian V | R. Jeffreys | C. Bell | R. Lamb |
| 1978 | King Con | G. Renilson | G. Renilson | P. Craggs |
| 1979 | Fighting Fit | Mrs. L. Carr | K. Oliver | C. Hawkins |
| 1980 | Salkeed | E. Bell | N. Crump | D. Atkins |
| 1981 | Astral Charmer | H. Bell | H. Bell | J. L. Goulding |
| 1982 | Cockle Strand | Colonel D. Greig | K. Oliver | D. Dutton |
| 1983 | Canton | S. Lycett Green | N. Crump | K. Whyte |
| 1984 | Androma | Wickersley Ltd. | J. Fitzgerald | M. Dwyer |
| 1985 | Androma | Wickersley Ltd. | J. Fitzgerald | M. Dwyer |
| 1986 | Hardy Lad | Mrs. J. Milligan | B. Wilkinson | M. Hammond |
| 1987 | Little Polveir | M. Shone | J. Edwards | P. Scudamore |
| 1988 | Mighty Mark | Mrs. F. Walton | F. Walton | B. Storey |
| 1989 | Roll-A-Joint | R. T. Williams | C. Popham | B. Powell |
| 1990 | Four Trix | Mrs. S. Catherwood | G. Richards | D. Byrne |

# THE CHELTENHAM GOLD CUP

| | | | | |
|---|---|---|---|---|
| 1946 | Prince Regent | J. Rank | T. Dreaper | T. Hyde |
| 1947 | Fortina | Lord Grimthorpe | H. Christie | R. Black |
| 1948 | Cottage Rake | F. Vickerman | M. V. O'Brien | A. Brabazon |
| 1949 | Cottage Rake | F. Vickerman | M. V. O'Brien | A. Brabazon |
| 1950 | Cottage Rake | F. Vickerman | M. V. O'Brien | A. Brabazon |
| 1951 | Silver Fame | Lord Bicester | G. Beeby | M. Molony |
| 1952 | Mont Tremblant | Miss D. Paget | F. Walwyn | D. Dick |
| 1953 | Knock Hard | Mrs. M. Keogh | M. V. O'Brien | T. Molony |
| 1954 | Four Ten | A. Strange | J. Roberts | T. Cusack |
| 1955 | Gay Donald | P. Burt | J. Ford | A. Grantham |
| 1956 | Limber Hill | J. Davey | W. Dutton | J. Power |
| 1957 | Linwell | D. Brown | C. Mallon | M. Scudamore |
| 1958 | Kerstin | G. Moore | C. Bewicke | S. Hayhurst |
| 1959 | Roddy Owen | Lord Fingall | D. Morgan | H. Beasley |
| 1960 | Pas Seul | J. Rogerson | R. Turnell | W. Rees |
| 1961 | Saffron Tartan | Colonel G. Westmacott | D. Butchers | F. Winter |
| 1962 | Mandarin | Mme. K. Hennessy | F. Walwyn | F. Winter |
| 1963 | Mill House | W. Gollings | F. Walwyn | W. Robinson |
| 1964 | Arkle | Anne, D. of Westminster | T. Dreaper | P. Taaffe |
| 1965 | Arkle | Anne, D. of Westminster | T. Dreaper | P. Taaffe |
| 1966 | Arkle | Anne, D. of Westminster | T. Dreaper | P. Taaffe |
| 1967 | Woodland Venture | H. Collins | F. Rimell | T. Biddlecombe |
| 1968 | Fort Leney | J. Thomson | T. Dreaper | P. Taaffe |
| 1969 | What A Myth | Lady Weir | Ryan Price | P. Kelleway |
| 1970 | L'Escargot | R. Guest | D. Moore | T. Carberry |
| 1971 | L'Escargot | R. Guest | D. Moore | T. Carberry |
| 1972 | Glencaraig Lady | P. Doyle | F. Flood | F. Berry |
| 1973 | The Dikler | Mrs. D. August | F. Walwyn | R. Barry |
| 1974 | Captain Christy | Mrs. J. Samuel | P. Taaffe | H. Beasley |
| 1975 | Ten Up | Anne, D. of Westminster | J. Dreaper | T. Carberry |
| 1976 | Royal Frolic | Sir E. Hanmer | F. Rimell | J. Burke |
| 1977 | Davy Lad | Mrs. J. McGowan | M. A. O'Toole | D. T. Hughes |
| 1978 | Midnight Court | Mrs. O. Jackson | F. Winter | J. Francome |

| | | OWNER | TRAINER | JOCKEY |
|---|---|---|---|---|
| 1979 | Alverton | Snailwell Stud Co. Ltd. | M. H. Easterby | J. J. O'Neill |
| 1980 | Master Smudge | A. Barrow | A. Barrow | R. Hoare |
| 1981 | Little Owl | R. J. Wilson | M. H. Easterby | A. J. Wilson |
| 1982 | Silver Buck | Mrs. C. Feather | M. Dickinson | R. Earnshaw |
| 1983 | Bregawn | J. Kennelly | M. Dickinson | G. Bradley |
| 1984 | Burrough Hill Lad | R. Riley | Mrs. J. Pitman | P. Tuck |
| 1985 | Forgive'N'Forget | T. Kilroe & Sons Ltd. | J. Fitzgerald | M. Dwyer |
| 1986 | Dawn Run | Mrs. C. Hill | P. Mullins | J. J. O'Neill |
| 1987 | The Thinker | T. McDonagh Ltd | W. A. Stephenson | R. Lamb |
| 1988 | Charter Party | Mrs. C. Smith | D. Nicholson | R. Dunwoody |
| 1989 | Desert Orchid | R. Burridge | D. Elsworth | S. Sherwood |
| 1990 | Norton's Coin | S. Griffiths | S. Griffiths | G. McCourt |

# THE CHAMPION HURDLE

| | | | | |
|---|---|---|---|---|
| 1946 | Distel | Miss D. Paget | C. Rogers | R. O'Ryan |
| 1947 | National Spirit | L. Abelson | V. Smyth | D. Morgan |
| 1948 | National Spirit | L. Abelson | V. Smyth | R. Smyth |
| 1949 | Hatton's Grace | Mrs. M. Keogh | M. V. O'Brien | A. Brabazon |
| 1950 | Hatton's Grace | Mrs. M. Keogh | M. V. O'Brien | A. Brabazon |
| 1951 | Hatton's Grace | Mrs. M. Keogh | M. V. O'Brien | T. Molony |
| 1952 | Sir Ken | M. Kingsley | W. Stephenson | T. Molony |
| 1953 | Sir Ken | M. Kingsley | W. Stephenson | T. Molony |
| 1954 | Sir Ken | M. Kingsley | W. Stephenson | T. Molony |
| 1955 | Clair Soleil | G. Judd | Ryan Price | F. Winter |
| 1956 | Doorknocker | C. Nicholson | W. Hall | H. Sprague |
| 1957 | Merry Deal | A. Jones | A. Jones | G. Underwood |
| 1958 | Bandalore | Mrs. D. Wright | J. Wright | G. Slack |
| 1959 | Fare Time | G. Judd | Ryan Price | F. Winter |
| 1960 | Another Flash | J. Byrne | P. Sleator | H. Beasley |
| 1961 | Eborneezer | Dr B. Paigar | Ryan Price | F. Winter |
| 1962 | Anzio | Sir T. Ainsworth | F. Walwyn | W. Robinson |
| 1963 | Winning Fair | G. Spencer | G. Spencer | A. Lillington |
| 1964 | Magic Court | J. McGhie | T. Robson | P. McCarron |
| 1965 | Kirriemuir | Mrs. D. Beddington | F. Walwyn | G. Robinson |
| 1966 | Salmon Spray | Mrs. J. Rogerson | R. Turnell | J. Haine |
| 1967 | Saucy Kit | K. Adler | M. H. Easterby | R. Edwards |
| 1968 | Persian War | H. Alper | C. Davies | J. Uttley |
| 1969 | Persian War | H. Alper | C. Davies | J. Uttley |
| 1970 | Persian War | H. Alper | C. Davies | J. Uttley |
| 1971 | Bula | Capt. E. E-Heathcote | F. Winter | P. Kelleway |
| 1972 | Bula | Capt. E. E-Heathcote | F. Winter | P. Kelleway |
| 1973 | Comedy of Errors | E. Wheatley | F. Rimell | W. Smith |
| 1974 | Lanzarote | Lord H. de Walden | F. Winter | R. Pitman |
| 1975 | Comedy of Errors | E. Wheatley | F. Rimell | K. White |
| 1976 | Night Nurse | R. Spencer | M. H. Easterby | P. Broderick |
| 1977 | Night Nurse | R. Spencer | M. H. Easterby | P. Broderick |
| 1978 | Monksfield | Dr. M. Mangan | D. McDonogh | T. Kinane |
| 1979 | Monksfield | Dr. M. Mangan | D. McDonogh | D. T. Hughes |
| 1980 | Sea Pigeon | P. Muldoon | M. H. Easterby | J. J. O'Neill |
| 1981 | Sea Pigeon | P. Muldoon | M. H. Easterby | J. Francome |
| 1982 | For Auction | P. Heaslip | M. Cunningham | C. Magnier |
| 1983 | Gaye Brief | Sheikh Ali Abu Khamsin | Mrs. M. Rimell | R. Linley |
| 1984 | Dawn Run | Mrs. C. Hill | P. Mullins | J. J. O'Neill |
| 1985 | See You Then | Stype Wood Stud Ltd. | N. Henderson | S. Smith Eccles |
| 1986 | See You Then | Stype Wood Stud Ltd. | N. Henderson | S. Smith Eccles |
| 1987 | See You Then | Stype Wood Stud Ltd. | N. Henderson | S. Smith Eccles |
| 1988 | Celtic Shot | D. Horton | F. Winter. | P. Scudamore |
| 1989 | Beech Road | A. Geake | T. Balding | R. Guest |
| 1990 | Kribensis | Sheikh Mohammed | M. Stoute | R. Dunwoody |

# QUEEN MOTHER CHAMPION CHASE

| | | | | |
|---|---|---|---|---|
| 1959 | Quita Que | Mrs. D. Brand | D. Moore | J. Cox |
| 1960 | Fortria | G. Ansley | T. Dreaper | P. Taaffe |
| 1961 | Fortria | G. Ansley | T. Dreaper | P. Taaffe |
| 1962 | Piperton | A. Thomlinson | A. Thomlinson | D. Dick |
| 1963 | Sandy Abbot | Mrs. J. McKechnie | G. Owen | S. Mellor |

| | OWNER | TRAINER | JOCKEY |
|---|---|---|---|
| 1964 **Ben Stack** | Anne, D. of Westminster | T. Dreaper | P. Taaffe |
| 1965 **Dunkirk** | W. Whitbread | P. Cazalet | D. Dick |
| 1966 **Flyingbolt** | Mrs. T. Wilkinson | T. Dreaper | P. Taaffe |
| 1967 **Drinny's Double** | P. Mellon | R. Turnell | F. Nash |
| 1968 **Drinny's Double** | P. Mellon | R. Turnell | F. Nash |
| 1969 **Muir** | W. Willis | T. Dreaper | B. Hannon |
| 1970 **Straight Fort** | G. Ansley | T. Dreaper | P. Taaffe |
| 1971 **Crisp** | Sir C. Manifold | F. Winter | P. Kelleway |
| 1972 **Royal Relief** | E. Courage | E. Courage | W. Smith |
| 1973 **Inkslinger** | Mrs. M. Jenny | D. Moore | T. Carberry |
| 1974 **Royal Relief** | E. Courage | E. Courage | W. Smith |
| 1975 **Lough Inagh** | A. Martin | J. Dreaper | S. Barker |
| 1976 **Skymas** | M. Magee | J. Lusk | M. Morris |
| 1977 **Skymas** | M. Magee | J. Lusk | M. Morris |
| 1978 **Hilly Way** | J. Sweeney | P. McCreery | T. Carmody |
| 1979 **Hilly Way** | J. Sweeney | P. McCreery | T. M. Walsh |
| 1980 **Another Dolly** | I. Urquhart | F. Rimell | S. Morshead |
| 1981 **Drumgora** | d. Monahan | A. Moore | F. Berry |
| 1982 **Rathgorman** | J. Lilley | M. Dickinson | K. Whyte |
| 1983 **Badsworth Boy** | D. Armitage | M. Dickinson | R. Earnshaw |
| 1984 **Badsworth Boy** | D. Armitage | M. Dickinson | R. Earnshaw |
| 1985 **Badsworth Boy** | D. Armitage | Mrs. M. Dickinson | R. Earnshaw |
| 1986 **Buck House** | Mrs. S. Purcell | M. Morris | T. Carmody |
| 1987 **Pearlyman** | Mrs. P. Shaw | J. Edwards | P. Scudamore |
| 1988 **Pearlyman** | Mrs. P. Shaw | J. Edwards | T. Morgan |
| 1989 **Barnbrook Again** | M. Davies | D. Elsworth | S. Sherwood |
| 1990 **Barnbrook Again** | M. Davies | D. Elsworth | H. Davies |

# THE KING GEORGE VI CHASE

| 1947 **Rowland Boy** | A. Boley | F. Walwyn | B. Marshall |
|---|---|---|---|
| 1948 **Cottage Rake** | F. Vickerman | M. V. O'Brien | A. Brabazon |
| 1949 **Finnure** | Lord Bicester | G. Beeby | R. Francis |
| 1950 **Manicou** | H.M. Queen Elizabeth | P. Cazalet | B. Marshall |
| 1951 **Statecraft** | Mrs. J. White | P. Cazalet | A. Grantham |
| 1952 **Halloween** | Contessa di S'Elia | W. Wightman | F. Winter |
| 1953 **Galloway Braes** | Lady Orde | A. Kilpatrick | R. Morrow |
| 1954 **Halloween** | Contessa di S'Elia | W. Wightman | F. Winter |
| 1955 **Limber Hill** | J. Davey | W. Dutton | J. Power |
| 1956 **Rose Park** | G. Lawrence | P. Cazalet | M. Scudamore |
| 1957 **Mandarin** | Mme. K. Hennessy | F. Walwyn | G. Madden |
| 1958 **Lochroe** | Mrs. J. M.-White | P. Cazalet | A. Freeman |
| 1959 **Mandarin** | Mme. K. Hennessy | F. Walwyn | G. Madden |
| 1960 **Saffron Tartan** | Colonel G. Westmacott | D. Butchers | F. Winter |
| 1963 **Mill House** | W. Gollings | F. Walwyn | W. Robinson |
| 1964 **Frenchman's Cove** | S. Joel | H. T. Jones | S. Mellor |
| 1965 **Arkle** | Anne, D. of Westminster | T. Dreaper | P. Taaffe |
| 1966 **Dormant** | Mrs. D. W-Kendrew | J. W-Kendrew | J. King |
| 1969 **Titus Oates** | P. Cussins | G. W. Richards | S. Mellor |
| 1971 **The Dikler** | Mrs. D. August | F. Walwyn | B. Brogan |
| 1972 **Pendil** | Mrs. C. Swallow | F. Winter | R. Pitman |
| 1973 **Pendil** | Mrs. C. Swallow | F. Winter | R. Pitman |
| 1974 **Captain Christy** | Mrs. J. Samuel | P. Taaffe | R. Coonan |
| 1975 **Captain Christy** | Mrs. J. Samuel | P. Taaffe | G. Newman |
| 1976 **Royal Marshal II** | J. Sumner | T. Forster | G. Thorner |
| 1977 **Bachelor's Hall** | P. Harris | P. Cundell | M. O'Halloran |
| 1978 **Gay Spartan** | M. Armstrong | A. Dickinson | T. Carmody |
| 1979 **Silver Buck** | Mrs. C. Feather | A. Dickinson | T. Carmody |
| 1980 **Silver Buck** | Mrs. C. Feather | M. Dickinson | T. Carmody |
| 1982 **Wayward Lad** | Mrs. S. Thewlis | M. Dickinson | J. Francome |
| 1983 **Wayward Lad** | Mrs. S. Thewlis | M. Dickinson | R. Earnshaw |
| 1984 **Burrough Hill Lad** | R. Riley | Mrs. J. Pitman | J. Francome |
| 1985 **Wayward Lad** | Mrs. S. Thewlis | Mrs. M. Dickinson | G. Bradley |
| 1986 **Desert Orchid** | R. Burridge | D. Elsworth | S. Sherwood |
| 1987 **Nupsala** | Mme. R. Fougedoire | F. Doumen | A. Pommier |
| 1988 **Desert Orchid** | R. Burridge | D. Elsworth | S. Sherwood |
| 1989 **Desert Orchid** | R. Burridge | D. Elsworth | R. Dunwoody |

* 1961, 1962, 1967, 1968, 1970, 1981 – No races.

# INDEX